Motown Evangelization

Global Perspectives on
the New Evangelization

Volume 4

Series Introduction

Then he sat down and taught the crowds from the boat. After he had
finished speaking, he said to Simon, "Put out into deep water and lower
your nets for a catch." Simon said in reply, "Master, we have worked hard
all night and have caught nothing, but at your command I will lower the
nets." When they had done this, they caught a great number of fish and
their nets were tearing.

—Luke 5:3–6

"How beautiful upon the mountains are the feet of the one bringing good news, announcing peace, bearing good news, announcing salvation, saying to Zion, 'Your God is King!'"
(Isaiah 52:7). Evangelization is something beautiful. Derived from the Greek word, *euaggelion*, evangelization means to bear a "happy/blessed message." It is safe to say that every
human being longs for good news, and the entire drama of salvation history, as revealed
especially in Scripture and Tradition, hinges on a claim to the best news there is. In a word,
salvation through divine intimacy—Emmanuel, God with us (see Isaiah 7:14; Matthew
1:23). And as for the essence of this salvation? Isaiah's witness makes it clear: a return to
goodness, peace, and the lordship of God.

The bridge of meaning between Isaiah's text and the life and teachings of Jesus of
Nazareth is unmistakable: "After John had been arrested, Jesus came to Galilee proclaiming
the gospel (*euaggelion*) of God: 'This is the time of fulfillment. The kingdom of God is at
hand. Repent, and believe in the gospel'" (Mark 1:14–15). Jesus not only proclaims the good
news indicated by Isaiah—"Your God is King!"—he manifests and embodies it. Jesus is the
good news of God in person: "And the Word became flesh and made his dwelling among
us" (John 1:14). In Jesus's humanity united with his divinity, the good news of God becomes
sacrament through the perpetual liturgy of incarnation. Yet the totality of God's revelation
in Jesus is laced with paradox. He is a servant king. His royal garments are stark naked-
ness. His crown is woven of thorns. His ministry is unconcerned with the accumulation of
material wealth but, to the contrary, is about giving all away. His queen is a vestal virgin, the
Church, *in persona Mariae*, and he reigns from a wooden throne of suffering.

In the twenty-first century, the paradoxical message of the Gospel is no less shocking than it was two thousand years ago. If anything, it is even more riveting to scientific
sensibilities and to a surging expansion of secularism taking root in virtually every cultural
setting of the world. As Pope Paul VI put it in his 1975 apostolic exhortation, *Evangelii
nuntiandi*, we have entered definitively "a new period of evangelization (*feliciora evange-
lizationis tempora*)" (2). In other words, today we find ourselves in a happy and profitable
season to evangelize.

This book series, *Global Perspectives on the New Evangelization*, aims to contribute
to the mission field of this "New Evangelization." By offering fresh voices from a diversity
of perspectives, these books put Catholic theology into dialogue with a host of conversation partners around a variety of themes. Through the principle of inculturation, rooted
in that of incarnation, this series seeks to reawaken those facets of truth found in the
beautiful complementarity of cultural voices as harmonized in the one, holy, catholic, and
apostolic Church.

John C. Cavadini and **Donald Wallenfang,** *Series editors*

Motown Evangelization

Sharing the Gospel of Jesus in a Detroit Style

EDITED BY

John C. Cavadini

AND

Donald Wallenfang

GLOBAL PERSPECTIVES ON THE
NEW EVANGELIZATION

PICKWICK *Publications* · Eugene, Oregon

MOTOWN EVANGELIZATION
Sharing the Gospel of Jesus in a Detroit Style

Global Perspectives on the New Evangelization 4

Pickwick Publications
An Imprint of Wipf and Stock Publishers
199 W. 8th Ave., Suite 3
Eugene, OR 97401

www.wipfandstock.com

PAPERBACK ISBN: 978-1-6667-0781-6
HARDCOVER ISBN: 978-1-6667-0782-3
EBOOK ISBN: 978-1-6667-0783-0

Cataloguing-in-Publication data:

Names: Cavadini, John C., editor. | Wallenfang, Donald, editor.

Title: Motown evangelization : sharing the gospel of Jesus in a Detroit style / edited by John C. Cavadini and Donald Wallenfang.

Description: Eugene, OR : Pickwick Publications, 2022 | Series: Global Perspectives on the New Evangelization 4 | Includes bibliographical references and index.

Identifiers: ISBN 978-1-6667-0781-6 (paperback) | ISBN 978-1-6667-0782-3 (hardcover) | ISBN 978-1-6667-0783-0 (ebook)

Subjects: LCSH: Catholic Church—Doctrines. | Evangelistic work—Catholic Church.

Classification: BX2347.4 M68 2022 (print) | BX2347.4 M68 (ebook)

07/12/22

The editors would like to dedicate this volume
to the memory and legacy of

Deacon Alex C. Jones, Jr.,

Former Roman Catholic Deacon at Prince
of Peace Catholic Church in Detroit,

Former Coordinator of Evangeliztion for the Archdiocese
of Detroit, and Founder of Alex Jones Ministries

"It is a tremendous hindrance to tell someone seeking
the truth to stay where he is."

—From Alex Jones's 2006 book, *No Price Too High:
A Pentecostal Preacher Becomes Catholic*

And to the leadership and vision of

Archbishop Allen H. Vigneron

Archbishop of the Archdiocese of Detroit

"The book of Acts ends in chapter 28 with Paul under house
arrest in Rome, still boldly preaching the Gospel. Luke ends
without finishing the story because the story of the Church's
mission continues in every age. We are living the 29th chapter
of Acts! The ecology of the New Testament by which the Gospel
was unleashed in the ancient world is the ecology of the
Church today. It thus includes the same elements of repentance
and faith; signs and wonders."

—*Unleash the Gospel,* 2017 Pastoral Letter
of Archbishop Vigneron

Contents

IV. Diversified Evangelization

V. Sanctified Evangelization

Acknowledgments

It is a loving obligation to recognize those whose support has made this book possible. First, the editors would like to acknowledge the McGrath Institute for Church Life at the University of Notre Dame and, especially, the unsparing hearts of Robert and Joan McGrath. Second, we thank Sacred Heart Major Seminary for sponsoring the 2019 Detroit symposium dedicated to the theme: "Enter through the Narrow Gate: The Urgency of the New Evangelization in the Third Milennium." Special thanks must be given to Msgr. Todd Lajiness, former seminary Rector, Fr. Stephen Burr, current seminary Rector, and Fr. Timothy Laboe, seminary Dean of Studies, who made this symposium possible. And third, we thank Wipf and Stock Publishers, especially Charlie Collier and Matt Wimer, for continuing to support the *Global Perspectives on the New Evangelization* book series by seeing it through to print. May the essays collected herein contribute to making Jesus Christ known and loved all the more in people's hearts throughout the world today and in the days to come.

List of Contributors

Cary Dabney, Assistant Professor of Theology, Walsh University

Robert Fastiggi, Bishop Kevin M. Britt Chair of Dogmatic Theology and Christology, Sacred Heart Major Seminary

Most Rev. Daniel E. Flores, Bishop of Brownsville, Texas

Scott Hahn, Fr. Michael Scanlan Chair of Biblical Theology and the New Evangelization, Franciscan University of Steubenville, and Founder and President of the Saint Paul Center for Biblical Theology

Mary Healy, Professor of Sacred Scripture, Sacred Heart Major Seminary

Ralph Martin, Professor of Theology and Director of Graduate Programs in the New Evangelization, Sacred Heart Major Seminary

Michael McCallion, Rev. William Cunningham Chair of Catholic Social Analysis, Sacred Heart Major Seminary

Rev. John McDermott, SJ, Professor of Theology, Sacred Heart Major Seminary

Rev. Peter Ryan, SJ, Professor of Theology and Spiritual Director, Sacred Heart Major Seminary

Donald Wallenfang, OCDS, Professor of Theology and Philosophy, Sacred Heart Major Seminary

Introduction

But how can they call on him in whom they have not believed?
And how can they believe in him of whom they have not heard?
And how can they hear without someone to preach? And how
can people preach unless they are sent? As it is written, "How
beautiful are the feet of those who bring the good news!" . . .
Thus faith comes from what is heard, and what is heard comes
through the word of Christ.

—Rom 10:14–15, 17

WHY THE TITLE *Motown Evangelization: Sharing the Gospel of Jesus in a
Detroit Style*? It is because the gospel of Jesus Christ is destined to be mobilized in a perpetual motion of healing, forgiveness, reconciliation, conversion, and empowerment. It is meant to be "a gospel with wheels" and "a
gospel with soul!" Good news on-the-go, on-the-move. It is a message of a
mystery not meant to be kept to oneself. The secret of the gospel of Jesus is
that it is no secret. The intention of this book's title is to give indication that
the United States's city of Detroit may serve as a provocative hermeneutical
key for Catholic evangelization today. Typically, when someone mentions
the city of Detroit in conversation, at least one negative reaction comes to
surface. "You're moving to Detroit? I'm sorry." "You're travelling through
Detroit? Be careful." "You're from Detroit? Oh." The city of Detroit is remarkably similar to that unsung biblical city of Nazareth. "Can anything
good come from Nazareth?" (John 1:46). Apparently, yes indeed.

Yet this book is not only about the city of Detroit, but about every little
corner of the world that is a potent receptor of the gospel of Jesus. The meaning of "sharing the gospel of Jesus in a Detroit style" points to the urgency and
fortitude that mark the vision of the New Evangelization. The history and demographics of Detroit are instructive for understanding Catholic teaching on

how to evangelize in a postmodern and post-pandemic atmosphere. Detroit symbolizes so many things related to Catholic evangelization by connecting the dots of a great constellation of meaning. First, the geographical area is referred to as *Waawiiyaataanong,* by the native Anishanabee people. *Waawiiyaataanong* translates to "where the water curves around." From a Christian perspective, one cannot help but think of the sacrament of baptism, where the water curves around body and soul. Further, the French name Detroit originated with the French settlers' reference to *le détroit du lac Érié* ("the strait of Lake Erie"). Detroit means "strait"—a narrow, constricted passageway. Following the economic boom caused by the rise of the twentieth-century automotive industry, the recent history of Detroit involves a great deal of economic distress and rampant poverty. Tens of thousands of vacant homes, properties and buildings checker the cityscape, now known as greyfield. Detroit has been in dire straits for the past several decades.

But, at the same time, Detroit is home to a rich diversity of cultures and ethnicities, including the largest percentage of Black Americans by city in the United States, that altogether communicate Catholicism. It is reminiscent of the vision of Saint John the Evangelist: "I had a vision of a great multitude, which no one could count, from every nation, race, people, and tongue. They stood before the throne and before the Lamb, wearing white robes and holding palm branches in their hands" (Rev 7:9). Referring to the narrow strait of water running from Lake Saint Clair to Lake Erie, the name Detroit signifies an abundance of theological meanings. The name at once calls to mind the narrow road that leads to heaven and the desperation of shattered lives and dreams. Such narrow corridors are precisely where God the Holy Spirit desires to be at work redeeming what was lost. Detroit conveys the final countdown, the eleventh hour, the fourth quarter, the third period, the ninth inning, overtime, the evening of opportunity. Even the two mottos of Detroit echo corresponding meanings: *Speramus meliora* ("We hope for better things") and *Resurget cineribus* ("It shall rise from the ashes"). Detroit is a setting that showcases the sufficiency of divine grace in a weak place (see 2 Cor 12:1–10) and reveals a "treasure in earthen vessels, that the surpassing power may be of God and not from us" (2 Cor 4:7). The city's area code—313—also is symbolic. For instance, with imaginative reference to the mystery of the Most Holy Trinity: three Persons, one divine Substance, and the three-act structure of salvation history, including creation, fall and redemption, and parousia. Detroit, in terms of its abstract theological meaning and concrete lived history, is a paradigmatic phenomenon through which to view the universal vocation of the New Evangelization.

This book originated with the 2019 symposium of scholars hosted by Sacred Heart Major Seminary at the Westin Book Cadillac hotel in Detroit, entitled "Enter through the Narrow Gate: The Urgency of the New

Evangelization in the Third Milennium." The chapters of this book are composed of presentations from that symposium, as well as a couple of additional essays to round out the collection. Authors include one bishop, two Jesuit priests, and seven laypeople. This demographic distribution of the essays is indicative of the resurgence of the lay vocation in the Church today, the Jesuit impetus of missionary evangelization, and the need for all authentic Catholic evangelization to be accountable to the bishops of the Church—the successors of the twelve Apostles. The essays are divided into five groups, under five headings: (1) Merciful Evangelization, (2) Urgent Evangelization, (3) Sacrificial Evangelization, (4) Diversified Evangelization, and (5) Sanctified Evangelization. These respective headings demonstrate the unique blend of elements emphasized both at the 2019 Detroit symposium and at Sacred Heart Major Seminary in general. On the whole, these essays form an implicit dialogue with one another, each essay not always putting the theological accent on the same point, or at times what seem to be opposite or even contradictory points.

Bishop Flores leads off the chapters with his meditations on evangelization and the charity of Christ. With his deliberate turn to the poor and the Eucharistic connotations of the gospel of Jesus, Bishop Flores sets the tonic key for all the essays to follow. Mercy is patient and Bishop Flores underscores this fact: "that with the Lord one day is like a thousand years and a thousand years like one day. The Lord does not delay his promise, as some regard 'delay,' but he is patient with you, not wishing that any should perish but that all should come to repentance" (2 Pet 3:8–9; cf. Ps 90:4). A counterpoint follows with Ralph Martin's and Fr. Peter Ryan's essays concentrating on the urgency of evangelization and the necessary consequence of hell in the wake of unrepented mortal sin. After all, Jesus insists on "how narrow the gate and constricted the road that leads to life. And those who find it are few" (Matt 7:14). The gospel of Jesus is at once urgently decisive and forbearingly merciful. The juxtaposition of these three essays underscores the impossibility of evacuating the paradoxical tension between divine mercy and divine justice.

Fr. John McDermott and Scott Hahn deliver essays on the concepts of suffering and sacrifice in relation to evangelization, asking the question, what role do suffering and sacrifice play in the process of evangelization? Fr. McDermott puts forth the essential doctrinal truth about the redemptive potential of suffering, while Scott Hahn, for his part, offers a biblical reflection on the theological concept of sacrifice in relation to Eucharistic liturgy that is meant to color the entire work of evangelization. These two essays powerfully convey the mystical pedagogy of suffering and sacrifice. The next set of essays by Cary Dabney and Michael McCallion accentuate the personal particularities of Catholic evangelization. After all, evangelization is not merely a matter of abstract concepts applicable to anonymous persons, but an incarnate message given to people with faces and names through the missionary course of inculturation and day-to-day parish communal life. Cary Dabney recounts the history of the Black Catholic experience vis-à-vis recent US Bishops' documents about racism, and Michael McCallion calls into question the typical zealousness of the universal movement of the New Evangelization by suggesting the occassional (and perhaps often unintended) alienating effects of this movement on certain people already present and active in parish communities. Evangelization is simultaneously universal and particular, global and contextualized.

Finally, Donald Wallenfang and Robert Fastiggi present essays at the intersection of the saints and the New Evangelization. An incarnate gospel can be perceived in its actual fullness only through attentiveness to the witness of its embodied emissaries. Donald Wallenfang ponders the postmodern milieu of the New Evangelization with responses from Saint Augustine and Saint Teresa of Ávila, in the end recommending his original notion of "montage ministry." Robert Fastiggi surveys and synthesizes several noteable magisterial texts demonstrating the indissoluble unity between the Blessed Virgin Mary and the New Evangelization. Catholic evangelization depends on the real intercession and intervention of the communion of angels and saints, without which the message of the gospel would remain practically immobilized. The book concludes with a transcript of the panel presentation from the 2019 Detroit symposium, including responses to five questions posed by the symposium audience.

Detroit. A narrow, constricted passageway. And this is the purpose of the gospel of Jesus Christ: to enter what is constricted and restricted only to make it convicted of a life afflicted by sin and yet ever depicted in the *imago Dei*. "For God did not send his Son into the world to condemn the world, but that the world might be saved through him" (John 3:17). "For the Son of Man has come to seek and to save what was lost" (Luke 19:10). We need only think of the parables of the lost sheep, the lost coin, the prodigal son, the generous sower of seeds, and the grain of wheat that dies in order to remember the overwhelming face of divine mercy. *Motown Evangelization* hopes to testify to this radical mercy of God the Father, revealed in God the Son and God the Holy Spirit, so that Catholic evangelization would be mobilized to the ends of the earth, all the way back into the heart of the Church—the Sacred Heart of Jesus.

Ex voto suscepto,

John C. Cavadini and Donald Wallenfang

I. Merciful Evangelization

1

Meditations on Evangelization and the Charity of Christ

Most Rev. Daniel E. Flores

Prologue

I do not intend to offer a complete scheme of evangelization, nor even an argument about a particular aspect. I will offer a few word-drawings. I invite you to consider calmly either a particular point, a quoted text, or a provoked image. My hope is that fragmented stained glass also admits light. The meditations are seven in number, with an epilogue at the end saving space for the eighth day.

What Is Grace?

In a simple but profound sense, in the human experience grace is something that is given *without having to*. It is something not deserved, not bought, not contracted: it is a gift freely given. It does not seek payment, nor does it care about claiming debts. Grace is as spontaneous as a smile, or an embrace between friends. We have all lived the greatness of the completely free gift, of the donation given without requiring anything. In the natural course of life, realizing that we have received a grace generates within us a spontaneous desire to want to respond in some way: to return the smile, return the embrace, to say thank you. Thus, grace shows forth its own dynamic, much like friendship does. Grace engenders grace.

Nevertheless, confronted with the generosity of others, we have also lived the experience of surreptitiously asking: *What does this person want from me, giving me so much?* We learn as children that not everything that comes with the countenance of grace is given free of charge. It is the cynicism that entered with Original Sin that has taught us to suspect that what is presented as a gift, can soon turn into indebtedness. The devil was presump-tuous enough to offer Jesus the kingdoms of the world, but the offer con-cealed a debt incurred: *tomorrow you owe me*. Despite the bitter experience of a business deal hidden behind a face of grace, the invitation of authentic grace retains its own splendor, one which calls us to breathe an air beyond sales and payments. By recognizing that we have received freely, grace asks us to give freely, as the Lord Himself says (Matt 10:7–8). Speaking of grace, as we will see throughout these reflections, Pope Benedict favored the word *gratuitousness*, and Pope Francis speaks incessantly of grace as a *self-giving* (*entrega*). In a vigorous yet no less simple theological sense, grace is what saves us through this dynamism of generosity generating generosity.

Grace and Charity

In order to follow this thread of grace, I would like to highlight a text of Saint Thomas taken from the third part of the *Summa Theologiae*. In question 46, article 3, the Saint asks about the *why* of the Passion of the Lord. Why did the Lord want to accept the Cross in order to save us? The question provides him an opportunity to summarize the teaching of the Scriptures on the work of Christ and the grace that saves us. "In the first place, by this means man knows how much God loves him and by this he is provoked to love Him in return, in which consists the perfection of human salvation. Thus, the Apostle says in Rom 5:8–9: "God proves his love for us in this, that while we were yet sinners, Christ died for us."

The passion of the Lord Jesus shows forth the love of God freely offered. According to Saint Thomas, it is the effective sign of the gift that is the Incar-nation and life of the Son of God. Through this sign we know the love of God the Father. Of course, the sign of the Cross admits of a variety of interpreta-tions. Not everyone sees in it the extreme love of God directed towards us. It is a grace to be able to see the Cross and understand what we see.

Catholic anthropology presupposes that in the encounter with the Lord Jesus, grace insinuates itself as a light in the mind, giving us to per-ceive what we could call the author's intention while offering himself in this way. The Scriptures testify to this intention understood by the first disciples. The mind perceives by grace the essentials of this grand dis-play as a manifestation of love freely given, of complete self-surrender, of charity poured-out. As the Dominican Olivier-Thomas Venard says in his book *A Poetic Christ*: "On the cross the incarnate Word speaks the most meaningful language there is when it comes to love: not the language of words, nor that of acts, but the language of the body."[1]

Grace manifests itself as something given for us to understand through the language of the crucified flesh of the Lord. Faith believes in this love, and it is a presence in the soul. Faith contains within itself the dynamism of grace. It engenders within us a spontaneous and completely free desire to want to give love in return, *in which consists*, Saint Thomas says, *the perfection of human salvation*. This desire is provoked through the charity manifested on the Cross and is identical with receiving the love of the Holy Spirit poured out into our hearts.

It is significant that in this context Saint Thomas invokes the authority of Saint Paul in chapter 5 of his Epistle to the Romans. If one consults the commentary of Saint Thomas on that chapter, you will discover that this is where he explains in great detail the relationship between the death of Christ on the Cross, faith in this manifestation of gratuitous love, and the movement of the Holy Spirit within us. The response of the soul to Christ is the response of love, the fruit of that love poured into our hearts.

Grace saves us. God gives us his love by giving us his Son; faith captures the reality of this love under the sign of the Cross, and the Holy Spirit reaches the heart to save us. Grace saves us through an interior renewal which capacitates us to love Christ *as he has loved us*. This love, the culmination of God's grace, the participation in God's own life, is called charity. Let us recall the words of Pope Francis in *Evangelii gaudium*, 37, where the Holy Father, quoting Saint Thomas tells us: "The foundation of the New Law is in the grace of the Holy Spirit, who is manifested in the faith which works through love (ST, 1–2, 108, 1)."

The Response of Love

In the visible source of the Cross, Christ reveals in a way accessible to us that the love of God is a grace of love offered, recognized and returned: 1 John 4:16: "We have come to know and to believe in the love God has for us. God is love, and whoever remains in love remains in God and God in him." Evangelization proposes to the human being the grace of Christ, inviting us to recognize in the Crucified One the manifestation of the charity of God, and in his resurrection our hope born of this charity. It is necessary to emphasize, especially today, that faith does not reach its end if it does not engender within us the same charity poured out: we respond to the Lord with grace and in grace. The charity of Christ does not save us

---

1. Venard, *A Poetic Christ*, 365.

by being recognized, it saves us by being returned; it saves us through our charity put into play within history. First John 3:16: "The way we came to know love was that he laid down his life for us; so we ought to lay down our lives for our brothers."

The laying down of our lives, referenced by Saint John gives concise expression of what the Lord commands and asks concerning the form of our response to him. On this point, Pope Benedict XVI tells us in his social encyclical *Caritas in veritate*, 5: "As objects of God's love, men and women become subjects of charity, they are called to make themselves instruments of grace, so as to pour forth God's charity and to weave networks of charity." And in *Evangelii gaudium*, 10, Pope Francis expresses himself in this way: "For here we discover a profound law of reality: that life is attained and matures in the measure it is offered up in order to give life to others. That is definitely the mission."

In the new life of grace, the very dynamic of the free gift of Christ requires us personally to formulate within ourselves the most exigent question of our lives as Catholics: *Lord, where are you that I might respond to you, to be able to love you as you have loved me?* The Lord himself indicates precisely the *where* of his presence, the *where* of our deepest longings as believers. When he spoke of the Eucharist, the Lord Jesus identified his real presence in his surrendered body and in his blood poured out at the supper of his own sacrifice. Furthermore, and with no less clarity, he personally identified himself with the poor: "Truly I tell you that what you did to one of these littlest ones, you did to me" (Matt 25:40).

Within this question that arises spontaneously from the dynamics of the grace of Christ, and from within the responsive outline the Lord offers, we find what we could call *the grace of the encounter offered* by God: with God himself *sacramented* among us, and with God present in the people with whom we share the human path. I stress again that this opening to the encounter is not presented as an option among options in the life of a Catholic; it is as essential as faith itself because it is the way of the response offered back to Christ. Faith itself, working through charity, seeks Christ with a hunger to respond to him. *His charity urges us.*

The Catholic faith, expressed in the Tridentine council, and in contrast to Lutheran doctrines, does not profess *sola fide*, a doctrine that teaches that by faith alone we are saved. I do not think that many Catholics would present themselves today to advocate for the *sola fide*, but I do think that in this age of comfortable individualisms and lifestyles, we run the risk of living faith with indifference, leaving aside the proposal of charity. In practice, we can live as if we only need to believe and profess the faith in order to be saved.

Such a way of appropriating faith reduces the horizon of salvation to the paltry space of my own life; that is to say, to thank God for making me know his love, but to worry little about the condition of those who walk with me on the paths of life, or to take lightly the importance of participating in the Eucharistic sacrifice. It is as if we were to say, *I have faith, I wish others had it.* We can live the faith with a condescending attitude mixed with a vague and distracted desire to promote the good for others. The grandeur of charity can be reduced to inoperable sentiments, when in fact it is the action of God within us enabling us to respond humanly, generously, gratuitously to the person who appears on our paths of life. Grace engenders grace or it dies in the stony ground of self-preoccupation.

The evangelical reality is otherwise. The grace of charity received invites us insistently to seek Christ in order *to love him in return, within which is found the perfection of human salvation*, as Saint Thomas says. To that seeking the scandal of the Cross provokes us. The work of Christ reveals the open heart of God where churns the Spirit of gratuitous communion and life-giving surrender. Only grace immerses us in the transforming waters that move us out of ourselves, to seek, find and taste this love that smells of Christ.

This provocation of the Cross is suitable for us precisely because without it we cannot develop a taste for the Kingdom. As Saint John Henry Newman said: "we live in this world to learn, by grace, to taste the things of God, and to savor what God savors."[2] If we do not learn to enjoy the taste of the charity of Christ while God grants us life, it is difficult to imagine how we could enjoy the eternal charity of God. Charity saves us by changing what and how we love. If we do not learn how to come out of ourselves to love Christ in the communion of his Body-Church around the altar of his Body-Sacrament, neither could we enjoy the eternal communion of saints. In the same way, if we cannot savor the self-gift of Christ in his mission on behalf of the rejected of this world, neither would we have hope of truly enjoying their heavenly company. In such cases, the eternal communion of the Saints around the Lamb who was slain would become a hell for us. Grace guides us to love what Christ loves, and through this transformation it makes us fit for glory. This point is also a basic element of the Catholic faith.

The Eucharistic Interruption

Here it would be good to pause for a moment to acknowledge the grandeur of the Eucharist in the life of a Catholic wishing to live the fullness of the life

2. Newman, *Parochial and Plain Sermons*, "Holiness Necessary for Future Blessedness."

of grace. In divine worship we receive the charity of Christ poured out from the altar. The Mass communicates the mystery of the love given by Christ in an intense narrative, using material signs and canonized words to make present the unfolding of the Trinitarian work on our behalf. It is the Father who sends us his Son through the work of the Holy Spirit. The Mass is a complete recapitulation and actual re-presentation of that saving work. The love of God is not communicated to us as something in the past, it is transmitted now through the language of the body, that language of which Venard spoke: Body and Blood present in the act of offering itself. Just as faith captures the charity of God under the sign of the Cross, this faith captures the same work of Christ interrupting time to be present in the elevated Host and in the Chalice presented to our sight. The few sacred words pronounced before the elevations effect what is silently manifested.

By presenting ourselves as recipients of his gratuitous self-giving, the Lord offers us communion in his charity. Manifesting himself as charity is one thing but offering himself to be taken—living body entering to give life to those who need it most—is the unsurpassable sign/presence of the dynamics of God's grace: life given, for charity's sake, that we might have life within his own charity. This enables us to be his *life-giving-over* people. The Eucharist is the sacrament of Charity just as the New Testament itself is the revelation of charity poured out. This is what Saint Thomas teaches, and what Pope Benedict XVI explains in *Sacramentum caritatis*.

But it would be a distortion if we do not understand that the action of the altar urges us to charity with the same force and vigor as the historical fact of the Passion and Resurrection of the Lord. It asks us for a response to the Lord enacted in our lives and unleashed in today's world. This dynamic is the same one Saint Thomas explained when discussing the reasons for the Passion. The Lord presents himself in this sacramental way precisely to provoke and renew within us the response of love. This grace saves us if we allow it to bring us to its intentional end in the charity of Christ operating within us. The charity of Christ makes us subjects, (agents) of charity, and from this charity arises the pressing concern of the Church and of every Christian to announce the Gospel and to serve the poor. We could say that if the Eucharistic mystery does not move us to go out and look for the Christ to whom we can offer a response of love, then we have been little touched by what we have seen in the Christ lifted up, and with little benefit have we received his offer of communion. Grace saves if we let it move us.

The Evangelization of the Poor and Being Evangelized by Them

The ecclesial renewals initiated by the grace of the Holy Spirit have always arisen through an evangelizing impulse and aimed in different ways to announce the gospel with clearer reference to the Lord Jesus, recognizing that his lifestyle and his mission completely coincide. Undoubtedly, the reform movements in the history of the Church born of an evangelical spirit confirm the decisive importance of the poverty of Christ as a point of reference. The Franciscans and the Dominicans are outstanding examples of this, although not the only ones.

I recommend to you a novel entitled *La confesión: El diario de Esteban Martorus*, written by the Mexican novelist Javier Sicilia. It is a provocative novel written with profound Catholic sensibility. It presents the poverty of Christ as an essential light for the Church today. The priest Esteban Martorus, the protagonist of the novel, is a poor curate, quite limited in his abilities; he is, though, a dedicated priest. In the first section I will cite, the priest is received by his cardinal archbishop. The cardinal has decided to send the priest to a village in the mountains, a poor and peripheral village. Within what is a dialogue between poverty and power, the priest says the following to the cardinal:

> Do you know what amazes me [Eminence] about the Incarnation?—I continued—, that it is altogether contrary to the modern world: the presence of the infinite in the limits of the flesh, and the fight, the fight with no quarter, against the temptations of the devil's excesses. You do not know how much I have meditated on the temptations in the desert. "Take up the power", the devil told him; that power that gives the illusion of being able to disrupt and dominate everything. But he maintained himself in the limits of his own flesh, in his own poverty, in his own death, so poor, so miserable, so hard. Our age, nevertheless, showing a face of enormous kindness, has succumbed to those temptations. "They will be like gods, they will change the stones into bread, and they will dominate the world" . . . to such an age we have handed over the Christ, and we do not even realize it.[3]

What is most actual about Javier Sicilia's analysis is the clear identification of poverty with limitation and lack of power. It is the opposite of the cultural current of excess that seeks to overcome the inherent limitation of the human condition; the culture of excess seeks to establish a limitless

---

3. Sicilia, *La confesión*, loc. 176; translation mine.

condition that can define and constitute its own reality. We have ordered *having* to the purposes of power, and *power* to ends of self-sufficiency. The relentless pursuit of potent freedom is largely the pursuit of total independence. Not having to depend on anyone, and not having to suffer that others depend on us, has become the ideal of socioeconomic progress. Poverty disturbs the conscience of the world that today enjoys its economic and political power. However, if we are honest, the poverty of material resources horrifies us precisely because the limitations of *not having* are limitations of power, and remind us of the interdependence of humanity, the need for the relationships without which we cannot survive.

In contrast Sicily identifies the poverty of Christ with the condition that embraces the limited and powerless state, unable, in the end, to overcome the interrelated dependence of the human being. It is a poverty that does not consider the limitations of the flesh to be a curse. On the contrary, God the Father decides to save the world through the poverty of his incarnate Son who renounces the path of manipulative power: *altogether contrary to the modern world.* And the culmination of this poverty (the dark light) is his death *so poor, so miserable, so hard.* Christ asked the Samaritan woman for water and he asked for it also from the Cross. Christ in his poverty, (what Saint Paul says makes us rich), gives of himself precisely by offering himself as needing something, and from this limitation, he gives us life. This man, wounded and vulnerable, who is God, appeals to our conscience, seeking how to provoke in us a response of charity. The mystery of not being self-sufficient beings, being able to respond to this condition in our neighbor opens us to salvation through exposing us to the possibility of freely receiving and freely giving.

If Father Martorus gives the cardinal a lesson about the dignity of the poor Christ and that of his people, later in the novel the priest receives a lesson from a trusted friend, an elderly woman religious living in the poverty of the peripheral village. She says the following:

> If misery exists, Father, and the statistics do not lie, it is because the dream of the rich has contaminated the dreams of the poor. At the bottom of things, poverty no longer exists, dear Father. The only thing that exists is wealth and misery. . . . Do you know why? I know well that you know. . . . Because they have been made to believe that their poverty is a shameful disease, a wound unworthy of the world. Never before has humanity, and here, excuse me, Father, I also included our Holy Mother Church, spit so much on the face of Christ, as if his poverty were a filth, that

unclean filth that they hung from the cross and which we, as did his detractors, make fun of.[4]

The dream of the rich has contaminated the dreams of the poor, she says, indicating that poverty and misery are different conditions. The dream of the rich is to dream of being able to manipulate everything, to have everything, to dominate everything. It becomes misery precisely when limitation shows itself as resistant to the dream of control and dominance.

Poverty of resources is not a disease, a plague that should cause us to flee from the poor. The world blames the poor for their poverty as if we had no responsibility. Meanwhile, a world culture dedicates itself to sustaining the dream of the rich, that is, a culture unmeasured in its consumption of the goods of the world. Remedies exist to improve the condition of the poor, but they start with seeing the poor as human beings, and not seeing their suffering as collateral damage that the world of measureless consumption laments even as it continues pursuing its dreams.

It turns out, then, that the coldness and indifference of the human being when faced with the need of the poor is the poorest possible condition for us as human beings; the indifference eclipses the opening to that love that wants to see the neighbor and respond with grace, humanely and gratuitously. Perhaps this point helps us to understand what Pope Francis means when he proposes in *Evangelii gaudium*, 198, that it is necessary that we all let ourselves be evangelized by the poor: "We need to let ourselves be evangelized by them. The new evangelization is an invitation to acknowledge the saving power at work in their lives and to put them at the center of the Church's pilgrim way." The saving force of their lives is the force that calls us to respond to suffering with a heart of flesh and not of stone. Without this opening, faith cannot save us.

The poor know one thing for certain: without the help of others, they cannot survive. Speaking with immigrants who have survived an extremely dangerous road, leaving Honduras, for example, and crossing all of Mexico to reach McAllen, Texas, one constantly hears how the help of people or the lack of help has determined the course of their journey. In this sense, the immigrant, representative of a human reality of suffering and rejection that many in the world do not want to recognize, is, in his person, dignified and in need. The poor offer us a grace, an opportunity, perhaps the last, to respond gracefully and overcome the indifference that is killing us.

4. Sicilia, *La confesión*, loc. 1669; translation mine.

A World That Questions Us

A key text on evangelization in the modern era is the 1975 apostolic letter of Pope Saint Paul VI, *Evangelii nuntiandi*. I would like to direct myself to a particular text where he speaks of a new evangelization. In paragraph 3 of the letter, he says the following:

> On June 22, 1973, we said to the Sacred College of Cardinals: "The conditions of the society in which we live oblige all of us therefore to revise methods, to seek by every means to study how we can bring the Christian message to modern man. For it is only in the Christian message that modern man can find the answer to his questions and the energy for his commitment of human solidarity."

I do not wish to focus on the question of methods and means, but on the simple and concise way in which the Holy Father describes the Christian message. He refers to the kerygma and to catechetical formation in grace when he says: *it is only in the Christian message that modern man can find the answer to his questions and the energy for his commitment of human solidarity.*

Speaking of questions and solidarity, the Pope develops the thread of the Second Vatican Council's document *Gaudium et spes*. For example, his words echo the language of *Gaudium et spes*, 3:

> Though mankind is stricken with wonder at its own discoveries and its power, it often raises anxious questions about the current trend of the world, about the place and role of man in the universe, about the meaning of its individual and collective strivings, and about the ultimate destiny of reality and of humanity. . . . For the human person deserves to be preserved; human society deserves to be renewed. Hence the focal point of our total presentation will be man himself, whole and entire, body and soul, heart and conscience, mind and will.

People today have many questions. Now then, there are questions of the intellect and questions of the heart. The mind affects the heart, and the heart affects the mind. It is necessary, therefore, to avoid a restricted interpretation that sees the Gospel as offering a response to only intellectual questions. Even the question about the existence of God is not simply an intellectual question; much less questions about salvation. The question about God and salvation arises from within the historical moment. And although one admits that human beings have an enormous capacity to forget what has been lived in other times, and for that reason think that our doubts are original, even so today's questions touch on new circumstances, requiring adequated responses.

There are many studies on the historical movements, cultural phenomena and intellectual roots that have come together to create the historical, cultural and intellectual air we breathe today. Among those studies, I greatly appreciate the description of our era offered by George Steiner in his book *Real Presences*, when he says that we have entered the time of the epilogue: "Throughout, my question is: what is the status and meaning of meaning, of communicative form, in the time of the 'after-Word'? I define this time as that of the epilogue (again, the term houses Logos)."[5] The time of the epilogue accepts the deconstructive critique (even without examining it thoroughly and critically), and despairs of the possibility of knowing the truth. It is the time that distrusts the truth of words; it is the time of the Word exiled from the city. This time coincides with the time of words multiplied meaninglessly, and of the word manipulated. The aggressive cynicism of today sees every expressive elaboration as a game of power and control. The diagnosis of Steiner and others is not far from the sense expressed by Javier Sicilia in the texts I earlier quoted, where the specter of power eclipses every other human aspiration.

It is worthwhile to note the actual response of the magisterium in recent years. I believe that we have been seeing a hermeneutic development, addressed to persons living in the time of the epilogue, of the after-Word, that is, of signification torn apart. Pope Benedict XVI published two encyclicals on the theological virtues with the intention of publishing the third. He began with charity (*Deus caritas est*), and continued with *Spe salvi* concerning hope. The third was already in preparation, on faith, when he made the humble decision to resign from the papacy. Pope Francis, also with humility, reviewed and published this third encyclical, *Lumen fidei*, on faith, by his own authority. The great schematic of these encyclicals affirms that the human being today has difficulties capturing faith in response to his questions if he does not first confront his identity as a human being in relation to other human beings, and if he does not face the root of the spontaneous human desire to sacrifice for and receive a worthwhile future.

The order of presentation of the encyclicals shows a deep continuity with what Pope Saint Paul VI teaches in *Evangelii nuntiandi* about the human questions to which the Gospel is directed. The papal magisterium has well diagnosed that doubts and confusion about the *reason for love* and the *reason for hope* afflict us deeply today. Without facing these, we cannot really understand what the gift and faith offers us. The sustained

5. Steiner, *Real Presences*, 94.

reflection on charity and hope before considering faith suggests something significant about today's path to Christ. Charity and hope are expressions of grace that give credibility to faith, and by extension give credibility to the *meaning of meaning*, to use Steiner's phrase.

Saint Thomas clearly teaches that hope and charity are the fruit of the dynamic encounter with the Crucified and Risen Christ, and that the coherent movement of grace within the human being begins with faith in God's love manifested in Christ. The order itself of the three encyclicals tells us that today we need to attend to the credibility of this dynamic of grace. Today's circumstances suggest that some cultures with a long Christian presence within them have lost the sense of the unity of this dynamic of grace. Instead of being seen as a coherent development within the believer, faith, hope and charity are perceived and appropriated by individuals in fragments and pieces. Likewise, there is little appreciation of the impact of the grace of theological virtues within society.

We could say that today the path to the truth of faith begins with addressing the credibility and the need for charity and hope in human life. As human beings, love and hope preoccupy us more in concrete life than does the truth. Obviously, the truth ought to preoccupy us more, but today's indifference in the face of the question of truth dominates the cultural space in much of the world. We are not in a position to recover a healthy concern about the truth without, at the same time, saying and manifesting something about love and hope, charity and pathways to the future. The human crisis today is not only a crisis of the credibility of faith; the human crisis today is worse than that: the human being no longer believes in love. This is quite grave. Evangelization, then, requires a sustained focus on the credibility of love. In particular it requires a focus on love as more than a game of power and control, disguised behind beautiful words. The gift of self, the free surrender in favor of those *who cannot repay* us, as the Lord tells us (Luke 14:14), is the path to the future of faith.

Obviously, an effort to evangelize in this social environment needs to recover the *saving power at work in the lives* of the poor. I will conclude this section by quoting Pope Francis again in *Evangelii gaudium*, 195:

> When Saint Paul approached the apostles in Jerusalem to discern whether he was "running or had run in vain" (Gal 2:2), the key criterion of authenticity which they presented was that he should not forget the poor (cf. Gal 2:10). This important principle, namely that the Pauline communities should not succumb to the self-centered lifestyle of the pagans, remains timely today, when a new self-centered paganism is growing. We may not always be able to reflect adequately the beauty of the Gospel,

but there is one sign which we should never lack: the option for those who are least, those whom society discards.

The End of History

Gaudium et spes, 39:

> Hence, while earthly progress must be carefully distinguished from the growth of Christ's kingdom, to the extent that the former can contribute to the better ordering of human society, it is of vital concern to the Kingdom of God. For after we have obeyed the Lord, and in His Spirit nurtured on earth the values of human dignity, brotherhood and freedom, and indeed all the good fruits of our nature and enterprise, we will find them again, but freed of stain, burnished and transfigured, when Christ hands over to the Father: "a kingdom eternal and universal, a kingdom of truth and life, of holiness and grace, of justice, love and peace." On this earth that Kingdom is already present in mystery. When the Lord returns it will be brought into full flower.

The kingdom which it is said to be *present in mystery* is the kingdom of grace, of the charity of Christ forging bonds of communion and self-gift within history. The parables of the Lord speaking of the end times, like the apocalyptic vision of Saint John, commit us to this vision of communion. Visions of the Holy Ones around the Lamb, images of the eternal banquet, of the wedding feast of the Son, and of the woman clothed with the sun, announce a transformation of the world from within. This eschatological vision remains on the periphery of the current conversation about evangelization. The human horizon reduced to the individual who believes he is self-sufficient to build his future, cannot do more than reduce the few thoughts he gives to eternity to a mere pittance. Even if the human being living in the epilogue thinks of eternity, it is imagined as a perpetual state where he can fulfill his personal desires and whims. An eternity conceived in this way becomes the perpetual boredom adumbrated by Sartre and other anxious existentialists of the twentieth century.

In this sense it is urgent for us to recover the sense of evangelization as a mission of the Spirit and of the Church intimately united with the end of time. I use the phrase *end of time* in two senses: the time that will come to an end, a terminus, and *the end* in the sense of its intentional purpose or finality. God moves history to an end, that end of charity and communion announced in the Gospel itself. Evangelization prepares this end precisely by unleashing the force of the Gospel within history. The charitable work of a people evangelized is the effective sign in time that already participates and thus announces what God has planned for creation transformed.

The teaching of the Church after the Council has moved to express itself more clearly about evangelization as a force and event in history, and about its relation to the scriptural eschatological vision. Specifically, this clarification manifests itself in the recent development of the social doctrine of the Church. I could cite several examples in the teaching of Saint Paul VI, Saint John Paul II, Benedict XVI, and Pope Francis. Each speaks of the relationship between evangelization, social doctrine and the eschatological vision in terms beyond what *Gaudium et spes* says. As an invitation for you to look further into teachings of this line, I will only cite a few examples. One aspect of this advance in the Church's social doctrine is the way Pope Benedict XVI speaks *the political path of charity*. The evangelical mission of the Church, the mission of charitable service in the world, and the final goal of history are tightly linked here:

> When animated by charity, commitment to the common good has greater worth than a merely secular and political stand would have. Like all commitment to justice, it has a place within the testimony of divine charity that paves the way for eternity through temporal action. Man's earthly activity, when inspired and sustained by charity, contributes to the building of the universal city of God, which is the goal of the history of the human family.... Underdevelopment has an even more important cause than lack of deep thought: it is "the lack of brotherhood among individuals and peoples." Will it ever be possible to obtain this brotherhood by human effort alone? As society becomes ever more globalized, it makes us neighbors but does not make us brothers. Reason, by itself, is capable of grasping the equality between men and of giving stability to their civic coexistence, but it cannot establish fraternity. This originates in a transcendent vocation from God the Father, who loved us first, teaching us through the Son what fraternal charity is.[6]

These texts, and many others in *Caritas in veritate*, advance Saint Paul VI's teaching on *the strength necessary for the commitment to human solidarity*. The issue of the necessity of grace touches the issue of societal relations precisely here. Yes, there exist aspirations and impulses in the lives of human beings and society that encourage us toward solidarity and hope. These human efforts aimed at inculcating relationships and conditions favoring common association and fraternity beyond family ties

---

6. Benedict XVI, *Caritas in veritate*, 7, 19.

have always existed in the cultures and histories of the world. Nevertheless, Benedict XVI's teaching notes that the human aspiration seeking to establish fraternity is weak and fragile without that charity which is manifested in the concrete application of gratuity, mercy and the spirit of communion. In addition, the Pope continues, without fraternal ties based on charity, not even justice can be achieved.

Paragraph 38 of *Caritas in veritate*, in fact, resonates with extraordinary force when he says the following: "Solidarity is first and foremost a sense of responsibility on the part of everyone with regard to everyone, and it cannot therefore be merely delegated to the State. While in the past it was possible to argue that justice had to come first and gratuitousness could follow afterwards, as a complement, today it is clear that without gratuitousness, there can be no justice in the first place." Even in a social context where the Church is perceived as a minority, the charitable work of the community is still enormously important for the evangelizing mission. Charity has the smell of Christ and can gradually infiltrate the social dynamics of the world. Communities and peoples counting themselves as unbelievers cannot fail to be influenced by this grace. Of course, in particular times and places this work inspires rejection and even persecution; but still, we see that it can inspire cooperation and great common efforts in favor of the poor and suffering. This reality is an essential part of the mission, since in a latent and mysterious way it tends to the final triumph of the Lamb who was slain and of his charity.

And here, Pope Francis, in *Evangelii gaudium*, 279, writes:

> It may be that the Lord uses our sacrifices to shower blessings in another part of the world which we will never visit. The Holy Spirit works as he wills, when he wills and where he wills; we entrust ourselves without pretending to see striking results. We know only that our commitment is necessary. Let us learn to rest in the tenderness of the arms of the Father amid our creative and generous commitment. Let us keep marching forward; let us give him everything, allowing him to make our efforts bear fruit in his good time.

In the end, while we work to share the grace and charity of the Gospel, and while promoting justice sustained by charity, we must maintain the ecclesial vision of the end, of a world transformed by charity, the gratuitous gift of self. This is the very same grace poured out upon believers through the Passion of Christ and the Holy Spirit infused in our hearts: May he *make our efforts bear fruit in his good time.*

Epilogue

I appreciate being invited to share these thoughts with you; it has been a great grace for me. Before finishing, I would like to give the last word to the Saint Oscar Romero. The martyr is the premier eschatological sign. The martyred archbishop gave his life for Christ. His life, his preaching and his martyrdom are a response of love to Christ, and at the same time a response given with love to the disquiets and tragedies lived in our time. His life and teaching testify to the intimate relationship between the Lord's life and gift, the Mass, the poor, the social doctrine of the Church, and the eschatological vision of the Gospel itself. I ask the Saint for his intercession frequently, asking him to help me, the bishops of the country, and of the whole world to give a faithful witness. I will cite two texts taken from his liturgical sermons. The first is taken from his sermon at the funeral Mass of Father Rutilio Grande, SJ, celebrated in the Cathedral of San Salvador (March 14, 1977). Father Rutilio was killed shortly after the arrival of Monsignor Romero to the archdiocese.

> The social doctrine of the Church [that] tells men that the Christian religion is not a solely horizontal, spiritualist sense, forgetting the misery that surrounds it. It is a gaze at God, and from God a gaze at the neighbor as a brother and to sense that "everything you did to one of these you did to me." A social doctrine that hopefully the movements sensitized on the social issue would know about. They would not expose themselves to failures, or to myopia, to a myopia that does not see more than temporal things, the structures of time. And as long as there is no living of a conversion in the heart, a doctrine that is illuminated by the faith to organize life according to the heart of God, everything will be flimsy, revolutionary, passing, violent.[7]

And then, a month later, on the II Easter Sunday 1977, of the sermon preached in the parish of the Resurrection, in the village of Miramonte:

> [We seek] to make pilgrimage (with the Lord) so that this Paschal Feast that is celebrated every year in the parish might be an invitation to work to make this world more human, more Christian; but to know that there is no paradise here on earth, not to be seduced by the redeemers who offer paradises on earth—they do not exist—but rather [to seek what] is beyond, with a very firm hope in the heart: to work the present, knowing

---

7. Romero, "Meditation of Love."

that the reward of that Easter will be in the measure in which we have here also made the earth, the family, the earthly, happier.

Saint Oscar Romero,

Pray for us.

Amen.[8]

Bibliography

Benedict XVI, Pope. *Caritas in veritate*. http://www.vatican.va/content/benedict-xvi/en/encyclicals/documents/hf_ben-xvi_enc_20090629_caritas-in-veritate.html.
———. *Deus caritas est*. http://www.vatican.va/content/benedict-xvi/en/encyclicals/documents/hf_ben-xvi_enc_20051225_deus-caritas-est.html.
———. *Sacramentum caritatis*. http://www.vatican.va/content/benedict-xvi/en/apost_exhortations/documents/hf_ben-xvi_exh_20070222_sacramentum-caritatis.html.
Francis, Pope. *Evangelii gaudium*. http://www.vatican.va/content/francesco/en/apost_exhortations/documents/papa-francesco_esortazione-ap_20131124_evangelii-gaudium.html.
———. *Lumen fidei*. http://www.vatican.va/content/francesco/en/encyclicals/documents/papa-francesco_20130629_enciclica-lumen-fidei.html.
Newman, John Henry. *Parochial and Plain Sermons*. San Francisco: Ignatius, 1997.
Paul VI, Pope. *Evangelii nuntiandi*. http://www.vatican.va/content/paul-vi/en/apost_exhortations/documents/hf_p-vi_exh_19751208_evangelii-nuntiandi.html.
Romero, Óscar A. "The Easter Church." http://www.romerotrust.org.uk/sites/default/files/homilies/ART_Homilies_Vol1_4_EasterChurch.pdf.
———. "The Motivation of Love." http://www.romerotrust.org.uk/sites/default/files/homilies/ART_Homilies_Vol1_1_Motivation_Love.pdf.
Sicilia, Javier. *La confesión: El diario de Esteban Martorus*. Barcelona: Debolsillo, 2016. Kindle.
Steiner, George. *Real Presences*. Chicago: University of Chicago Press, 1989.
Thomas Aquinas. *Summa Theologiae*. https://www.corpusthomisticum.org/sth0000.html.
———. *Summa Theologica*. Translated by the Fathers of the English Dominican Province. 5 vols. Notre Dame: Ave Maria, 1981.
Vatican II. *Gaudium et spes*. http://www.vatican.va/archive/hist_councils/ii_vatican_council/documents/vat-ii_const_19651207_gaudium-et-spes_en.html.
Venard, Olivier-Thomas. *A Poetic Christ: Thomist Reflections on Scripture, Language, and Reality*. Translated by Kenneth Oakes and Francesca Aran Murphy. New York: T. & T. Clark, 2019.

8. Romero, "The Easter Church."

II. Urgent Evangelization

2

Enter through the Narrow Gate

THE FOLLOWING TEXT FROM Luke 13 was the theme of the *Enter Through the Narrow Gate: The Urgency of the New Evangelization in the Third Millennium* symposium but, surprisingly, it wasn't directly commented on until the final panel. This is a very important text and it has serious implications for evangelization.

> **Luke 13:22–30 (RSV)**
>
> [22] He went on his way through towns and villages, teaching, and journeying toward Jerusalem. [23] And someone said to him, "Lord, will those who are saved be few?" And he said to them, [24] "Strive to enter by the narrow door; for many, I tell you, will seek to enter and will not be able. [25] When once the householder has risen up and shut the door, you will begin to stand outside and to knock at the door, saying, 'Lord, open to us.' He will answer you, 'I do not know where you come from.' [26] Then you will begin to say, 'We ate and drank in your presence, and you taught in our streets.' [27] But he will say, 'I tell you, I do not know where you come from; depart from me, all you workers of iniquity!' [28] There you will weep and gnash your teeth, when you see Abraham and Isaac and Jacob and all the prophets in the kingdom of God and you yourselves thrust out. [29] And men will come from east and west, and from north and south, and sit at table in the kingdom of God. [30] And behold, some are last who will be first, and some are first who will be last."

While Jesus was talking to his own people and warning them that they could actually be excluded from the heavenly kingdom if they didn't enter into relationship with him, believing in him and obeying his word, this passage obviously has wider application which we will consider as we continue this study.

And, of course, it is not an isolated text. Many of Jesus's parables and direct teachings repeat the point. Matthew 7 does so in a particularly direct way.

Matt 7:13–29 (RSV)

[13] "Enter by the narrow gate; for the gate is wide and the way is easy, that leads to destruction, and those who enter by it are many. [14] For the gate is narrow and the way is hard, that leads to life, and those who find it are few. . . . [21] Not everyone who says to me, 'Lord, Lord,' shall enter the kingdom of heaven, but he who does the will of my Father who is in heaven."

Recently there has been an upsurge of publications aggressively advocating the doctrine of universalism—the belief that all or almost all will in the end be saved. David Bentley Hart's recent book is a prime example of this, where he asserts that if only one soul is lost, God is a "monster."[1] The "new universalism" goes beyond the already questionable "hope that all be saved" that Balthasar had made popular to a bold assertion that all must be saved or God is not good.[2] Michael McClymond[3] and many others have ably refuted this argument in various publications but in the minds and hearts of many of our fellow Catholics a universalistic worldview has taken hold, even among many who have never read a theological article about it. It is spreading as it were, almost by osmosis, propelled by the collapse of Christian culture and a radical secularism which is hostile to Christ and the Church, and, in particular, the absolute claims of Jesus to be *the* way. Uncertain trumpet sounds from within the Church are adding to the spread of what the main stream Christian tradition has always considered a condemned heresy. Partial readings of the documents of Vatican II and statements of famous theologians in their regard contribute to the confusion as well. And, of course, the corrosive effect of post-modernism and its ironically absolute claims that there is no absolute truth and no way of knowing it if there was, has deeply penetrated the culture. "That may be your truth but it's not mine."

---

1. Hart, *That All Shall Be Saved*, 191–92. Likewise, see multiple books by Ilaria Ramelli and Robin Parry that argue for universalism. See also its influence on popular Catholic spirituality, for example, in Rohr, *The Universal Christ*.

2. Although Balthasar comes close to the "new universalism" when he intimates that if even one soul ends up being lost God has lost his "gamble."

3. McClymond, "Opiate of the Theologians"; Gomes, "Shall All Be Saved?"; Martin, "Review."

As a result of this, if I were to describe how many of our fellow Catholics look at the world today, I would describe it like this: Broad and wide is the gate that leads to heaven and many are traveling that way; narrow is the gate and difficult the road that leads to hell and hardly anyone is going there. No need to strive; chill.

Where did this energetic and widespread sympathy for universalism come from? In Catholic theological circles Karl Rahner's theory of the "anonymous Christian," while certainly nuanced in his own articulation of the theory, led many to believe that most people were anonymous Christians even if they didn't explicitly believe, and were in fact saved. Hans Urs von Balthasar's book, *Dare We Hope "That All Men Be Saved"?*, has had a big impact and has been championed by major media figures like Bishop Robert Barron. Even though Balthasar affirms time and time again that he is not formally teaching universalism, he makes his sympathies very clear and people understandably get the impression from reading the book that probably all will be saved.

In his last major work, *Dare We Hope "That All Men Be Saved"?*, he very clearly states his conclusion on the issue of universal salvation by citing a text of Edith Stein which she never published, and which, he affirms, "expresses most exactly the position that I have tried to develop." [4]

Balthasar recounts how she speculates on how grace can secretly work in the souls of apparent unbelievers as "all-merciful love" descends to everyone:

> And now, can we assume that there are souls that remain perpetually closed to such love? As a possibility in principle, this cannot be rejected. *In reality*, it can become infinitely improbable—precisely through what preparatory grace is capable of effecting in the soul. . . . Human freedom can be neither broken nor neutralized by divine freedom, but it may well be, so to speak, outwitted. [5]

He also insists that we only meditate on the possibility of hell for ourselves and not think about it as a possibility for others, which, of course, undermines perhaps the major motivation of 2,000 years of Christian missionary efforts. Every papal missionary document up until the very eve of Vatican II spoke of the need to save souls from hell, the default situation of the human race, being lost. This was the explicit motivation of the greatest missionary saints such as Saint Francis Xavier and the many now nameless priests who packed their belongings in coffins as they went to disease

4. Balthasar, *Dare We Hope*, 218.

5. Stein, *Welt und Person*, 158, cited by Balthasar, *Dare We Hope*, 219–21.

infested regions of Africa, knowing they would die soon, but willing to sacrifice their very lives for the salvation of souls.

The Catholic theologian, John Sachs, in a lengthy article on universal salvation that appeared in *Theological Studies*, expresses what he claims is the current Catholic theological consensus about eschatology and gives credit for this to Rahner and Balthasar:

> We have seen that there is a clear consensus among Catholic theologians today in their treatment of the notion of apocatastasis and the problem of hell. . . . It may not be said that even one person is already or will in fact be damned. All that may and must be believed is that the salvation of the world is a reality already begun and established in Christ. Such a faith expresses itself most consistently in the hope that because of the gracious love of God whose power far surpasses human sin, all men and women will in fact freely and finally surrender to God in love and be saved.
>
> When Balthasar speaks of the duty to hope for the salvation of all, he is articulating the broad consensus of current theologians and the best of the Catholic tradition. Like other theologians, notably Rahner, he intentionally pushes his position to the limit, insisting that such a hope is not merely possible but well founded. . . . I have tried to show that the presumption that human freedom entails a capacity to reject God definitively and eternally seems questionable. And, although this presumption enjoys the weight of the authority of Scripture and tradition, it would seem incorrect to consider this possibility as an object of faith in the same sense that the ability of human freedom in grace to choose God is an object of faith.[6]

While this view may not actually be the consensus of Catholic theologians it is indisputably hugely influential. So much so that as the Church turned towards a reemphasis on the need for the Church to evangelize, it has had to counter the presumption of universal salvation in virtually every document it has published on the subject.

In every major post-conciliar document on evangelization[7] explicit reference is made, by popes and the Congregation for the Doctrine of the

6. Sachs, "Current Eschatology," 252–53.

7. Just as over a period of decades a body of teaching that came to be known as the Church's "social teaching" developed, so too we are seeing a body of teaching develop concerning the Church's teaching on evangelization. Pope Francis's *Evangelii gaudium* is a significant contribution to this literature although it focuses more on attitudinal and spiritual obstacles to evangelization rather than doctrinal. There also seems to be a shift

Faith (CDF), to the doctrinal confusion that is undermining evangelization. Whether it be Paul VI's 1975 *Evangelii nuntiandi* or John Paul II's
1990 *Redemptoris missio*, or the CDF's 2000 *Dominus Iesus* or the CDF's
2007 *Doctrinal Note on Some Aspects of Evangelization*, each attempt by
the magisterium to resolve the confusion seems to be met with failure.
So much so that we read once again in the 2007 *Doctrinal Note* about this
"growing confusion":

> There is today, however, a growing confusion which leads many
> to leave the missionary command of the Lord unheard and inef-
> fective (cf. Mt 28:19). . . . It is enough, so they say, to help people
> to become more human or more faithful to their own religion;
> it is enough to build communities which strive for justice, free-
> dom, peace and solidarity. Furthermore, some maintain that
> Christ should not be proclaimed to those who do not know him,
> nor should joining the Church be promoted, since it would also
> be possible to be saved without explicit knowledge of Christ and
> without formal incorporation in the Church.[8]

While the *Doctrinal Note* addresses in a thorough manner the question of whether preaching the Gospel is an imposition on people's freedom,
it doesn't thoroughly address the doctrinal confusion lurking around the
truth of it being possible for people to be saved without hearing the Gospel
and the common temptation to presume such people are saved, as stated in
the above citation. It was my concern to address this recurring issue that led
to my book *Will Many Be Saved? What Vatican II Actually Teaches and Its
Implications for the New Evangelization.*[9]

Perhaps the best use of this short chapter would be to summarize the
argument of the book which, as far as I know, is the most in-depth treatment of this conciliar teaching and which is frequently cited in studies

in Pope Francis's concerns from an early concern with encouraging evangelization to a
later concern in warning against proselytism which has not yet been clearly defined, as
of this writing, by him, but has been understood by some to include an encouragement
to silent witness and not explicit proclamation or efforts to bring people to conversion.

8. Congregation for the Doctrine of Faith, *Doctrinal Note*, 3.

9. Martin, *Will Many Be Saved?* See also Martin, *Mission of the Redeemer*; Martin,
Urgency of the New Evangelization; Martin, "Ad Gentes," in Lamb and Levering, *Recep-
tion of Vatican II*, 266–91; Martin, "The Pastoral Strategy of Vatican II: Time for an Adjustment?" in D'Costa and Harris, *The Second Vatican Council*, 137–63. And see articles
on related topics: Martin, "Will Many Be Saved? What Vatican II Actually Teaches and
Its Implications for the New Evangelization: A Response to Some Criticism," in Shaw,
Eschatology, 175–215; Martin, "The Pastoral Strategy of Vatican II"; Martin, "Doctrinal
Clarity for the New Evangelization." I am drawing from these previously published
works for the current article.

related to this question. It provides the doctrinal and magisterial under-
pinning for our interpretation of texts such as "enter by the narrow gate."
This teaching of course concerns the Church's mission *ad gentes* ("to the
nations"). We will also consider in much briefer form the application of
the teaching to baptized Catholics.

As is clear from my book's title, my main concern is to focus attention
on a text from Vatican II that sums up in succinct form, both in the text itself
and in its important footnotes, what the Catholic Church actually teaches
about the possibility of people being saved without hearing the Gospel and
the significant limitations on these conditions.

That's why in my book, while clearly affirming the teaching of the
Catholic Church based on Romans 1 and Romans 2, and subsequent doctrinal clarifications, that it is indeed possible under certain conditions for
people to be saved without hearing the Gospel, I primarily focused on how
the Council teaches that "very often" (the Latin is *at saepius;* the translation
I'm using is Flannery's) these conditions aren't in fact met, and, for the sake
of people in this situation and their salvation, the Gospel urgently needs to be
preached, not just to "enrich" their lives or "give meaning to their lives," but
to save their lives (see *Lumen gentium*, 16). Of course, my book unreservedly
affirms the clear teaching of the Church that since God wills the salvation of
the whole human race, each person is given the possibility of being saved in
ways known only to God (see *Ad gentes*, 7; *Gaudium et spes*, 22).

Here are the sentences of *Lumen gentium* 16 in question—first of all
those sentences that affirm the possibility of being saved without hearing
the Gospel:

> Those who, through no fault of their own, do not know the
> Gospel of Christ or his Church, but who nevertheless seek God
> with a sincere heart, and moved by grace, try in their actions
> to do his will as they know it through the dictates of their con-
> science[10]—those too may achieve eternal salvation. Nor shall
> divine providence deny the assistance necessary for salvation
> to those who, without any fault of theirs, have not yet arrived
> at an explicit knowledge of God, and who, not without grace,
> strive to lead a good life. Whatever good or truth is found
> amongst them is considered by the Church to be a preparation

---

10. The following footnote is inserted here as part of the Council text: Cfr. Epist.
S.S.C.S. Officii ad Archiep. Boston.: Denz. 3869–72. The reference to the *Letter of the
Holy Office to the Archbishop of Boston*, which offers doctrinal clarifications on the is-
sues raised by Fr. Leonard Feeney in his strict interpretation of *Extra Ecclesiam Nulla
Sallus*, provides important insight to the proper understanding of the text as we will see.

for the Gospel[11] and given by him who enlightens all men that they may at length have life.

It is important to pay attention to the conditions under which it is possible for someone to be saved without hearing the Gospel: an inculpable ignorance of the Gospel, a sincere seeking of God, and a response to grace that enables one to live in accordance with the dictates of conscience. It is also important to pay attention to the very important footnote that references the response of the Holy Office to the Fr. Feeney case. This doctrinally important letter makes clear that, indeed, even an unconscious desire for God and His Church may be salvific, but not just any kind of unconscious desire. The letter makes clear that it is not enough just to simply "believe in God," and "be a good person" in order to be saved, but there must be a personal response to the light of revelation which involves a surrender in faith to the person revealing—a supernatural faith—and a change of life that is enabled by an infusion of supernatural charity.

And here are the final three sentences which speak about the obstacles to the possibility of salvation being realized without hearing the Gospel:

> But very often (*at saepius*),[12] deceived by the Evil One, men have become vain in their reasonings, have exchanged the truth of

11. The following footnote is inserted here by the Council Fathers as backing for this text: "See Eusebius of Caesarea, *Praeparatio Evangelica*, I, 1: PG 21, 28 AB." Joseph Ratzinger, "La Mission d'Après Les Autres Textes Conciliaires," in Dewailly et al., *Vatican II*, 129n11, indicates that this reference to Eusebius does not really support the point being made, but, of course, the point can be supported in other ways. "The reason for this allusion is not very clear, since in this work Eusebius, in treating of the non-Christian religions, has another emphasis than our text: Eusebius underlines the aberrations of the pagan myths and the insufficiency of Greek philosophy; he shows that Christians are right in neglecting these in order to turn to the sacred writings of the Hebrews which constitute the true 'preparation for the gospel.' (La raison de cette allusion n'est pas très claire, car dans cet ourvrage l'orientation d'Eusèbe, par rapport aux religions non chrétiennes, est tout autre que dans notre texte: Eusèbe signale les égarements des mythes païens et l'insuffisane de la philosophie grecque; il montre que les chrétiens voint juste en les négligeant pour se tourner vers les liveres saints des Hébreux qui constituent las véritable 'préparation évangélique.) The Sources Chrétiennes translation of this text, *La Préparation Évangélique: Livre I*, 97–105, shows that Euesbius, in the chapter cited, only mentions the non-Christian religions and philosophies as being in dire need of conversion. He speaks of them as representing a piety that is "lying and aberrant," (*mensongère et aberrante)* and cites the Scripture that speaks of "exterminating all the gods of the nations" and making them "prostrate before Him."

12. The Walter Abbott translation that appeared in 1966 translates the Latin phrase as "But rather often." The commonly used Flannery translation of the Council documents translates the Latin *at saepius* as "very often." This is the translation we are using. Other English translations use "but often," (the translation of the National Catholic Welfare Conference, the precursor of the National Council of Catholic

God for a lie and served the world rather than the Creator (cf. Rom. 1:21, 25). Or else, living and dying in this world without God, they are exposed to ultimate despair. Hence to procure the glory of God and the salvation of all these, the Church, mindful of the Lord's command, "preach the Gospel to every creature" (Mk. 16:16) takes zealous care to foster the missions.

Because sustained attention hasn't been paid recently to the doctrinal truths that the last three sentences of *Lumen gentium* 16 reaffirm, many Catholics—and many Protestants as well, including a growing number of Evangelicals[13] (and this includes many theologians and pastoral leader)—as we have pointed out, have made a hugely unwarranted leap from "possibility" to "probability" to a "practical universalism" that presumes that virtually everybody will be saved, except perhaps some exceptionally evil historical figures. What are these doctrinal truths that *Lumen gentium* 16 reaffirms? The conciliar text reaffirms the foundational doctrinal truths that affirm that we don't live in a neutral environment and that the spiritual realities referred to in the Scriptures as the world, the flesh, and the devil present great obstacles to fulfilling the conditions under which it is possible to be saved without the Gospel. Everyone is subject to the weakness of mind and will as a result of original sin, made worse by actual sin; everyone is vulnerable to the "world"—the international pagan culture that aggressively is attacking respect for God and his Word and that dominates the media and universities; and everyone without the protection of the "spiritual armor" is subject to the deceptions of the evil one who sends forth his "fiery darts" multiple times a day.

Because these sober texts have been virtually ignored—even by well-known theologians who deal with this issue—a presumption in favor of almost universal salvation has permeated the culture, even that of the Church. Cardinal Dulles explicitly recognizes, in somewhat shocking words, Balthasar's influence in communicating a universalist mentality:

Bishops, contained in Trouvé, *The Sixteen Documents of Vatican II*). The Vatican website translation also uses "but often." The English translation (by Clarence Gallagher) of *Lumen gentium* in Norman Tanner's two volume collection of the *Decrees of the Ecumenical Councils* uses "more often, however." The French translation of the text that Congar collaborated on translates *at saepius* as "mais trop souvent" (*L'Église de Vatican II, Tome I*). The Vatican website French translation uses "bien souvent." The Italian translation on the Vatican website is "ma molto spesso." The Spanish translation on the Vatican website is "pero con mucha frecuencia."

13. Rob Bell's *Love Wins* is perhaps the best known of the popular evangelical books adopting stances similar to Balthasar's regarding the possibility of eternal separation from God.

Hans Urs von Balthasar popularized the idea that we may hope that no one ever goes to hell. Rightly or wrongly, he is often interpreted as though he believed that in the end all men and women attain to the joys of heaven. Priests and theologians frequently give the impression that the doctrine of hell is a medieval superstition rather than an essential component of the gospel. In so doing, they may well be doing Satan's work because the fear of hell occupied a central place in the preaching of Jesus.[14]

The claim of my book is that while Balthasar's hope for universal salvation is perhaps logically possible, given the weight of Scripture and Tradition, it is so only in the sense that it is logically possible that a major league baseball team would win every one of its games in any season. It has never happened and to use his language, it is "infinitely improbable" that it ever will. Is a theological speculation that is contrary, as Fr. Sachs puts it, to the weight of Scripture and Tradition really well founded? And if it isn't well founded, as I will argue, how pastorally wise is it to teach such a thing?

Cardinal Dulles summarizes the clear consensus of the dogmatic tradition:

> The constant teaching of the Catholic Church supports the idea that there are two classes: the saved and the damned. Three General councils of the Church (Lyons I, 1245; Lyons II, 1274; and Florence, 1439) and Pope Benedict XII's bull *Benedictus Deus* (1336) have taught that everyone who dies in a state of mortal sin goes immediately to suffer the eternal punishments of hell. This belief has perdured without question in the Catholic Church to this day, and is repeated almost verbatim in the *Catechism of the Catholic Church* (CCC 1022, 1035).[15]

The Council of Trent, in teaching carried forward and affirmed by Pope John Paul II in *Veritatis Splendor*, affirms the reality of eternal punishment for unrepented mortal sins:

> It must be asserted, against the subtle modes of thinking of certain people, who *by fair and flattering words deceive the hearts of the simple-minded* (Rom 16:18), that the grace of justification once received is lost not only by apostasy, by which faith itself is lost, but also by any other mortal sin, though faith is not lost. Thus is defended the teaching of the divine law which excludes from God's kingdom not only unbelievers, but also the faithful

14. Dulles, "Current Theological Obstacles to Evangelization," in Boguslawski and Martin, *New Evangelization*, 19–20.

15. Dulles, "The Population of Hell," 37.

if they are guilty of fornication, adultery, wantonness, sodomy, theft, avarice, drunkenness, slander, plundering, and all others who commit mortal sins from which, with the help of divine grace, they can refrain, and because of which they are severed from the grace of Christ (1 Cor 6:9-10; 1 Tim 1:9-10).[16]

This section of the Council's teaching on justification ends with the warning that "unless each one faithfully and firmly accepts it, he cannot be justified."[17]

Jesus, John, Matthew, Luke, Mark, James, Peter and Paul, in the multiple texts that talk of the final judgment of the human race, are unmistakably declaring that if people persist in unbelief and immorality to the end, they will be eternally lost. To suppose that when they taught God's universal will of salvation they thought they were teaching something that wasn't in harmony with the specific criteria for the final judgment or were unaware that they were, lacks all credibility. There is nothing in the Scriptures to indicate that there are second chances after death, but rather, just the opposite.[18] Life is emptied of its meaning if our choices do not end up really mattering for our eternal destinies. As the International Theological Document on eschatology puts it:

In revealing the Father's secrets to us, Jesus wants to make us his friends (cf. Jn 15:15). But friendship cannot be forced on us. Friendship with God, like adoption, is an offer, to be freely accepted or rejected. . . . This consummated and freely accepted friendship implies a concrete possibility of rejection. What is freely accepted can be freely rejected. [No one who] thus chooses rejection "has any inheritance in the kingdom of Christ and of God" (Eph 5:5). Eternal damnation has its origin in the free rejection to the very end of God's Love and Mercy. The Church believes that this state consists of deprivation of the sight of God and that the whole "being" of the sinner suffers the repercussion of this loss eternally. . . . This doctrine of faith shows equally the

16. Decrees of the Council of Trent, Session 6, "Decree on Justification," Chapter 15, in Tanner, *Decrees*, 677.

17. Decrees of the Council of Trent, Session 6, "Decree on Justification," Chapter 16, in Tanner, *Decrees*, 678.

18. International Theological Commission (ITC), "Some Current Questions in Eschatology," in Sharkey and Weinandy, *International Theological Commission*, 85–91. The widespread belief in "second chances," in the form of various theories of reincarnation, caused the ITC to devote substantial attention to this issue in their document on eschatology.

importance of the human capacity of freely rejecting God, and the gravity of such a freely willed rejection.[19]

While we cannot judge the state of anyone's soul and what transpires at the moment of death, it certainly appears—from the view of human resistance to grace, and subsequent judgment, contained in the Scriptures and from empirical observation—that many people persevere to the end in their rejection of God and/or in a life of immorality. Balthasar acknowledges as much, but then posits the possible chance(s) after death, for which there is no basis in the Scriptures or the Magisterium. He claims that those who take the traditional interpretation of these texts on judgment—following Augustine (but also Aquinas and the entire theological/magisterial mainstream!), that there will be a definitive separation of the human race based on how people have responded to the grace of God—have "transformed," and indeed "vitiated," the Scriptures which, he claims, only warn of a possibility and do not teach that there will indeed be a division of the human race into the saved and damned. Such an interpretation seems strained.

Cardinal Dulles summarizes the meaning of the "two destination" New Testament passages like this:

> As we know from the Gospels, Jesus spoke many times about hell. Throughout his teaching, he holds forth two and only two final possibilities for human existence: the one being everlasting happiness in the presence of God, the other everlasting torment in the absence of God. He describes the fate of the damned under a great variety of metaphors: everlasting fire, outer darkness, tormenting thirst, a gnawing worm, and weeping and gnashing of teeth. . . . Taken in their obvious meaning, passages such as these give the impression that there is a hell, and that many go there; more in fact, than are saved.[20]

Even if one does not want to claim that these passages indisputably reveal that there are people in hell, or that there are more in hell than in heaven, despite the strength of this opinion in the theological tradition's understanding, one would at least have to say that from the weight of the Scriptures and the historical testimony of final rejection of God or embrace of immorality, both in the Scriptures and contemporary history and experience, that it is not just a theoretical possibility but very probable that many end up in hell.[21] Fr. Kevin Flannery, SJ, former Dean of the Philosophy

19. International Theological Commission (ITC), "Some Current Questions in Eschatology," 89.

20. Dulles, "The Population of Hell," 36.

21. When the ITC, in their document, "Some Current Questions in Eschatology,"

Faculty at the Gregorian, and current professor, acknowledges that a case can be made that the Scriptures do not imply with the force of logical necessity that there are people in hell. He argues, though, that the overwhelming weight of Scripture and Tradition "approach logical necessity."[22] As Fr. James O'Connor puts it, these passages and how they have been interpreted by the theological tradition and the Magisterium lead us to *presume* that there will be many in hell, a presumption that the Holy Spirit who inspired the Scriptures intends us to have, a presumption imparted to us by a God who is utterly truthful and cannot deceive:

> In the light of what it has been given us to know, we must presume that (in numbers completely unknown to us) humans will be included in "the eternal fire prepared for the devil and his angels" (Matt. 25:41), and that we ourselves could be among that number. It is such a presumption that the words of Jesus and the teaching of the Church would appear to have as their own, and better guides in this matter we cannot have. Against such a presumption one cannot have what is properly defined as theological hope, but we can and must have a human hope, a wish which expresses itself in prayer and zealous efforts, for the salvation of all.[23]

This "presumption" which is given to us in Scripture and Tradition, by a God who is utterly truthful and will not deceive, is the opposite of the prevailing "presumption" that everybody or almost everybody will be saved, and that finite human freedom is unable to finally resist the grace of God. The current "theological consensus," as Sachs has stated it, that he attributes to the huge influence of Rahner and Balthasar, is precisely the reverse of what has been revealed to us as it has been understood by the Church throughout the ages. With this as our doctrinal and magisterial

---

90–91, attempts to assess the efficacy of the universal offer of salvation, it cautiously says that it has "ample efficacy." It then warns: "But, since hell is a genuine possibility for every person, it is not right—although today this is something which is forgotten in the preaching at exequies—to treat salvation as a kind of quasi-automatic consequence. . . . The Christian ought to be aware of the brevity of life since he knows we have one life only. As we 'all sin . . . in many ways' (Jas 3:2) and since there often was sin in our past lives, we must 'use the present opportunity to the full' (Eph 5:16) and throwing off every encumbrance and the sin that all too readily restricts us, run with resolution the race that lies ahead of us, our eyes fixed on Jesus, the pioneer and perfector of faith' (Heb 12:1–2). 'We have not here a lasting city, but seek one that is to come' (Heb 13:14). The Christian then as an alien and a pilgrim (cf. 1 Pet 2:11) hurries in holiness of life to his own country (cf. Heb 11:14), where he will be with the Lord (cf. 1 Thess 4:17)."

22. Flannery, "How to Think about Hell," 477.

23. O'Connor, "Von Balthasar and Salvation," 20.

foundation, let's return now to our consideration of the theme of this symposium, the Luke 13 text:

Luke 13:22–30 (RSV)

22 He went on his way through towns and villages, teaching, and journeying toward Jerusalem. 23 And someone said to him, "Lord, will those who are saved be few?" And he said to them, 24"Strive to enter by the narrow door; for many, I tell you, will seek to enter and will not be able. 25 When once the householder has risen up and shut the door, you will begin to stand outside and to knock at the door, saying, 'Lord, open to us.' He will answer you, 'I do not know where you come from.' 26 Then you will begin to say, 'We ate and drank in your presence, and you taught in our streets.' 27 But he will say, 'I tell you, I do not know where you come from; depart from me, all you workers of iniquity!' 28 There you will weep and gnash your teeth, when you see Abraham and Isaac and Jacob and all the prophets in the kingdom of God and you yourselves thrust out. 29 And men will come from east and west, and from north and south, and sit at table in the kingdom of God. 30 And behold, some are last who will be first, and some are first who will be last."

It is clear that people were shocked by Jesus's words and thought they were on friendly terms with him and of course should be admitted to his house. Jesus makes clear, though, that familiarity with his teaching, attendance at his healing sessions, or even eating and drinking with him do not constitute the relationship with him that will admit people to his house. It's clear that faith, repentance and obedience are necessary, and actually becoming part of Jesus's family before the door closes, is essential. Just knowing about Jesus and being positively disposed to him is not enough. It is necessary to enter into relationship with him, obey his teachings and persevere to the end. It is necessary to "strive" (the underlying Greek word is where we get the English word "agonize") to enter the kingdom of God as the kingdom suffers "violence" and the violent enter it. The violence of conversion, of repentance, of taking up our cross and following Jesus, the violence of crucifying the flesh, of being crucified to the world, falling into the ground and dying, losing our life in abandonment to Jesus so as to truly find it for all eternity in the Father's house. And then, the text from Matthew which also speaks of entering by the narrow gate:

Matt 7:13–29 (RSV)

13 "Enter by the narrow gate; for the gate is wide and the way is easy, that leads to destruction, and those who enter by it are

many. [14] For the gate is narrow and the way is hard, that leads to life, and those who find it are few. [15] Beware of false prophets, who come to you in sheep's clothing but inwardly are ravenous wolves. [16] You will know them by their fruits. Are grapes gathered from thorns, or figs from thistles? [17] So, every sound tree bears good fruit, but the bad tree bears evil fruit. [18] A sound tree cannot bear evil fruit, nor can a bad tree bear good fruit. [19] Every tree that does not bear good fruit is cut down and thrown into the fire. [20] Thus you will know them by their fruits. [21] Not every one who says to me, 'Lord, Lord,' shall enter the kingdom of heaven, but he who does the will of my Father who is in heaven. [22] On that day many will say to me, 'Lord, Lord, did we not prophesy in your name, and cast out demons in your name, and do many mighty works in your name?' [23] And then will I declare to them, 'I never knew you; depart from me, you evildoers.' [24] Every one then who hears these words of mine and does them will be like a wise man who built his house upon the rock; [25] and the rain fell, and the floods came, and the winds blew and beat upon that house, but it did not fall, because it had been founded on the rock. [26] And every one who hears these words of mine and does not do them will be like a foolish man who built his house upon the sand; [27] and the rain fell, and the floods came, and the winds blew and beat against that house, and it fell; and great was the fall of it." [28] And when Jesus finished these sayings, the crowds were astonished at his teaching, [29] for he taught them as one who had authority, and not as their scribes.

The world and Church are full of false prophets who tell us that virtually everyone will be saved or even more boldly, that everyone will be saved. Denial of the truths connected to Jesus's urgent warnings to enter by the narrow gate or door, in my opinion, has contributed mightily to the accelerating institutional collapse of the Church that we are now experiencing in the developed countries. The whole witness of the Scriptures is to the two ways, one of which leads home to the Father's house and one of which leads to the "outer darkness" where there is "weeping and gnashing of teeth." Jesus's clear and urgent warnings are spoken out of love, wanting us all to be in the Father's house and part of his body, before the door closes. The truth of the narrow door is not only relevant for the urgency to preach the gospel to those who haven't heard it, but also a truth that's relevant for the baptized who aren't living as disciples of Christ, the primary "target audience" of the New Evangelization.

Although it is very important to understand the actual situation of non-Christians in regard to salvation and the necessity of preaching the

Gospel, it is also important to understand what the Council (and the Scriptures!) teach about the salvation of baptized Catholics. Based on some of the same and similar scriptural passages we have been considering, the Church teaches that it is not enough just to be baptized or even go to church on Sundays, but that unless we actually obey the teachings of Jesus in thought, word and deed, not only will we not be saved but we will be the more severely judged. *Lumen gentium* 14 makes this stunningly clear:

> Even though incorporated into the Church, one who does not however persevere in charity is not saved. He remains indeed in the bosom of the Church, but "in body" not "in heart." All children of the Church should nevertheless remember that their exalted condition results, not from their own merits, but from the grace of Christ. If they fail to respond in thought, word and deed to that grace, not only shall they not be saved, but they shall be the more severely judged.

This text is repeated by Saint John Paul II at the end of chapter 1 of *Redemptoris missio*.

Just like the Jews boasting about having the Temple in their midst was not enough to save them from severe judgment, nor the Jews in Jesus's time claiming to be children of Abraham was enough to save them from condemnation, just claiming we are Catholic is not enough to save any of us from severe judgement. In fact, in Jesus's time, those who were most proud of being "children of Abraham" were so deeply deceived in their prideful presumption that they were blind to the fact that they were, in fact, children of the devil (John 8:44)! God forbid this would be the case with us because of a diabolical presumption or false ethnic pride. May we all take to heart the solemn warnings that Jesus gives us in Luke 13 and in Matt 7, and in multiple other texts, and strive to humble ourselves, and help others, to enter through the narrow gate and return to paradise, and find ourselves in the Father's house. The gate of course is Jesus.

Bibliography

Balthasar, Hans Urs von. *Dare We Hope "That All Men Be Saved"? With a Short Discourse on Hell.* Translated by David Kipp and Lothar Krauth. San Francisco: Ignatius, 1988.

Baraúna, Guilherme, and Yves Congar, eds. *L'Église de Vatican II, Tome I, Texte Latin et Traduction.* Translated by P. Th. Camelot. Paris: Cerf, 1966.

Bell, Rob. *Love Wins: A Book about Heaven, Hell, and the Fate of Every Person Who Ever Lived.* San Francisco: Harper, 2011.

Boguslawski, Steven, and Ralph Martin, eds. *The New Evangelization: Overcoming the Obstacles*. New York: Paulist, 2008.

Congregation for the Doctrine of Faith. *Doctrinal Note on Some Aspects of Evangelization*. https://www.vatican.va/roman_curia/congregations/cfaith/documents/rc_con_cfaith_doc_20071203_nota-evangelizzazione_en.html.

D'Costa, Gavin, and Emma Jane Harris, eds. *The Second Vatican Council: Celebrating Its Achievements and the Future*. London: Bloomsbury T. & T. Clark, 2013.

Dewailly, Louis Marie, et al., eds. *Vatican II: L'Activité Missionnaire de l'Église*. Paris: Cerf, 1967.

Dulles, Avery. "The Population of Hell." *First Things* 133 (2003) 36–41.

Eusebius of Caesarea. *La Préparation Évangélique: Livre I*. Translated by Jean Sirinelli and Édouard des Places. Paris: Cerf, 1974.

Flannery, Austin, ed. *Vatican Council II: The Conciliar and Post Conciliar Documents*. *New Revised Edition, Vol. I*. Northport, NY: Costello, 1996.

Flannery, Kevin. "How to Think about Hell." *New Blackfriars* 72.854 (1991) 469–81.

Gomes, Alan W. "Shall All Be Saved? A Review of David Bentley Hart's Case for Universal Salvation." *Credo*, December 2, 2019. https://credomag.com/article/shall-all-be-saved/.

Hart, David Bentley. *That All Shall Be Saved: Heaven, Hell, and Universal Salvation*. New Haven: Yale University Press, 2019.

International Theological Commission. "Some Current Questions in Eschatology." http://www.vatican.va/roman_curia/congregations/cfaith/cti_documents/rc_cti_1990_problemi-attuali-escatologia_en.html.

Lamb, Matthew L., and Matthew Levering, eds. *The Reception of Vatican II*. New York: Oxford University Press, 2017.

Martin, Ralph. "Doctrinal Clarity for the New Evangelization: The Importance of Lumen Gentium 16." *Fellowship of Catholic Scholars Quarterly* (2011) 9–17.

———. *The Mission of the Redeemer: A Commentary by Ralph Martin*. Boston: Pauline Books and Media, 2015.

———. "The Pastoral Strategy of Vatican II: Time for an Adjustment?" *Josephinum Journal of Theology* 19.1 (2012) 70–90.

———. "Review: The Devil's Redemption." *Homiletic and Pastoral Review* (2019). https://www.hprweb.com/2019/11/review-the-devils-redemption/.

———. *Will Many Be Saved? What Vatican II Actually Teaches and Its Implications for the New Evangelization*. Grand Rapids: Eerdmans, 2012.

———. *The Urgency of the New Evangelization: Answering the Call*. Huntington, AL: Our Sunday Visitor, 2013.

McClymond, Michael. "Opiate of the Theologians." *First Things*, December, 2019. https://www.firstthings.com/article/2019/12/opiate-of-the-theologians.

O'Connnor, James. "Von Balthasar and Salvation." *Homiletic and Pastoral Review* 89.10 (1989) 10–21.

Rohr, Richard. *The Universal Christ*. New York: Convergent, 2019.

Sachs, John R. "Current Eschatology: Universal Salvation and the Problem of Hell." *Theological Studies* 52 (1991) 227–54.

Sharkey, Michael, and Thomas Weinandy, eds. *International Theological Commission: Texts and Documents 1986–2007, Vol. II*. San Francisco: Ignatius, 2009.

Shaw, Elizabeth, ed. *Eschatology: Proceedings of the Fellowship of Catholic Scholars 37th Annual Convention (Sept 26–27, 2014)*. Notre Dame: Fellowship of Catholic Scholars, 2015.

Stein, Edith. *Welt und Person. Beitrag zum christlichen Wahrheitsstreben* [World and Person. A Contribution to Christian Truth Seeking]. Edited by Lucy Gelber and Romaeus Leuven. Freiburg: Herder, 1962.

Tanner, Norman, ed. *Decrees of the Ecumenical Councils*. Washington, DC: Georgetown University Press, 1990.

Trouvé, Marianne Lorraine, ed. *The Sixteen Documents of Vatican II*. Introductions by Douglas G. Bushman. Boston: Pauline Books and Media, 1999.

Vatican II. *Lumen gentium*. https://www.vatican.va/archive/hist_councils/ii_vatican_council/documents/vat-ii_const_19641121_lumen-gentium_en.html.

3

The *Spectacular* Joy of Heaven and the Real Possibility of Missing out on It

REV. PETER RYAN, SJ

TWO PROBLEMS UNDERMINE OUR efforts to evangelize: We not only fail to communicate the marvelous appeal of heaven, but we give people the impression that they need not strive for it anyway because missing out on salvation is practically impossible. Evangelization will succeed only if we help people see that heaven is a supremely wonderful gift, but one we will exchange for everlasting sadness unless we respond to grace.

I will now make the point even more strongly. It is my contention that our efforts to evangelize not only will not fail, but will be wildly successful if we can convince people of those two truths—first, that heaven[1] is a stupendous blessing that no one in his right mind would want to miss out on, and second, that it is dangerously easy to miss out on it, for many people do. It is essential that we convince people of not just one but both of those truths.

Consider what prevents a great many people in our culture from embracing the faith. If they read the New Testament and come to understand the love of God manifested in Jesus Christ and handed down in the Church, they cannot help but be attracted to the faith, for a stunningly loving God who not only becomes one of us but pours out his very lifeblood for us is undeniably appealing! But they soon find a stumbling block, namely, the requirements of Christian moral living.

Some of these requirements have to do with the Church's teaching on, for example, the wrongness of being selfish with the goods of this world—we are, after all, obliged to use not just some but all of our excess

---

1. I speak of *heaven* because the term is both scriptural and commonly understood as "what God has prepared for those who love him" (1 Cor 2:6; all Scripture passages are taken from the Revised Standard Version). As I explain, I do not mean a purely spiritual reality, but the fullness of the definitive kingdom of God.

wealth to benefit others rather than for luxuries and needless investment for ourselves and those near and dear.[2] That is a very challenging teaching! Yet teachings like that are not what alienates people from the faith. We know very well what does alienate them—the Church's teachings on sexual morality. People imbued with the values of contemporary secular culture recoil from the teaching that sexual activity outside of marriage is always gravely wrong and separates one from Christ. The idea that to remain in the state of grace and find salvation, those who are divorced and remarried must forgo all sexual activity, and those who experience same-sex attraction must not act on that attraction, and the unmarried must be celibate until they get married, and even married couples must reject contraception—all of this strikes people as being too much, a bridge too far.[3]

According to the ethos of contemporary culture, Church teachings on sexual morality are a strange bit of bad news within the Good News—so bad, in fact, that many people are inclined to reject the Good News rather than accept the seemingly bad part. For the secular culture rightly regards intimacy as essential to happiness, but wrongly assumes that sexual activity is essential to intimacy. The culture therefore treats enjoying sex as a right and a requirement of happiness.

Marriage is, of course, a great good, and the sexual embrace is integral to it and distorted outside of it. It is because the Church recognizes these truths that she teaches what she does about sex.[4] That teaching is challenging indeed, but if we can convince people that the definitive kingdom of God, the marriage feast of the Lamb, offers us far greater intimacy than any experience of sexual union in this life—that the kingdom offers not only intimate communion with the divine Persons themselves, which we can't begin to imagine, but also the human intimacy of the blessed as a communion of friends in the Lord, friends enjoying rich and varied fulfillment in the whole range of human goods—we will be well on our way

2. Vatican II, *Gaudium et spes*, 69, teaches: "God intended the earth with everything contained in it for the use of all human beings and peoples," and "attention must always be paid to this universal destination of earthly goods. In using them, therefore, man should regard the external things that he legitimately possesses not only as his own but also as common in the sense that they should be able to benefit not only him but also others." Indeed, after affirming the right to "a share of earthly goods sufficient for oneself and one's family," the document affirms the teaching of Church Fathers and Doctors "that men are obliged to come to the relief of the poor and to do so not merely out of their superfluous goods [note omitted]."

3. For a summary of the Church's teaching on chastity, see *Catechism of the Catholic Church*, 2337–59.

4. For a summary of the Church's teaching on marriage, see *Catechism of the Catholic Church*, 2360–400.

to winning their hearts. If we can help people see that this fulfillment is beyond wonderful when it begins and keeps getting better and better forever, but that they can easily miss out on this joy, and will indeed miss out and instead experience everlasting sadness unless they responds to God's grace, then many will surely be motivated to respond wholeheartedly, no matter what the cost, to the One who so earnestly desires our salvation that he poured himself out for us.

The so-called bad news within the good news will not phase them. They will not care what sacrifices they have to make. Even the sacrifice of living a holy and sexually pure life will not seem to be too much if only they can win the pearl of great price, the definitive kingdom of God. But, again, we need to convince people of not just one but both truths: the kingdom to which God graciously invites me is a gift of supreme joy, and I'll miss out on it if I fail to cooperate with grace.

To bring the point home, permit me to tell a story from my childhood. When I was in the sixth grade, I sang in the school choir, and I recall a rehearsal we had shortly before Christmas. We must have had catechism class earlier that day—we used the *Baltimore Catechism*, which did not, shall we say, go in for felt banners and collages, but was instead very strong and good medicine—for I remember being preoccupied with the Church's teaching on heaven and hell. I began thinking about hell and was of course horrified at the prospect of going there! The thought of experiencing misery forever and ever brought home the importance of never doing anything that might result in that outcome. I tried to imagine what it would mean for something to last forever, and it was mind boggling! And it was utterly appalling to imagine everlasting misery!

Then I started thinking about heaven. It had been presented to us as the vision of God—as the experience of gazing at him forever and ever. Although that prospect was enormously preferable to the alternative, it was not particularly appealing. In fact, the more I thought about it, the more I wondered how it would be possible to be happy forever if that is what heaven consists of. Looking at God every day, 24/7. Forever! I found myself plunged into a seemingly inescapable sadness as I thought about it. Even the beautiful Christmas hymns we were singing proved powerless to draw me out of it.

That evening, as my brothers and sisters were wrapping presents, trimming the tree, playing with the train set, and generally experiencing the joy of the season, my mother noticed that I wasn't myself. She asked if anything was the matter. She pressed me about it, and with all the eloquence of an eleven-year-old, I communicated my troubling thoughts and concluded with distress: "You just keep looking at God every day, all day long, forever and ever, and it will never end!"

My mother—what would I have done without her?—knew how to respond. "But you won't want it to end!" she said. Those words broke the spell. I knew they were true, even though I didn't understand *how* they could be true given the account of heaven I had been taught. Still, I knew that once I experienced heaven, I would not want it to end.

Notice that my problem was not that of taking salvation for granted. I was convinced that hell was real. My problem was that I did not find heaven, as it had been explained to me, appealing. So, let's begin there. Let's first consider the problem of helping people see how wonderfully appealing heaven—the definitive kingdom of God—really is, and then we'll discuss, more briefly, the other very serious problem of taking salvation for granted. There are significant theological reasons for affirming both truths.

I. We Need to Communicate the Great Appeal of the Kingdom.

My mother's words assured me that people in heaven will not be bored but, quite to the contrary, will be so happy that they won't want it to end. Indeed, as St. Thomas Aquinas teaches, they *can't* want it to end.[5] But neither my dear mother nor the great St. Thomas have helped me see *how* heaven could be forever appealing. And it seems to me extremely important to help people see that, because the mere conviction that it *will* in fact be appealing only takes us so far. James T. O'Connor explains the problem in a comment on the tendency to deemphasize the realism of the new heavens and new earth:

> A danger in all such spiritualizing tendencies—proper as they are in their efforts to avoid a grossly materialistic view of the life ahead of us—is that they deprive the imagination and the conceptualizing intellect of any object upon which to focus and nourish themselves. This deprivation ultimately influences the will. Since the intellect has nothing concrete to offer the will as a motive for action, the volitional faculty will lack motivation sufficient to move it toward the future. As a result, it will be directed even more naturally toward what is immediate and tangible. Likewise, the virtue of hope is attenuated since it is given as a goal something that can only be indistinctly apprehended.[6]

Consider an analogy. A man tempted to sexual infidelity is far more likely to be deterred if he imagines the wife and children he loves and the

---

5. "Now it is impossible for anyone seeing the Divine Essence, to wish not to see It." Aquinas, *Summa Theologiae*, I-II.5.4c.

6. O'Connor, *Land of the Living*, 37.

hurt that such a choice would cause them than if he merely reminds himself of the fact that such a choice is morally wrong. And he will be far more motivated to act uprightly by a good he can imagine, such as his family remaining intact and enjoying each other's company, than by an abstract idea of good. So also, a person will be far more motivated to cooperate with Jesus's plan of salvation and store up for himself treasure in heaven if he is able to imagine what heavenly treasure is, than if what he is storing up is, as far as he is concerned, a mere abstraction. Unless we effectively communicate the appeal of heaven, people will find it all too easy to stop seeking the kingdom first and turn instead to things they *do* find appealing—even things that can prevent a person from entering heaven.

How then can we help people appreciate the appeal of the kingdom? If it included only the beatific vision—which we rightly understand as divine intimacy—communicating the appeal of the kingdom would seem to me an impossible task. For divine intimacy is not a human good transformed, but an utterly supernatural reality and therefore beyond our ability to imagine. This is what St. Paul refers to when he speaks of "What no eye has seen, nor ear heard, nor the heart of man conceived, what God has prepared for those who love him" (1 Cor 2:9). We could quite rightly affirm that heaven *will* in fact be wonderfully fulfilling, but it is by no means clear that we could help people see *how* it is appealing.[7]

But, of course, the kingdom does include elements—essential elements—besides the beatific vision, namely, resurrection life, the new heavens and new earth, and the communion of saints. Of course, sharing in divine life, precisely because it is a supernatural blessing, is infinitely greater than these other elements of the kingdom. But these other elements are nevertheless essential, and they have the advantage of being at least to some degree imaginable.

How do we know that heaven cannot be reduced to the beatific vision? It is abundantly evident from Scripture and Church teaching. The Old Testament makes it clear that the Jews of Jesus's time hoped for the coming of God's kingdom and understood it on the basis of the Scriptures they heard read in their synagogues and the psalms they prayed there. They did not understand the kingdom as only spiritual, but as a concrete, bodily reality. It is described as a feast in which the broken world is healed, sin and death are overcome, and God's people are consoled. Isaiah makes this especially clear when he prophesies:

7. Some of the ideas that follow are given fuller expression in Grisez and Ryan, "Sketch of a Projected Book about the Kingdom of God," in Weigel, *Moral Good*, 149–65.

On this mountain the Lord of hosts will make for all peoples a feast of fat things, a feast of wine on the lees, of fat things full of marrow, of wine on the lees well refined. And he will destroy on this mountain the covering that is cast over all peoples, the veil that is spread over all nations. He will swallow up death for ever, and the Lord God will wipe away tears from all faces. (Isa 25:6–8)

The New Testament goes further. Jesus does not just awaken hope for God's kingdom, but directs us to that kingdom as our true ultimate end: "Seek first the kingdom of God!" he says (Matt 6:33; Luke 12:21). Jesus does not preach a purely spiritual, otherworldly kingdom, for he fulfills the hope expressed in the Old Testament.

The kingdom does, of course, include the beatific vision, or divine intimacy. As the Eternal Word, Jesus is united with the Father and the Holy Spirit, and by being united to Jesus, we are able to enjoy divine intimacy. But the kingdom also involves human fulfillment. It includes bodily resurrection and the company of friends. By being united to Jesus, we also experience those blessings, since as members of His Body we share in His resurrection and are united with one another. There are, of course, many New Testament passages about resurrection, and here I quote two of the more important: "He who eats my flesh and drinks my blood has eternal life, and I will raise him up at the last day" (John 6:54); and "If we have become united with Him in the likeness of His death, certainly we shall also be in the likeness of His resurrection" (Rom 6:5).

Paul makes it very clear that the definitive kingdom will also include a renewal of all creation: "The creation itself will be set free from its bondage to decay and obtain the glorious liberty of the children of God." Another essential aspect of the kingdom, one very much connected with the fact that it will be bodily, is that it will be a real community of the blessed with Jesus. Jesus promises companionship to all the Twelve: "As my Father appointed a kingdom for me, so do I appoint for you that you may eat and drink at my table in my kingdom, and sit on thrones judging the twelve tribes of Israel" (Luke 22:29–30; cf. Matt 19:28). This *being with* is community. It is evident again in Jesus's reply to the thief on the cross, who asks to be remembered when Jesus comes into his kingdom: "Today you will be with me in Paradise" (Luke 23:43).

In short, when Jesus says we should seek first the kingdom, he is urging us to take the kingdom, with all its essential elements—bodily resurrection, the communion of friends, the new heavens and the new earth, and the vision of God—as our ultimate end.

Church teaching confirms that the kingdom is our true ultimate end, and that its essential elements are not only the beatific vision, but also bodily life in the new heavens/new earth and the communion of friends. This is evident in the words from the Nicene Creed, which we proclaim every Sunday: "I look forward to the resurrection of the dead." In accord with the whole New Testament and the Creed itself, the *Catechism of the Catholic Church* treats (1) living forever as bodily persons (2) with the risen Lord Jesus as distinct objects of Christian faith and hope: "We firmly believe, and hence we hope that, just as Christ is truly risen from the dead and lives forever, so after death the righteous will live forever with the risen Christ and he will raise them up on the last day."[8] They are objects of faith and hope distinct from the beatific vision. This point is especially obvious in the case of the resurrection of the body, since those who are perfectly purified have the beatific vision even before being raised.

The *Catechism* also teaches: "Those who die in God's grace and friendship and are perfectly purified live for ever with Christ. They are like God for ever, for they 'see him as he is,' face to face."[9] This passage teaches two distinct things about those who die in grace and are perfectly purified: (1) They live forever with Jesus, and (2) They have the beatific vision. The *Catechism* justifies those statements by quoting Benedict XII's *Benedictus Deus*, which defined that the saved enjoy the beatific vision before they are raised from the dead.[10]

Why is it so important to hold that those human blessings and not only the beatific vision are essential to the kingdom? There are various reasons, but the one especially relevant for evangelization is that the prospect of those human blessings helps us see how the kingdom is truly fulfilling. If human goods are not essential to the kingdom, it is not clear how the kingdom can be a fitting fulfillment for human nature or how human beings can be adequately motivated to desire it.

We are given a share in the divine nature at baptism when we are born again. But the *we* who are given that divine gift come to be at our first birth (that is, at our conception), when each of us becomes a unique human person with a human nature. With respect to our sharing in the divine nature, we are oriented to Trinitarian intimacy, and if we remain faithful we will enjoy it forever in the kingdom. But with respect to our human nature, we are oriented to fulfillment in human goods. This enables us to say that the blessed will enjoy actual participation in specifically human goods.

---

8. *Catechism of the Catholic Church*, 989.

9. *Catechism of the Catholic Church*, 1023.

10. See Denzinger and Schönmetzer, *Enchiridion Symbolorum*, 1000.

Someone might ask, "Can we not hold instead that the blessed will be fulfilled in specifically human goods inasmuch as these are present—and in a more eminent way—in God?" After all, persons having the beatific vision will hardly be likely to set it aside to attend to specifically human goods.

But that problem arises only if one assumes that the beatific vision is an act of the human intellect or some other specifically human capacity. Such a view, though traditional, focuses on our union with God at the expense of our otherness from him. Yet God himself wills our otherness from him! In fact, that otherness makes our union with him possible—just as the differences between husband and wife make their union possible, and the differences between the divine Persons make it possible for God to be a communion of love rather than a monolith. Our otherness is found in our humanity, and in the uniqueness of the humanity of each. That otherness is relevant not just with respect to our initial creation but also with respect to the completion of our creation in the kingdom.

To properly account for the otherness of created persons in the kingdom, we must consider their perfection in the goods proper to their nature. Our unique perfection in human goods is what each created human person brings to the communion of the kingdom so as to be a really distinct participant in it. The uniqueness of our selves depends on the path God calls us to walk, the particular choices he wants us to make, and how we respond. I submit that it is not just a question of living this life so one can have a better vision of God by having more charity. Rather, one needs to live this life in order to become more and more the unique person God created one to be forever in the kingdom.

If our ultimate fulfillment required only having human goods in an eminent way by having the beatific vision, then neither having one's risen body, nor being with Jesus, Mary, the angels, and other saints, nor anything else could add anything at all to the beatitude provided by the beatific vision. But *actually* having one's body and *actually* being with Jesus, Mary, the angels, and the saints—not just having the good of those realities as it is present in God and already possessed by having the beatific vision—must have intrinsic worth. For if it had none, all those realities would be superfluous, and God in his wisdom would never have provided them for those who love him.

In short, the blessed experience the beatific vision, or specifically divine intimacy, not as a human act but as their fulfillment precisely as children of God. This enables us to understand divinization in a very real and strong sense rather than a merely metaphorical one, and also to see that our fulfillment in human goods is itself real and robust. Our specifically human fulfillment is not absorbed into our sharing in Jesus' divine life any more than Jesus's human nature is absorbed into his divine nature. In both cases, the two are inseparable but distinct, not in competition with each other but aspects of an integrated, unified whole.

Enjoying the beatific "vision" and living our human lives, we will not need to set aside one for the other. Indeed, we should bear in mind the teaching of Vatican II, in *Gaudium et spes*, 39, that human persons will not set aside their human fulfillment in the kingdom, but rather will find there all of the fruit of their promotion of human goods during the present age, and indeed all of the goods proper to human nature.[11]

There is cause for rejoicing here, for by explaining that in addition to the unimaginable good of divine intimacy, the blessed really do enjoy robust human fulfillment that we can at least begin to imagine, we can, with the Holy Spirit's help, awaken people to the joy of the kingdom and elicit their desire to seek it first no matter what the cost.

If I had been told about human fulfillment in the kingdom, my boyhood experience of reflecting on heaven would surely not have been marked by sadness. I would have rejoiced if someone had told me that in addition to divine intimacy, I would enjoy a wonderful *human* relationship with Jesus as man, similar to but far better than the human relationship we now have with him.

And if only I had been told that the bodies of the blessed will be radiantly beautiful, each with his or her own distinctive beauty, and that the blessed will not only experience no suffering, illness, injury, defect, or bodily decline of any kind, but will be perfectly equipped to experience ever-increasing joy, whether gradually increasing or punctuated by sudden bursts! I wish I had known that the memories, imaginations, and all the sensory capacities of the blessed will function marvelously well, and that they are able to move with ease and speed, and thus can be present to different people at different times—sometimes with Jesus and Mary, sometimes with others near and dear, and at still other times with new friends.

I wish I had been told that the blessed will be able to enjoy various activities that engage their unique and complementary gifts, activities like singing, dancing, making music, and perhaps even various kinds of sports. Or exploring the seemingly endless new heavens and new earth. Or that the

---

11. See Vatican II, *Gaudium et spes*, 39: "After we have promoted on earth, in the Spirit of the Lord and in accord with his command, the goods of human dignity, familial communion, and freedom—that is to say, all the good fruits of our nature and effort—then we shall find them once more, but cleansed of all dirt, lit up, and transformed, when Christ gives back to the Father the eternal and universal kingdom: 'a kingdom of truth and life, a kingdom of holiness and grace, a kingdom of justice, love, and peace'" (translated by Grisez and Ryan, "Hell and Hope for Salvation"; internal quotation from *Roman Missal*, "Preface of the Solemnity of Christ the King").

blessed might even enjoy eating and drinking as aspects of their bodily life in the kingdom—since the risen bodies of the blessed shall, as St. Augustine puts it, "be invested with so sure and every way inviolable an immortality, that they shall not eat save when they choose, nor be under the necessity of eating, while they enjoy the power of doing so."[12]

Would that someone had told me that the blessed will reign with Christ, as Scripture and Church teaching both make clear, and that this activity will involve deliberation and choice. And that it will be a fulfilling, joyful experience because Jesus will not reign as an autocrat but with the glad cooperation of every one of the blessed. And that because all of the blessed will love one another as they love themselves, governance of the kingdom, no matter how complex it may be, will go smoothly.

I would have been consoled to learn that friendships will begin whenever people meet; that everyone will be friends and will therefore appreciate others' accomplishments and be generous in sharing their gifts with others; that since everyone loves one another, each of the blessed is fulfilled when others are fulfilled and rejoices in being loved by all of the others, so that the blessed will share together in a glorious, ever-rising cycle of joy.

Perhaps I would have been too young to appreciate it at the time, but people who have adopted our secular culture's assumptions about sex would surely find it helpful to realize that resurrection life is a communal good that individuals somehow participate in together, in Christ and with each other. Contemporary people would find it especially beneficial to realize that one-flesh union with Jesus and all of his members is a far greater communion than the sexual union of spouses in the present age. They would benefit by insight into why this is so: In the conjugal act, spouses delight in the experience of their communion which is grounded in a single function, but the blessed will be united not with respect to a single function but with respect to life as a whole, so that they will somehow experience their bodily communion in *whatever* they do together. They will therefore experience a far greater delight in it than any married couple can experience in the present age. Moreover, unlike marriage, communion among the blessed will be inclusive rather than exclusive.

12. Augustine, *City of God*, xiii.22.

II. We Need to Help People See That It Is Easy to Miss out on the Great Joy of Salvation, for Many Do.[13]

In earlier times, some Christians held that (1) *God creates some people intending them to die in grace and enter into his kingdom, and creates others intending them to die in sin and end in hell.* Few hold that view today because it makes it difficult to believe in God's mercy and thus in God himself. Many Christian theologians and pastors affirmed, to the contrary, that (2) *God will see to it that every person he creates will enter into the heavenly kingdom,* hoping that this view, which emphasizes God's mercy, would encourage people to persevere in or embrace Christian faith. But that is not what happened. Instead, churches that proclaimed the message of universal salvation have generally experienced more defections from the faith and fewer conversions.

The question therefore arises: Does holding and preaching (2) no less than doing the same with (1) foster secularism and impede fruitful evangelization?

I answer in the affirmative because of what these views, though radically different in content, have in common: In neither case can a person make a choice that affects his eternal destiny. In the first, a person is predestined to either heaven or hell and will end there no matter what. In the second, every person is predestined to heaven.

Why should we think that common denominator fosters secularism and impedes evangelization? The answer is that a person who is convinced that his or her destiny is already determined realizes that it is impossible to make choices for the purpose of finding salvation. People who accept (1) may be worried that they are predestined to hell rather than heaven, and so, to stave off despair, may make choices—like doing good works or repenting from sin—to convince themselves that they are predestined to heaven. But they don't think those choices themselves in any way affect their destiny, or that any other choices they might make could do so. People who accept (2) are convinced that they are going to find salvation no matter what—that it is a sure thing. And it is impossible to hope for a sure thing; one can only take it for granted. In that case, one's choices to do good works or repent from sin are not made in order to find salvation but for some other reason—perhaps to help others in this world or to make oneself feel better.

Both of those views are very clearly at odds with Catholic teaching. Many Catholics instead hold either (3) *Only Satan, his demons, and a few extremely*

---

13. Much of what follows is a slightly adapted and abbreviated version of Grisez and Ryan, "Hell and Hope for Salvation."

wicked human beings will be damned, or (4) *We cannot know whether any human being will be damned.* Do those views fare any better?

It is not impossible for someone who holds (3) to be convinced that it would be unacceptably risky to assume that neither they nor any of their loved ones will be among the few extremely wicked human beings who will be damned. But it is far more likely for people who hold (3) to suppose that neither they themselves nor anyone they care about is or ever will become one of the few extremely wicked people—like, perhaps, Hitler or Stalin—who will be damned, and as a result to take salvation for granted rather than actually *seek* it, as Jesus urged us to do.

It is likewise not impossible for someone who holds (4) to be convinced that it would be unacceptably risky for they themselves and those they care about to take it for granted that God will save everyone. But it is far more likely for those who hold (4) to think that they can safely assume that all will be saved. They might reason that respected theologians hold (4). They might note that the Church prays that everyone will be saved, that God surely answers the Church's prayers, and that nothing is impossible for God.

Therefore, holding (3) or (4) is likely to have the same effects on people that holding (2) would have had: they can no longer hope for, and therefore cannot make any choice for the sake of, their own or others' salvation. If you think salvation is a sure thing, you can't shape your life or recommend that others shape theirs with a view to receiving it rather than missing out.

Views (3) and (4) are held by many Catholics today, including theologians, priests, and even bishops, some of whom seem quite orthodox and admirable in other ways. Yet it is evident that those views are absolutely toxic for evangelization. If we wanted to undermine our project to unleash the gospel, a very effective way to do so would be to promote the view that only the fallen angels and a few horrific people will be damned, or the view that we cannot know that any human being will be damned. No matter how effectively we communicate the appeal of the gospel, people are very unlikely to accept it and be faithful to it—to pay the cost of discipleship, which includes living a sexually pure life—if they hold those views. For they will surely ask themselves, "Why change my life if salvation is a sure thing anyway?"

But I do not propose that we reject those views only because of their deadly consequences. I propose that we reject them because they are false, and that we hold instead what the New Testament clearly teaches: first, that God wills everyone to be saved and that Christ died for everyone; and second, that more than a few will nevertheless be lost.

Consider what Jesus himself teaches: that many who acted in his name will be shocked to find themselves condemned by their failure to have done the Father's will (see Matt 7:21–23); that some who think they have fulfilled their responsibilities to him will be surprised to find themselves condemned for having failed to meet his pressing needs in the least of his brothers and sisters (see Matt 25:41–46); and that we should "Strive to enter by the narrow door," because many "will seek to enter and will not be able" (Luke 13:24). Without saying whether those saved will be few, Jesus makes it clear that more than a few will be lost.

Some claim that, while Jesus may well have said such things, he did not mean to provide information about what to expect when he returns but only to motivate people to repent, believe, and follow him. But Jesus would have been dishonest had he tried to motivate people by warnings that were not truthful information about their prospects if they failed to heed his warnings. And for well over a millennium, Christians realized that these sayings did indeed truthfully convey Jesus's teaching that more than a few will be lost, a teaching they considered important precisely because it continued motivating people as he plainly intended.

To hold that we cannot know whether any human beings will be damned—or that if any are damned, it will only be Satan and his minions and a few utterly wicked people—implies that the whole body of Christians misunderstood what Jesus intended, and thus also implies that the Holy Spirit failed to remind them of Jesus's teaching and complete it by teaching them all things, as he promised his disciples that the Spirit would do.[14] Such a view is also at odds with the teaching of Vatican II about the inability of the entire body of the faithful, which is anointed by God, to err in matters of belief.[15]

I take no joy in defending the view that more than a few people will end in hell, but our age surely deserves to hear what Scripture teaches about this and what the Church has understood it to mean. Some people think that any focus on the possibility of damnation is going to impede our efforts to unleash the Gospel. I think the opposite is true.

It seems to me that to evangelize successfully, we first need to help people grasp the staggering beauty of God's plan of salvation. He created us out of a sheer desire to communicate his goodness even beyond the Trinity. And when he saw us go astray, he sent his only Son to share our human nature—to

14. See John 14:26: "But the Counselor, the Holy Spirit, whom the Father will send in my name, he will teach you all things, and bring to your remembrance all that I have said to you."

15. Vatican II, *Lumen gentium*, 12, teaches: "The entire body of the faithful, anointed as they are by the Holy One, cannot err in matters of belief. They manifest this special property by means of the whole people's supernatural discernment in matters of faith when 'from the Bishops down to the last of the lay faithful' they show universal agreement in matters of faith and morals." The internal quotation is from St. Augustine, *De Praedestinatione Sanctorum*, 14, 27.

be like us in all things but sin—and pour out his very life for us. Jesus invites us to be intimately united with him, and to enjoy forever both unimaginably wonderful intimacy with the divine Persons and robust human fulfillment as members of his risen body. But effective evangelization also requires that we help people realize that receiving this wonderful gift of God's definitive kingdom is not automatic. It is a disastrous mistake to take heaven for granted, but we will find ourselves doing precisely that and leading others to do the same unless we receive and communicate the hard truth that many people miss out on heaven. We need to heed the words of St. Paul: "work out your own salvation with fear and trembling" (Phil 2:12). Far from being harsh, Paul is loving his people by alerting them to a truth they must appropriate in order to avoid disaster. He adds beautiful words that can inspire our efforts to evangelize: "Do all things without grumbling or questioning, that you may be blameless and innocent, children of God without blemish in the midst of a crooked and perverse generation, among whom you shine as lights in the world, holding fast the word of life" (Phil 2:14–16).

Bibliography

Aquinas, Thomas. *Summa Theologiae.* https://www.corpusthomisticum.org/sth2001. html.

Augustine of Hippo. *City of God.* http://www.newadvent.org/fathers/120113.htm.

Catechism of the Catholic Church. https://www.vatican.va/archive/ENG0015/_INDEX. HTM.

Denzinger, Heinrich, and Adolf Schönmetzer, eds. *Enchiridion Symbolorum: Definitionum et Declarationum de rebus fidei et morum.* 36th ed. Freiburg in Breisgau: Herder, 1965.

Grisez, Germain, and Peter Ryan. "Hell and Hope for Salvation." *New Blackfriars* 95 (2014) 606–15.

O'Connor, James T. *Land of the Living.* New York: Catholic Book Publishing, 1992.

Vatican II. *Gaudium et spes.* http://www.vatican.va/archive/hist_councils/ii_vatican_ council/documents/vat-ii_const_19651207_gaudium-et-spes_en.html.

———. *Lumen gentium.* https://www.vatican.va/archive/hist_councils/ii_vatican_ council/documents/vat-ii_const_19641121_lumen-gentium_en.html.

Weigel, Peter J., ed. *Moral Good, the Beatific Vision, and God's Kingdom: Writings by Germain Grisez and Peter F. Ryan, S.J.* New York: Peter Lang, 2015.

III. Sacrificial Evangelization

4

Suffering and the New Evangelization

REV. JOHN MCDERMOTT, SJ

AMERICANS LIVE IN THE world's most technologically advanced society, and technology aims at facilitating the human life's daily tasks in the home and at work, abolishing their dreariness and monotony, and lightening the load of decisions for those responsible for them. Moreover, medicine and hospital care have attained ever new heights of professional expertise; many a disease or injury which in previous ages would have involved permanent impairment or even death can now be treated, assuaged, and healed. The greatest strides in the alleviation of pain have seemingly been accomplished. Is mankind returning to a fabled golden age when all will live without suffering at peace with nature and themselves?

One can doubt it for several reasons. First, Christians believe that original sin has not only alienated men from God and from each other but has also warped human perceptions of reality. Concupiscence reigns in our interior motions. What St. Paul wrote two millennia ago still holds true:

> I do not understand my own actions. For I do not do what I want, but I do the very thing I hate. Now if I do what I do not want, I see that the law is good. So then it is no longer I that do it, but sin which dwells within me. For I know that nothing good dwells within me, that is, in my flesh. I can will what is right, but I cannot do it. For I do not do the good I want, but the evil I do not want is what I do. Now if I do what I do not want, it is no longer I that do it, but sin which dwells within me. So I find it to be a law that when I want to do right, evil lies close at hand. For I delight in the law of God in my inmost self, but I see in my members another law at war with the law of my mind and making me captive to the law of sin which dwells in my members. Wretched man that I am! Who will deliver me from this body of death? (Rom 7:15–24)

Secondly, St. Paul's dire view of humanity seems to be confirmed by empirical evidence in our increasingly technologically perfected, medically advanced society. Almost twenty million Americans—that involves almost 7 percent of the population over the age of twelve—suffer from some form of substance abuse, be it drugs or alcohol.[1] That means that they cannot do what they want to do. Moreover, one in four people (27 percent) rarely or never feel as though there are people who really understand them, and the degree of loneliness is highest among those in the 18–37 age group.[2] Millennia earlier Aristotle remarked, "Without friends no one would choose to live."[3] No wonder that the suicide rate among youth 17–25 has been climbing even faster than in the general population. Approximately forty-seven thousand suicides occur annually in our country, and it is the second leading cause of death among youth 10–34. Almost 2 percent of youth 18–25 contemplated suicide in 2017. The suicide rate increased 31 percent in the period 2001–17.[4] While the divorce rate has been gradually lessening from the 1990s, when over half of marriages seemed doomed to dissolution, one main reason for that is the decline in the over-all number of marriages. People enter in various types of cohabitation instead. Unfortunately, these temporary alliances are becoming ever more transient. Then, of course, we are reminded that children of divorce or abandoned cohabitation relations are four times more likely to suffer divorces in their own marriages than children from stable families, not to mention out-of-wedlock pregnancies, transient cohabitations, lower academic and professional achievements, and general insecurity and unhappiness.[5] How can anyone be happy when a basic human relation is destroyed, especially if solemn pledges of fidelity had been given? How can one overlook one's own neglected children? There must be a good many unhappy people, even guilty people, walking around America's cities and villages.

A technological world does not remove suffering; indeed, it may increase suffering. While medical advances can cure diseases and alleviate physical sufferings, they cannot destroy death or eliminate all the heartache which living with other human beings entails. Despite medical progress many people still live with daily pain due to incurable infirmities. The rational Utopias which various philosophers of unlimited progress proposed

1. Bose et al., "Key Substance Use."

2. Nemecek et al., "Cigna U.S. Loneliness Index," 2–7.

3. Aristotle, *Nic. Eth.* 8.1.

4. See Centers for Disease Control and Prevention, "Suicide"; National Institute of Mental Health, "Suicide."

5. See Anderson, "The Impact of Family Structure"; Parker, "Key Statistics about Kids from Divorced Families."

in the nineteenth century seem like pie in the sky with a bitter after-taste. Their pipe dreams caused millions to die on battlefields and in prisons for the implementation of totalitarian fantasies. These same humanists excoriate their imaginary God for letting wickedness and evil flourish upon the earth. How, they ask, can one believe in a God who purports to be a father to His children when He remains idly by while His children are tormented not only by humanly caused evils, but also by tremendous natural catastrophes like droughts, famines, hurricanes, tornadoes, etc.? The dilemma is all the more pressing when one considers how innocent children, who have not sinned, are subjected to sufferings caused by nefarious adult agents. Either God is impotent to change the world for the better, in which case He is neither omnipotent nor God. Or He does not really care for His alleged children, in which case humans need not be concerned about Him.[6]

The response to that protest entails analyzing its context, recognizing the presuppositions for this world's anguish, and proposing the Catholic faith's answer, which is both theoretical and practical. Only the Catholic faith can propose a wisdom which appeals to man's heart as well as to his mind. Given that so much pain, physical and psychological, permeates human existence, the proper understanding of suffering enables the Church to proclaim to the world the mystery of life, suffering, death, and love in which life's only satisfying sense is found. Her message can serve as the springboard for evangelization, meeting men where they are, in apparently senseless suffering, and summoning them to a higher destiny.

The Context of the Atheistic Protest

Paradoxically the protest against God arises most brazenly in the culture formed by the biblical tradition. Polytheism accepted sufferings more easily. If gods and goddesses suffered, how could mere mortals be precluded from such a fate? The Greek divinities had their disputes, affairs, and deceptions which entangled human beings in them willy-nilly. Woe betide you if Hera went into a huff or if, like Hippolytus, you did not take Aphrodite seriously enough. It was hazardous to live in a universe of squabbling gods, when the unexpected thunderbolt might emerge from the cloud at any moment.

---

6. The classical expression of the complaint is uttered by Ivan Karamazov in Dostoyevsky, *The Brothers Karamazov*, 242–55. Not only is Ivan's rant replete with contradictions but Dostoyevsky, a believing Christian, actually refutes Ivan's position in the rest of the novel. Camus, *The Plague*, took up the complaint and expanded it. It found expression also in the linguistic analytic school in Flew and MacIntyre, *New Essays in Philosophical Theology*, 96–130.

Monotheism offers a great advantage in simplifying human life. Moses's words form the daily prayer of pious Jews, "Hear, O Israel, the Lord our God is one Lord, and you shall love the Lord your God with all your heart and with all your soul, and with all your might" (Deut 6:4–5). If there is only one God, lives can be unified in serving that God; foreign forces wishing to derail men are reduced to a subordinate place. But monotheism's advantage soon raises a problem: why does God allow the good man to suffer? This question is all the more pressing when, unlike many variations of Buddhism and Hinduism, Jews and Christians believe in a personal God. Thence arises Job's dilemma, which is only intensified in view of all the innocent children made to suffer for the sins of others.

The Secular Impasse

It is always easier to complain than to propose and, especially, to implement a practical answer. Today's secularized world finds God otiose except when it wants to complain. By complaining it obscures its own inability to handle suffering. For suffering is secularism's Achilles heel. Secularism cannot respond adequately to suffering, and that incapacity is, I suspect, the deepest reason for the culture of death which John Paul II identified as the blight of our civilization (*Evangelium vitae*, 12–30). Because the world finds no sense in pain, it seeks to abolish suffering and frustration by all means possible: the scientific taming of nature, universal hospital coverage, unlimited "safe sex," no-fault divorce, abortion, euthanasia, "trigger warnings," "safe spaces," and wherever we go from there. As it has been rightly prophesized, "Compassion leads to the gas chamber."[7] The more we flee suffering, the more terrifyingly and intolerably it permeates our existence.

Atheists and agnostics frequently focus on innocent suffering to justify their repudiation of God. Surely complaints about God and His providence come easily to mind when bad things happen to good people. Yet a perusal of atheistic literature soon reveals that no matter how impassioned writers might be in rejecting God, they shed little light upon life's meaning. Human existence is a mystery. The world existed long before the human race came into it and it will probably endure long after its demise. What then is its purpose and what meaning has my individual existence in it?

7. The original version of the quote comes from Flannery O'Connor's "Introduction" of Dominican Nuns of Our Lady, *A Memoire of Mary Ann*: "When tenderness is detached from the source of tenderness [i.e., Christ], its logical outcome is terror. It ends in forced-labor camps and in the fumes of the gas chamber." Since the book is difficult to obtain, we rely for the quotation in Montgomery, "Walker Percy and the Christian Scandal," 38–39, who quotes Percy to the same effect from his *Thanatos Syndrome*.

The definitive answer to such immense questions surpasses every mortal mind, yet there are hints of meaning. Alongside all the suffering arise moments when the heart leaps up in gratitude and joy: at beholding a beautiful sunrise or sunset, at a friendship given, at truth's discovery, at courage and honesty manifested in fidelity, at parental sacrifices. Are these lasting values or just delusions? If there is no God, all these values crumble with mortal mankind into dust. If there is no God, to whom does one render thanks? If there is no God, why bother to sacrifice for anyone in a world condemned to suffering? Are life's positive experiences merely the carrot dangling before the dumb donkey to motivate mankind's endless motion on a purposeless evolutionary treadmill? Or are they omens of deeper meaning? Such is life's mystery. If there is meaning beyond mortal finitude, there is God. Yet within his horizon of meaning every believer should recognize why suffering is so intricately entwined in human life. As John Paul II wrote: "Suffering seems particularly proper to man's nature. It is as deep as man himself, precisely because it manifests in its own way the depth which is proper to man, and in its own way surpasses it" (*Salvifici doloris*, 2). Philosophical analysis and theological insight illuminate why suffering is intricately entwined in human life—a truth often bitter to bear but ultimately liberating.

Philosophy: Suffering Is Humanly Irradicable

No mortal can exterminate pain from human existence. Any attempt to do so is doomed to increase suffering. Consider first the human predicament and the conditions of possibility for suffering. All humans have sentient bodies. They require feelings to maneuver in a material world. Sensations not only cause pleasure, they also warn against danger. Physical pain derives from an excess of sensation. After coming inside on a cold winter day one can steer a frozen backside toward a great fire; its warmth is very enjoyable. But if one stays too close too long, warmed cheeks become burnt buns. Even in Paradise Adam could have stubbed his toe; that would be better than continually banging his brains against walls through which he was trying to walk. To abolish all possibility of physical pain one must abolish sensation and, with it, all bodies and physical pleasure. As Plato noted, pain and pleasure are practically inseparable: two beings fastened at their acme (*Phaedo*, 60b). But the total abolition of physical pain does not render men impervious to injury. Even angels can and do suffer. Human beings are limited in body and spirit, which means that they exist in relation to others and are dependent upon those others for weal and woe. This truth especially regards other people's freedoms. They can reject as well as accept each other. Further, finitude, when perceived, is always transcended; once a limit is recognized, the spirit is already beyond it. As long as a baby enclosed in a playpen does not recognize bars as restrictions, he does not feel constricted. Once he perceives them as limitation, he is already beyond them in knowledge and desire. Thence springs a desire for something more; but nothing finite can satisfy a desire for the always more, and the finite cannot reach the infinite on its own. Man can never be totally fulfilled on the basis of finite experience, and the more finite consciousness is elevated to awareness of its limitations, the more exquisite become its spiritual sufferings. For that reason, most variations of Buddhism and Hinduism aim at the total eradication of desire, which is seen as the cause of evil. Ultimately this view leads to the suppression of the self, the extinction of individual consciousness.[8]

Some preliminary conclusions offer themselves. First, the only sure-fire way to nullify all pain is to escape the body and either become the infinite God or at least reduce all others to automata controlled by oneself, a pure spirit. Hence it becomes clear that underlying many modern protests against God lurks the hidden desire to become God, to control good and evil by rendering one's own arbitrary freedom supreme. That is a very loveless world that humans aspire to create.

A second conclusion follows: because sufferings are tied to finitude, they can be relativized. Just as there is no best of all possible worlds, there can be no worst of all possible worlds. This affords a word of consolation to all Irish and Polish optimists: things can always get worse. Indeed, since many different viewpoints are possible on finite realities, a person's perspective on sufferings can increase or diminish them.[9] For example, if anyone were to raise a gun to the average citizen and threaten to kill him unless he ran 26 miles in less than four hours, he might well reply, "Just shoot me now; why should I bother with that agony?" If the same threat were delivered to a world-class marathon runner like Wilson Kipsang, he could reply, "Why, that is nothing; I do that before breakfast every other morning." Perhaps a reader remembers days of gridiron glory. Did you feel all the bruises when you were

8. Zaehner, *Hinduism*, 4–5, 59–63, 66–72, 74–79, 114–20; Hume, "An Outline of the Philosophy of the Upanishads," 66–69; Ch'en, *Buddhism*, 33–39, 41–47, 49–52, 54–60.

9. In modern civilization, pangs of childbirth are much anticipated and empathized. But Engelmann, *Labor among Primitive Peoples*, 7–10, noted how labor pains increase with civilization: among primitives "labor may be characterized as short and easy." An extreme version of the influence of subjectivity upon pain that is found in Schleiermacher, *Christian Faith*, 382–84, 397, 400, 408–9, 414–18, 458–59, whereby Jesus enjoyed the "imperturbable blessedness" of His God-consciousness even in His Passion. Schleiermacher lacks a proper understanding of the hypostatic union; he places Jesus's human nature, i.e., His human self-consciousness, in direct contact with the divine nature, which is understood as bliss.

smashing through the line for the greater glory of Hobash High? You might have been half-maimed, but the battle was exhilarating, and the adrenaline was pumping. The next day you might be groaning in the hospital, but on the field, you were unstoppable, Mr. Superman. But if Lois Lane or Sweet Suzie visited you in the hospital and gushed over your fabulous feats, what are the wounds of yesteryear on St. Crispin's day? At the opposite extreme are found both the fabled princess who excruciatingly feels the pea under twelve mattresses and the spoiled brat who, in intolerable torment, insists on his Wheaties instead of the Corn Flakes served by his mother.

A final conclusion flows from finitude: human beings are dependent upon each other. Even the most rugged individualist needs a Mommy and a Daddy, who gave him life, fed him, and taught him to talk. Scholars identify in the Old Testament the phenomenon of "corporate personality": an individual is not only a constitutive but also a representative member of the group to which he belongs.[10] Not only does the group influence him but also what he does affects the group: David's sin caused the plague to strike his people (2 Sam 24), Moses's prayer saved Israel from destruction (Exod 32:7–14; Ps 106:23), Abraham's fidelity explains why God so loves the Jews (Gen 23:15–18; Sir 44:19–22). The Israelites identified themselves with their ancestors and knew that their conduct had repercussions upon fellow Jews and their progeny. God punishes to the third and fourth generation but shows His mercy to the thousandth generation (Exod 20:5–6). Orthodox Jews today become upset with Conservative and Liberal Jews. One Jew's infraction of the Law has negative repercussions on all Jews (Deut 29:18–19). Corporate solidarity also explains how the Suffering Servant bore the sins of others and how Adam's sin affected all his children. However antithetical to modern susceptibilities, this biblical view contains a great truth. Men are their brothers' keepers. No one is a mere individual, responsible for himself alone. That insight reveals the inherent contradiction in the complaint of those protesting against the injustice whereby children suffer for their parents' sins. Can a child really be considered independent of all other human beings until he or she performs a free act? Can she be isolated from her parents? Can he be a new Adam at creation's beginning, responsible for himself alone? If such isolation were possible, how might anyone protest in the child's name, in solidarity with the child?

10. Robinson, *Corporate Personality*; Fraine, *Adam and the Family of Man*.

Suffering Is Humanly Unintelligible

Here the mystery of original sin is foreshadowed, to which this presentation later returns. Before that, suffering should be analyzed from a slightly different angle. No human can fully explain suffering. Suffering is unique to each person. It is *my* suffering or *yours* or *his* or *hers*. Even your sympathy for me does not let you suffer *my* sufferings. Suffering is individual, and the individual as such cannot be captured in any science. All scientific explanations must use universal concepts—"the soul knows bodies through the intellect with an immaterial, universal, and necessary knowledge" and "science is not with singulars."[11] Yet universal concepts cannot comprehend the individual in its individuality here and now. Goethe's axiom sums up science's predicament: *Individuum est ineffabile.*[12] Men are mysteries to themselves, especially in their freedom, individuality, and sufferings.

The limitations of human science become all the more obvious once the ultimate reason for unjust sufferings is sought. To seek the reason for something means to seek its cause, and to seek a cause presupposes a necessary connection between cause and effect; otherwise only an occasion or condition of an event is named, not a cause. Hence in seeking the cause one seeks a necessity. But if the reason, or cause, for injustice is discovered, injustice is made necessary. That is absurd. That would not only make God, the First Cause, responsible for injustice but also would insert men into a warped moral universe against which their moral sense protests. Actually, injustice presupposes freedom, a free act deliberately gone awry, whereas a cause's "necessity" removes freedom. Hence one rightly concludes that finite minds cannot understand evil choices in themselves. From a human perspective no total answer to the conundrum of unjust suffering or any suffering is to be expected. This conundrum undercuts particularly any philosophy based upon natures.[13] For pain indicates that a nature is not functioning properly, and what is contrary to nature falls outside the parameters of every natural philosophy. Clearly, if human intellects cannot understand evil, physical and moral, they can never banish it. No human plan, be it Social Security, Medicare, or Obamacare, can ever

---

11. Aquinas, *Summa Theologiae*, I.84.1c; Aquinas, *In post. Anal.* I.44.34.

12. Janke and Luther, "Individuum/Individualismus I," notes that although this expression has not been found in any medieval thinker, "it derives (*stammt*) from a good Aristotelian family."

13. Lest anyone conclude that man cannot know God's existence by his natural reason—contrary to Catholic doctrine (DS 3004; 3026)—he may consult a proof of God's existence based on freedom apart from revelation: McDermott, "Faith, Reason, and Freedom," 307–32.

liberate mortals from the need of suffering. If any answer to the dilemma of suffering is to be offered, it must come from beyond man.

Suffering's Positive Value

If suffering is not an absolute evil—sin alone is an absolute evil—some positive meaning can be discovered in suffering. First, suffering alerts against greater physical evil: being singed by fire warns one to step away and not be burned. Second, in order to grow physically stronger, athletes have to break down muscle tissue: no pain, no gain. Physical exercise hurts, but muscles are toned and strengthened by it. On the spiritual level, suffering stands at the service of growth. Men learn more quickly and more thoroughly through suffering. My father said that he was educated in the school of hard knocks, and he was just paraphrasing the popular adage, knowledge makes a bloody entrance, which reflects the wisdom of Aeschylus, "[Zeus] regularly (*kypios*: masterfully) joins learning to suffering."[14] Moreover, suffering can break down selfishness. The French Catholic Léon Bloy wrote consolingly to a friend upon the loss of his young daughter, "Man has places in his heart that as yet have no existence; pain has to enter before they can be."[15] At the very least suffering can function as a punishment for sin, recalling sinners to themselves and to concern for others. It can also awaken compassion and force men to live with others. Many times, in the case of economic depression, a family will stick close together in a common struggle whereas economic prosperity allows individuals to forget their real need for and appreciation of others. A maimed or mentally impaired child often brings his or her family to greater unity and mutual help.[16] That love in mutual self-sacrifice produces greater joy than all the material gadgets in the world. Finally, ordinary people often become aware of their value as free persons when they have to suffer for duty or an ideal. Nobility is shown when someone willingly dies for a belief. The examples of martyrs illustrate to what heights of courage and fidelity humanity is capable under

14. Aeschylus, *Agamemnon*, 177. A little later in the *Agamemnon*, 250–51, the thought is repeated: "Justice inclines the scale for those suffering to learn."

15. Cited by Congar, "The Problem of Evil," 401.

16. Schulman, *Coping with Tragedy*, describes how the tragedy of a maimed child often brings families closer together. In many cases (chapters 1, 6, 9, 10, 13, 15, 16, 17, 23) religious faith supplies a great support, in others (4, 7, 8, 14, 18–20) some support. Surprisingly most of the Catholic families (2, 5, 9, 12, 19, 20) did not receive great support from their faith. That may be explained by the date of publication, fourteen years after the beginning of Vatican II, a time of theological confusion when the joyboy theologians predominated with their mantra (falsely attributed to Augustine), "We are an Easter people, and Alleluia is our song!"

grace. Many people make smaller, analogous sacrifices in daily life, finding meaning in them and testifying to man's transcendence of merely natural tendencies to self-perpetuation and self-fulfillment.[17]

Imagine, for a moment, a world without the possibility of suffering. Every challenge and adventure would disappear. No dragons could be slain, nor princesses rescued. Scaling Mt. Everest would be as dangerous as scratching one's nose. Indiana Jones would yawn away his existence. Men would remain on their spiritual backsides all day, consuming the fruit dropping from the mango tree. A world of boredom would ensue since no risk could be involved. No one wins since no one loses. Men could not even commit suicide out of boredom lest they hurt themselves. In short, a finite world without the possibility of suffering cannot be tolerated.

The Mystery of Death

A word should be said about death, which most men fear mightily, and which is anticipated in suffering. Indeed, the devil employs fear of death as his principal means of enslaving men (Heb 2:14–15). Nonetheless death cannot be an absolute evil. First, insofar as this life is replete with sufferings, death liberates from them. On the occasion of his brother's death, St. Ambrose expressed a similar insight: "From the beginning God did not institute death, but He bestowed it as a remedy. . . . There ought to be an end to evils in order that death might restore what life lost."[18] Second, imagine, if possible, a world without death. It would be monotonous and boring. Bodies would gradually shrink away. Ancient Greek mythology recounts how Eos, or Aurora, the goddess of dawn, fell in love with the beautiful youth Tithonus and abducted him (*Homeric Hymn to Aphrodite*, 218–45). In the felicity of romantic love, she entreated Zeus to grant her beloved the gift of immortality. She eventually prevailed upon Zeus to render Tithonus immortal. Alas, she neglected to request perpetual youth. He constantly became older, continually diminishing in size. Eos locks him in her bedchamber, whence only his voice emerges, while she seeks out other lovers. That might explain another version in which he is transformed into a never ceasing, chirping cicada.[19] In retelling the myth, Tennyson has Tithonus pray for mortality and speak "of happy men that have the power to die, /

17. Kant, *Grundlegung der Metaphysik der Sitten*, 18–21, 61–63, 87–89; Kant, *Kritik der Praktischen Vernunft*, 95–98, 177–79, noted the connection between human dignity and moral freedom which suffers to fulfill the moral law.

18. Ambrose, *De excessu fratris*, 2.47.

19. Rose and Robertson, "Eos," in Hammond and Scullard, *The Oxford Classical Dictionary*, 385.

And grassy barrows of the happier dead." A similar fate befell the Cumaean Sibyll, who negligently besought immortality without eternal youth from Apollo and with time withered into a cicada. Kept in a cage in a tavern, she constantly repeats her chant, *thelo thanein, thelo thanein,* "I wish to die, I wish to die." That phrase served as the motto placed by T. S. Eliot at the beginning of "The Waste Land," describing modern culture which has no reason to live or perpetuate itself but cannot quite die. Before Elliot, Jonathan Swift concocted the race of Struldbruggs, humans born with a mark upon their foreheads indicating that they are immortal. These are condemned to "the dreadful project of never dying." For they grow old and become "opinionative, peevish, covetous, morose, vain, talkative." Then they gradually lose all their spiritual faculties, retain only envy and impotent passions, and wander friendless in a perpetual daze. These most pitiable of creatures lose their teeth and hair as well as their appetite for food, yet remain subject to diseases of all sorts.[20] Even if their spiritual faculties and bodies did not deteriorate, would they not become utterly bored as the same experiences keep on repeating themselves again and again without end, the eternal return of the same? In Tolkien's myths about Middle-earth the elves, who retain their powers and cannot die except by violence, ultimately grow weary of living there and, following their hearts' desire, depart freely for Valinor's Blessed Isles. Death is rightly called the Gift of Men as well as the Doom of Men.[21] Life without death would be dreary. As Ambrose remarked: "Immortality is more a burden than enjoyment unless grace breathes upon it."[22] In this life, death cannot be entirely bad.

In many ways, death bestows a poignant value on human life and those whom are loved. Shakespeare's sonnet 73 communicates that insight:

> That time of year thou mayst in me behold
> When yellow leaves, or none, or few do hang
> Upon those boughs which shake against the cold,
> Bare ruined choirs, where late the sweet birds sang.
> In me thou see'st the twilight of such day
> As after sunset fadeth in the west,
> Which by and by black night doth take away,
> Death's second self, that seals up all in rest.
> In me you see'st the glowing of such fire,

---

20. Swift, "Gulliver's Travels," III.X, in *The Writings of Jonathan Swift,* 181–83.

21. Tolkien, *The Return of the King,* 234, 308–10, 315, 342–43, 406; Tolkien, *The Simarillion,* 41–42, 88, 104–5, 264–65.

22. Ambrose, *De excessu fratris,* 2.47.

That on the ashes of his youth doth lie,
As the death-bed whereon it must expire,
Consum'd with that which it was nourish'ed by.
This thou perceiv'st, which makes thy love more strong,
To love that well which thou must leave ere long.

The very fragility of mortal things renders them all the more precious. A mother's or a father's love for a child endangered by sickness witnesses that truth. Indeed, their love grows through the sufferings which they share with their child.[23] The good and the beautiful have to be protected. The Roman forum in its dilapidated state is doubtless rendered more romantically and entrancingly beautiful because it no longer gleams like the neighboring, garish monument to Victor Emmanuel; its brokenness touches men's imaginations and feelings.

Finally, consider the relation of morality to suffering. As noted above, human beings often become aware of their worth when they are ready to suffer for an ideal or another person. In life there emerge conflicts between what one feels like doing and what one should do. Moral conscience opens men to a universe transcending the ordinary world with its search for self-fulfillment. Heroes give their lives for duty and love. Indeed, the very appeal for justice reveals that one suffers at recognizing injustice, how things should not be. Hence moral awareness, which differentiates man from the animals, is bound up with suffering. If justice utterly prevailed in this world and only the evil suffered, it would be all but impossible to distinguish self-interest from moral altruism. If morality received its just reward right away, only the invincibly stupid would be immoral.

God's Relation to Suffering

Denying God does not solve the problem of suffering. One can imagine God's extirpation, but the suffering remains, and the injustice remains, and there is no hope for a solution. If this world is all that is, what is justice? So many predators and swindlers escape punishment for their iniquitous actions. "Justice" becomes a phantasmagorical figment of imagination, a term employed by media moguls and political pundits to manipulate the masses. Justice does not exist in a world of injustice. Justice's standard must transcend this world. And "justice" cannot be an impersonal norm; it must be capable of judging human hearts. Only a personal God can afford any hope of making

---

23. Cf. Aristotle *Nic. Eth.* 9:7 1168a 21–27, who noted that we become more attached to those for whom we make sacrifices.

sense out of this piebald world. As my Irish grandmother prognosticated, "There has to be a heaven since there's no justice on this earth." But why does God allow the suffering of the innocent? That is the nub of the question. Only the Christian God supplies a satisfactory answer.

The Theology of Suffering

Two cautions must be issued at the beginning of the theological answer. First, suffering is real. Some religions deny the reality of suffering, as Christian Science does, and types of Buddhism and Hinduism see all finite realities as "appearance," *maya*. Nonetheless the appearances hurt. Therefore, there must be some reality to the appearances. All philosophies distinguishing appearance from reality face the impossible challenge of explaining how appearances, the non-real, somehow exist in the world or in the mind. Second, the immediate appeal to religion is short-sighted and contradictory. If anyone says, "Don't worry about all the sufferings here, God will make it up in the next life," he risks divorcing God from the world He created. If God can do justice in the next world, why doesn't He do it here now? If this world is a world abandoned to injustice, how can anyone know that a God of justice exists? Such knowledge cannot be based on human experience; it seems to contradict experience. The basis for affirming God's justice and love must therefore be discovered in this world.

Now the sufferings of the innocent can be confronted. Who are innocent? The modern world is conditioned to accept a juridical notion of innocence whereby no one is guilty before he or she performs a malevolent free act. So, it considers all children innocent. Nonetheless all cultures insist that they be trained to self-discipline and regard for others. No one wants to see little Johnny perpetually poop in his pants nor little Mary howl every morning for food and comfort at 2:00 a.m. Every child experiences inherent self-satisfying urges which must be conquered for the growth of freedom. That implies that some selfishness resides from the beginning in human nature. Every nature seeks the fulfillment of basic, inborn impulses before learning to love properly. Adults recognize that their best inspirations to do good and help others or to resist an evil temptation are at times suppressed by a fear of being hurt or seeming ridiculous or becoming too involved. That tendency to selfishness is inborn. St. Augustine recalled seeing a child howling with rage and hating his brother because that brother was sharing his mother's milk, even though the first child was already filled (*Confessions*, 1:7). That Freud managed to convince so many intelligent people that little boys want to kill their fathers and rape their mothers indicates that some evidence testifies that distorted passions have planted their roots in the depths of human psyches.[24] The Church recognizes concupiscence as an inborn tendency deriving from sin and inclining to sinful behavior (DS 1515). St. Paul's "indwelling sin" (Rom 7:17–23) afflicts humans from conception. It can it be restrained and overcome only through freedom's proper discipline under grace. That entails a struggle. Full innocence requires the proper use of freedom to master sinful tendencies. Who then are fully innocent in the sense that they do not succumb to selfish inclinations? According to Catholic theology only Jesus and His mother, both of whom went to the cross without recriminations.

On another point, a simple clarification refutes atheists' objections. According to the Bible, God is not the Father of all men. In the Old Testament, YHWH is Father to Israel, the king, and the just man, all by His election. In the New Testament Jesus alone is Son of God by nature, by His eternal birth from the Father. He alone dared to address YHWH as *Abba*, Dad or Daddy. Men are not sons by nature but become sons by adoption, by rebirth in baptism. Jesus gives them the courage to call His Father "Our Father." He always distinguished "my Father" from "your Father." Only once did He say, "Our Father," viz., when teaching his disciples how to pray (Matt 6:9).[25] Jesus, the sole revealer of the Father, enables men to become God's children. St. John stated it simply: "To those who received Him [Jesus], believing in His name, He gave the power to *become* God's children; they were born, not of blood nor of the will of the flesh nor of the will of man, but of God" (1:12–13). Human beings are not born God's children but have to become His children, reborn by faith and baptism. This reality is called by St. Paul "adoptive sonship" (Rom 8:15, 23; Gal 4:5; Eph 1:5). This means that they are bound to understand God as Father just as Jesus did. His innocent sufferings did not cause Jesus to deny God as His Father. Rather in His agony, foreseeing His torments, He affirmed both God's omnipotence and His fatherhood. He prayed, "Abba, Father all things are possible to you. Let this chalice pass me by. But not what I will but what you will" (Mark 14:36). On the cross His last words were, "Father, into your hands I commend my Spirit" (Luke 23:46). For Christian disciples, who have received Jesus's Spirit, innocent suffering does not contradict but reveals God's love.

---

24. Read the "Introduction" by A. A. Brill to *The Basic Writings of Sigmund Freud* to encounter the adulation ascribed to Freud's work. For a more convincing, saner view of children's psychology, see Bowlby, *A Secure Base*, 1–37, a good summary of more detailed studies.

25. Cf. Schrenk, *"pater,"* in *TDNT* 5:974–1014; Sparks, "The Doctrine of the Divine Fatherhood in the Gospels," in Nineham, *Studies in the Gospels*, 241–62; Marchel, *Abba, Père!*; Jeremias, "Abba," in *The Prayers of Jesus*, 11–65.

St. John affirmed God's love for the universe precisely "because He gave His only-begotten Son" (3:16), and St. Paul argued that because God sacrificed His only Son for us nothing in creation can separate us from God's love in Christ (Rom 8:28–39). It is a strange religion in which the suffering of the innocent proves not God's non-existence but His love for men. Yet such is basic Christian faith and the key to suffering's meaning.

Christian Suffering: Original Sin

What is the sense of Christian suffering? The Bible offers many reasons for suffering: the evil are punished while the good are rewarded—that is only justice; God brings men to a fall in order to convert them from sin; moreover, after conversion, they still must be purified; habits of sin must be eradicated, and that entails a painful going against the warped grain. Men are tested by God in the sense that God's love involves a choice, a preference of Him over all other goods, and the sacrifice involved can be painful. But there is something more, Christians do not suffer only for themselves just as they do not live for themselves alone. They suffer for others. That is implied in the doctrines of original sin and redemption. These deep mysteries require explanations.[26]

God created man in His image, male and female, in the image of His love. He wants to share His life with men, to divinize them. For God is tripersonal love, pure mutual self-giving from eternity to eternity. What other reason might move the philosphers' self-sufficient, entirely blissful, omniscient, omnipotent God to create a world that would only give Him trouble? Mankind's original parents' sin broke the primordial unity of love existing among men and between men and God. When there is no love in the world, no one can know the God who is Love. In a loveless world, men lose their freedom; they have no reason for any choice; every finite reason for acting can always be relativized and put into question. "Why should I love anyone else, i.e., prefer another person to myself?" Divorce and abortion are both available. Without love the world's meaning becomes at best ambiguous and opaque: Does God love us? Does God exist? What reason remains for living, for enduring so much pain, if death ultimately frustrates all plans and hopes?

After the primordial sin, all human beings are born into a world from which their first parents tried to banish God, a loveless world. As St. Paul wrote, "We were by birth (*physis*: nature) children of wrath, like the rest"

---

26. The biblical basis for these answers is explored in greater detail in McDermott, *The Bible on Human Suffering*.

(Eph 2:3). The continuation of such a world involves hell. No one has access to God, and since man was originally created out of love for love, fallen man is doomed to eternal frustration. God could have abandoned men to the world which they attempted to create exclusively for themselves. Does it seem very unjust that all human beings are condemned because of what Adam and Eve did? "Why should I have to suffer because of what someone else did so long ago? How unfair of God!" Such is mankind's plaint.

Another question responds to the first question. Who remembers the name of the wheel's inventor, the tamer of fire, the first shipbuilder? How many good things humans take for granted without gratitude, yet once something inconveniences them, how swiftly they groan and protest! Can anyone live in human society and expect to accept only good things from his predecessors while reviling them for whatever goes wrong? Put this in more personal terms. Suppose your father or mother committed a crime and everyone turned against him or her. What should your reaction be? Should you say: "I want nothing to do with him. Let him go his own way. He is not my father"? Are you then a dutiful, loving child or even a just person? Is not such a rejection parricide and ultimately the wish for self-annihilation? Into that predicament men are born as a result of original sin: either they love their parents and share their fate, or they reject them and prove ungrateful, unfaithful children. So springs the trap of original sin: either men identify with sinning parents or refuse to love them and repeat their sin, further polluting the world. They are damned if they do and damned if they don't. Who can redeem their sinful situation? Who can restore the human race's fractured unity and let men find love and God again?

Too often the modern world accepts an anthropology which concentrates on the individual human nature without recognizing that "man" never exists alone. Even rugged individuals depend on parents to be born, be nourished, and flourish. No one ever learns a language by himself, and without language, thought hardly comes to birth or quickly atrophies. Communality defines man primordially. Every individual exists in himself and in relation. Indeed, the very notion of finite being implies that it is limited (*finitum*) by others. As John Paul II's analysis of freedom indicates, the person is both in himself and in relation.[27] That is how man is created

---

27. Wojtyła, *Acting Person*, 276–300; Wojtyła, "The Person," esp. 283–306. Although Wojtyła, "The Person," 303, presupposes "the particular priority of the subject as person in regard to the community," that reflects his chosen starting point in individual consciousness; earlier, however, he admits (p. 273): "The whole process of understanding man must embrace both the others and my own self and . . . I may start from either." Also, in *Acting Person*, 276: "The person and the community may be said to coalesce together." Clearly the self-conscious subject's in-itself cannot be separated from his relation to others.

in the image of God, i.e., in freedom for love. "God created man in His own image, in the image of God He created him; male and female He created them" (Gen 1:27). By oscillating between the singular and the plural in his description of the culminating object of God's creation, the sacred writer recognizes the unity and plurality implicit in being human from the very beginning. Man cannot be fully human unless in relation to others, indeed only in loving others. St. Maximus Confessor recognized that "man" is primarily a concrete whole before the individuals constituting it: the individual only exists within that whole in relation to others. Further, in the hypostatic union he saw the basic principle of divine love which effects the greatest unity while maintaining the greatest diversity of natures. "Insofar as [the union] comes together it does not entirely obscure their essential and natural elements but perfectly preserves the difference."[28] His insight applies to the ontological structures of the Trinity and the Incarnation as well as to humanity itself. For husband and wife, the basic components of the family and society, are intended to be two in one flesh (Gen 2:24; Mark 10:7–10; Eph 5:31). Though each spouse desires to be fully one with the other, both wish the other to remain fully himself or herself. Love provides the greatest unity while maintaining the greatest diversity. Recent Thomistic thinkers like Rousselot, Przywara, and von Balthasar have also recognized the need to uphold the notion of mankind's fundamental, primordial unity.[29] That insight facilitates understanding not only original sin but also the eschatological Adam's redemption.

Redemption

No human being, no part of the broken whole, can reconstitute the whole. Mankind's shattered state is like Humpty Dumpty; all the king's horses and all the king's men can't put him back together again. No human being can provide the center or the new beginning by saying to everyone else: you have to love me, you have to give your lives for me. Besides, based on man's broken, selfish experience, who can assure the rest of mankind that God is love and really cares? Only He who is personally eternal Love can assure

---

28. Cf. Balthasar, *Cosmic Liturgy*, 159–65; Maximus the Confessor, *Epistola ad Nicandrum* (PG 91, 96D–97A); Maximus the Confessor, *Ambiguorum Liber* (PG 91, 1044D–1045A; 1056CD).

29. Rousselot, *L'Intellectualisme de saint Thomas*, 124–32; Przywara, *Analogia Entis*, 135–41, 199–210; Przywara, *Deus Semper Maior*, 1:54–61, 70; Balthasar, *Theodramatik*, 334–61; Balthasar, *Theo-logic*, 153–58, 168–70. Aquinas's polymorphic understanding of nature includes the notion of a concrete universal: see McDermott, "On Nature, Freedom, and Person in Aquinas and Beyond," 798–99.

men of Love's reality, and He assumed a human nature in order to communicate love in a language that men might understand. He called all to conversion, to follow Him, to unite themselves to Him and share His fate. He submitted to the conditions of creaturely limitation and suffered death since sinful men seek to avoid admitting their sinfulness and need. All except His mother betrayed, abandoned, and killed Him, but on Easter morning He rose from the dead to prove that Love is stronger than death and sin, to offer Himself to men again and convert their hearts to Him. When men love Jesus, God Himself in person, they are one with God where they are most themselves, in their personal freedom, where each says "I." In love human beings are most free, most themselves, yet most joined to their beloved, letting Him rule their lives. "Now live no longer I," wrote St. Paul, "but Christ lives in me" (Gal 2:20). "For me to live is Christ and to die is gain" (Phil 1:21). This most profound union with God banishes sin, the refusal of love. Jesus paid the price of redemption in His cross and resurrection, setting sinners free to love Him without fear.

All those who love Jesus are united with Him entirely, body and soul. Thus is established the Church, the Body of Christ (1 Cor 12:12–31; Eph 5:21–33), where Jesus remains present through all time, offering Himself in word and sacrament to sinners. Christians desire to be conformed to Christ crucified (Rom 8:17; Gal 2:20; Phil 3:8–11). The Church is the place of crucified love, where men should turn in conversion to let God's love penetrate their hearts. This is why the Eucharist stands in the Church's center, the place of love's concrete commitment and her daily nourishment. The Church is also the place of resurrected joy, for there love conquers human hearts, and when believers really live for Jesus, crucifying their flesh with all its selfish desires, they are set free to love (Rom 6:6–11; 8:2; Gal 5:1–24; Col 3:5–15). From such self-sacrificial Christians, a wonderful community results. But no one should join the Church just to enjoy a personally fulfilling human community; the ultimate reason for entering the Church should be that she is the way sinners are joined to Jesus; she is the ordinary means of salvation (DS 1351; 2865–67). Precisely because the Church embraces sinners, not rejecting her wayward children, living with ecclesial sinners often entails a heavy cross.

The liberating love of Jesus solves the dilemma of original sin. It no longer matters if men are sinners; they can confess their sins without fear; they can identify with their sinful parents, for God loves sinners (John 3:16; Rom 5:8; 1 John 4:10). They need no longer defend and justify themselves. Justification is God's gift in Jesus Christ (Rom 3:21–30; 5:1–2). Jesus has broken the vicious circle of sin, guilt, and recrimination. They can and should love their parents. If Jesus bears their sins, in union with Him they can and should bear their parents' sins.

Salvific Suffering

This union in love explains the meaning of Christian suffering. Christians suffer for their personal sins and to root out the habits of sin, which, congealed in concupiscence, have deformed them. For concupiscence arises out of fear of the vulnerability which love entails. In a fallen, hostile world men seek to protect and perpetuate themselves by heaping up money, property, and power. Since such things invariably distort friendships, they console themselves in the absence of love with purchased pleasures, love's sickly substitutes. But conformity to Christ reforms sinners into the image of God in which they were originally created. He is the eschatological Adam in whose image man was created (1 Cor 15:45; 2 Cor 4:4; Col 1:15–20; Eph 1:3–10). Consequently, they strive to overcome their inborn selfishness and gladly bear the sufferings entailed in the struggle.

Christians also suffer with Christ and for others. They are baptized into Christ's death in order to be crucified with Him, to die to sin, and to share His eternal life (Rom 6:3–11). They enjoy the communion which Christ's love creates. Looking upon Jesus crucified, suffering for their sins, how can they remain distant, neutral observers or just cheer Him on from the sidelines? "Just ten more yards to go, Jesus, and then you'll be on top of the hill. Hang tough." No! Love wants to suffer with the beloved. If God let His heart be broken to break the hardness of calloused human hearts, how can anyone refuse to share His crucified love?[30] If Jesus invited a doubting

---

30. That God suffers for men is in accord with Christian faith. Catholic doctrine defines God's immutability (DS 800; 3001), but that immutability need not depend upon Scholastic arguments from potency to act, where potency is understood as imperfection seeking perfection and God is identified with Pure Act. Change has to exist with God if He freely created the world, chose to redeem it, and responds to prayer (Luke 11:9–13). God is immutably infinite, tri-personal Love; He cannot be otherwise, and He will definitively conquer death and sin. John Paul II, *Dominum et vivificantem*, 39–40; Benedict XVI, *Spe salvi*, 39; Benedict XVI, *Deus caritas est*, 10, 12, allow for God's compassion due to man's sin. John Paul II approved the orthodoxy of the expression "one of the Trinity suffered" (DS 401; also 423.432). The suffering of the divine Persons belongs to Western popular piety's emphasis on the crucified Christ and finds its supreme artistic expression in El Greco's "Trinity" (Prado), when the artist reproduces the basic structure of Michelangelo's Roman Pieta with God the Father replacing Mary, God's Mother. For a speculative grounding of divine immutability allowing change, see McDermott, "Faith, Reason, and Freedom," 307–32. Protestant theologians Kitamorei, Pannenberg, Moltmann, and Jüngel have sought to reconcile becoming with God's being. For this history, see H. Hoping, *"Caritas est passio*: Das Sterben Jesu und die Frage nach dem leidendem Gott,"* in Augustin et al., *Mein Herr und mein Gott*, 334–46.

Thomas to place his hand into His wounded side (John 20:27), why do others hesitate to touch the heart of God?

Love creates communion. St. Paul uses the Greek word *koinonia* to describe the relationship between Jesus and the Christian and among Christians. It signifies community, communion (as in Holy Communion), participating in, and sharing actively with. He wrestled with the Greek language to express the novelty of the Christian mystery of love. For the first time *koinonia* involved a sharing in not just material realities or ideas but in persons: a communion in the Holy Spirit and in the Body and Blood of Christ; likewise, *koinonia* was employed for the first time to indicate an active giving a share in, not just a passive participation. Indeed, *koinonia* embraces material as well as spiritual realities; also, for the first time it indicated a monetary collection, the one destined for Jerusalem's poor. This word *koinonia*, pregnant with so many meanings, describes many aspects of life in the Body of Christ. It helps believers to understand their sufferings. At the beginning of the Second Letter to the Corinthians Paul wrote:

> Blessed be the God and Father of our Lord Jesus Christ, the Father of mercies and God of all consolation, who comforts us in all our tribulation, so that we might comfort others in all tribulation through the comfort with which we are comforted by God. For as Christ's sufferings superabound (*perisseuei*) upon us, so also through Christ our comfort superabounds. If we are troubled, it is for your comfort and salvation. If we are comforted, it is for your comfort active in the bearing of the suffering which we also suffer. And our hope for you is firm, since we know that as you are sharers (*koinonoi*) in the sufferings, so you are sharers in the comfort. (2 Cor 1:3–7)

Because Christians share Christ's life, His sufferings overflow upon them. They are being remade ever more into the image of incarnate Love. Christians are strange in this world. How many times the New Testament reports rejoicing in suffering, from the Beatitudes on! For in their suffering they are never alone. They are joined to Christ and His redemptive work. In Col 1:24, St. Paul writes, "Now I rejoice in sufferings for your sake, and I fill up what is lacking to the tribulations of Christ in my flesh for the sake of His Body, the Church." Not that anything is lacking to the perfection of Christ's redemptive work. The Greek word *hysteremata*, translated as "what is lacking," is generally used by St. Paul as the opposite of the word *perisseuma*, superabundance. Just as God's infinity does not exclude but creates finite men, just as God's omnipotence does everything to save mankind without destroying their response but rather creating it, so there is room for believers to contribute in love to the salvation of all others sharing in Christ's *koinonia*, His Body.[31]

This mystery is the mystery of love that is full yet grows. It is illustrated and lived daily. With their marriage vows, husband and wife intended to love each fully other without conditions, yet over the years they can confess that their love has grown. So also, religious intend to dedicate their whole lives to God without restrictions when they pronounce their vows. Their love is full, yet no one kills them immediately after the vow formula. Though full, their love, it is augured, should grow. This paradox is based upon the Christian mystery: in Jesus the kingdom of God was already fully present, yet still to come. Room is left for the superabundant accomplishment of God's will in Jesus's disciples. The indicative of love accomplished in Christ grounds the imperative for their response of love (1 John 4:7–11).[32] By free acceptance of sufferings they contribute to the salvation of all in the Church and over the Church to all human beings whom Christ calls to the fullness of His love. Thus the leaden dross of suffering is transmuted into the gold of love by the cross of Jesus Christ, a mystery far more transformative than any philosopher's stone and deeper than the wisdom of worldly philosophers.

The Church's Mission

This understanding of suffering also illuminates man's original task in the world. God enjoined on Adam the tilling of the Garden (Gen 2:15). Without a commission in the world to fulfill, man would have been reduced to the passivity of a welfare recipient, deprived of meaningful accomplishments. Instead his ingenuity and fortitude were challenged to improve the world and suffuse it with works of love, making it more hospitable to his fellow human beings and reflective of God's generous love. Despite the Fall, God's original plan to have men assist at the world's amelioration remains to be carried out. The task is now much more burdensome but also more imperative. Not only is material creation to be enhanced so that it might lend itself to mankind's acts of fraternal charity but also the sacrifices entailed in overcoming the results of sin and selfishness contribute spiritually and efficiently to the salvation of other humans. A world called to spiritual evolution, i.e., greater charity, challenges men to grow "to the measure of the stature of the fullness of Christ" (Eph 4:13–16).

In Christ's cross men confront the ultimate choice of faith and meaning. Either they close themselves in upon their sufferings, finding no

31. For further elaboration, see McDermott, "The Biblical Doctrine of KOINO-NIA," 64–77, 219–33.

32. McDermott, "Jesus and the Kingdom of God," 69–91. .

meaning in them—they are individual, unintelligible to human reason, and contrary to nature—and so embitter themselves, or else they let themselves be opened to a mystery of love far surpassing their minds and hearts. Evolution in both physical and spiritual spheres calls for sacrifice. Then Christian disciples join their sufferings to Christ's for the increase of love, mankind's redemption, and eternal sharing in divine life. They know that God can bring good out of evil as He did in His Son's Passion. Sometimes He wishes to open human hearts to Himself in order that He might respond to prayers for particular intentions. Then He provides a requested healing or bestows comfort and strength. If some suffer more than others, that is due to the humanly incalculable concatenation of physical conditions, the residue of past sins, and human freedom. Yet more, those suffering are being invited to conform themselves to His beloved Son, the perfect expression of selfless love. Although usually because of their weakness God treats His children more gently than they deserve, sometimes He summons them to heroism. When St. Paul repeatedly besought God for the removal of a particular "thorn in the flesh," he received the answer, "My grace is sufficient for you; for my power is made perfect in weakness." Then Paul proclaimed his faith, "I shall most gladly boast of my weaknesses, in order that the power of Christ may rest upon me. Therefore for Christ's sake I am content with weaknesses, insults, hardships, persecutions, and calamities; for when I am weak, then I am strong" (2 Cor 12:7–10). Some great saints, like Thérèse of Lisieux and John of the Cross, desired sufferings in order to join themselves ever more closely to Christ and increase divine love in their souls and in the world.[33] Such heroes by grace overcome the world, leaving the rest of humanity models of courage, patience, and fidelity. For this large remnant, God alone is the final judge of frail hearts summoned to love in challenging conditions. May He be merciful.

Catholic Christianity preserved this positive evaluation of suffering in its entirety. Before post-Vatican II theologies introduced confusion into Catholic life, it had been common practice for Catholics to recite daily the morning offering, in which are offered up prayers, works, joys, and sufferings in reparation for their sins and the sins of others. Thereby personal growth in love and holiness ensued. It may be time to renew that practice. Catholics knew that God wanted them to share in His redemptive work, not certainly as independent agents, but entirely governed by His omnipotent love. One can merit justification as little as one can earn love. Indeed, justification is the result of God's free love implanted and accepted in human hearts through Christ.

---

33. For example, see Thérèse of Lisieux, *Story of a Soul*, 214–20; John of the Cross, "The Dark Night," 2:5–12, in *Collected Works of St. John of the Cross*, 335–57.

The Christian faith tells us that natural powers alone do not suffice for salvation. Sinful creatures are called and empowered by God to surpass themselves. Ultimately God created them not for happiness or its pursuit, but for divinization, sharing in His eternal life of self-giving love. Men are challenged to surpass their nature. Only in dying to themselves do they live to God. That gives the answer to suffering in the concrete: when tragedy strikes you or someone whom you love, do not enter into a philosophical or theological analysis of suffering, as this essay attempts. Rather place yourselves and your loved ones under the cross with Mary, the mother of God, who accepted the Father's will for her Son and drank the redemptive cup to the dregs. Salvation was won on the cross, the definitive revelation of God in a fallen world.

The Church's doctrine alone can illuminate the meaning of suffering and give hope, consolation, and courage to people who must undergo sufferings in this world, i.e., everyone. Unfortunately, not everyone has heard the good news about suffering, and Catholic Christians should mediate knowledge of it by living their lives in joy, even when sufferings are inflicted upon them. They know not only that ascetical sufferings are required to overcome the concupiscence which lies deep in human hearts but also that sufferings freely accepted lead to ever greater union with their Savior, Jesus Christ. Knowing and living this mystery, they should be zealous to spread it to others who are suffering and seeking meaning in their lives. So, the same love which strengthens Catholics in bearing sufferings, Christ's love, should move them to bring its consolation and strength to others. For if someone is not strengthened to bear sufferings in this life, he shall sadly bear them in the next. There is a single hope for all: conversion to Christ's cross and encouragement of others to do the same. Planted in the Church's midst is the new tree of life, the blessed Eucharist, both challenge and consolation, sacrifice and joyous celebration.[34]

Bibliography

Aeschylus. *Agamemnon*. http://classics.mit.edu/Aeschylus/agamemnon.html.

Ambrose of Milan. *De excessu fratris sui Satyri libri duo*. http://www.documentacatholica omnia.eu/o3d/0339-0397,_Ambrosius,_De_Excessu_Fratris_Sui_Satyri_Libri_ Duo_[Schaff],_EN.pdf.

Anderson, J. "The Impact of Family Structure on the Health of Children: Effects of Divorce." *Linacre Quarterly* 81 (2014) 379–83.

---

34. This article was previously presented in lecture form in various milieux. I express a word of gratitude to Laura Ring, a former student, for her kindness in offering critique and suggestions for improvement. She is not in agreement with everything. Needless to say, the responsibility for errors is my own.

Aquinas, Thomas. *Expositio libri Posteriorum Analyticorum.* https://isidore.co/aquinas/PostAnalytica.htm.

———. *Summa Theologiae.* https://www.corpusthomisticum.org/sth0000.html.

Aristotle. *The Complete Works of Aristotle: The Revised Oxford Translation.* Edited by Jonathan Barnes. 2 vols. Princeton: Princeton University Press, 1984.

Augustin, G., et al., eds. *Mein Herr und mein Gott: Festschrift W. Kasper.* Freiburg: Herder, 2013.

Balthasar, Hans Urs von. *Cosmic Liturgy.* Translated by B. Daley. San Francisco: Ignatius, 2003.

———. *Theodramatik, II/1.* Einsiedeln: Johannes, 1976.

———. *Theo-logic, I.* Translated by A. Walker. San Francisco: Ignatius, 2000.

Benedict XVI, Pope. *Deus caritas est.* http://www.vatican.va/content/benedict-xvi/en/encyclicals/documents/hf_ben-xvi_enc_20051225_deus-caritas-est.html.

———. *Spe salvi.* http://www.vatican.va/content/benedict-xvi/en/encyclicals/documents/hf_ben-xvi_enc_20071130_spe-salvi.html.

Bose, J., et al. "Key Substance Use and Mental Health Indicators in the United States: Results from the 2017 National Survey on Drug Use and Health." https://store.samhsa.gov/system/files/pep19-5068.pdf.

Bowlby, John. *A Secure Base.* New York: HarperCollins, 1988.

Camus, Albert. *The Plague.* Translated by S. Gilbert. New York: Knopf, 1948.

Centers for Disease Control and Prevention. "Suicide." https://www.cdc.gov/vitalsigns/suicide.

Ch'en, K. *Buddhism.* Woodbury: Barron, 1968.

Congar, Yves. "The Problem of Evil." In *God, Man, and the Universe,* edited by Jacques de Bivort de la Saudee, 393–421. London: Burns & Oates, 1954.

Dominican Nuns of Our Lady of Perpetual Help Home. *A Memoire of Mary Ann.* Savannah: Beil, 1991.

Dostoevsky, Fyodor. *The Brothers Karamazov.* Translated by Constance Garnett. New York: Random House, 1996.

Engelmann, G. *Labor among Primitive Peoples.* St. Louis: Chambers, 1883.

Flew, Antony, and Alasdair C. MacIntyre. *New Essays in Philosophical Theology.* London: SCM, 1955.

Fraine, J. de. *Adam and the Family of Man.* Translated by D. Raible. Staten Island, NY: Alba, 1965.

Freud, Sigmund. *The Basic Writings of Sigmund Freud.* Translated by A. A. Brill. New York: Modern Library, 1938.

Hammond, N., and H. Scullard, eds. *The Oxford Classical Dictionary.* 2nd ed. Oxford: Clarendon, 1970.

Hume, Robert. "An Outline of the Philosophy of the Upanishads." In *The Thirteen Principal Upanishads,* translated by Robert Hume, 1–72. London: Oxford University Press, 1931.

Janke, Wolfgang, and Henning Luther. "Individuum/Individualismus I: Philosophisch." *Theologische Realenzyklopädie* 16 (1987) 117–27.

Jeremias, Joachim. *The Prayers of Jesus.* Translated by J. Bowden et al. Philadelphia: Fortress, 1978.

John of the Cross. *The Collected Works of St. John of the Cross.* Translated by K. Kavanaugh and O. Rodriguez. Washington, DC: ICS, 1979.

John Paul II, Pope. *Dominum et vivificantem.* http://www.vatican.va/content/john-paul-ii/en/encyclicals/documents/hf_jp-ii_enc_18051986_dominum-et-vivificantem.html.

————. *Evangelium vitae*. https://www.vatican.va/content/john-paul-ii/en/encyclicals/documents/hf_jp-ii_enc_25031995_evangelium-vitae.html.

————. *Salvifici doloris*. https://www.vatican.va/content/john-paul-ii/en/apost_letters/1984/documents/hf_jp-ii_apl_11021984_salvifici-doloris.html.

Kant, Immanuel. *Grundlegung der Metaphysik der Sitten*. Edited by B. Kraft and D. Schönecker. Hamburg: Meiner, 1999.

————. *Kritik der Praktischen Vernunft*. Edited by K. Vorländer. Hamburg: Meiner, 1928.

Marchel, W. *Abba, Père!* Rome: Pontifical Bible Institute, 1971.

McDermott, John. *The Bible on Human Suffering*. Middlegreen: St. Paul, 1991.

————. "The Biblical Doctrine of KOINONIA." *Biblische Zeitschrift* 19 (1975) 64–77, 219–33.

————. "Faith, Reason, and Freedom." *Irish Theological Quarterly* 67 (2002) 307–32.

————. "Jesus and the Kingdom of God in the Synoptics, Paul, and John." *Église et Théologie* 19 (1988) 69–91.

————. "On Nature, Freedom, and Person in Aquinas and Beyond." *Nova et Vetera* 9.3 (2011) 791–824.

Montgomery, Marion. "Walker Percy and the Christian Scandal." *First Things* 32 (1993) 38–44.

National Institute of Mental Health. "Suicide." https://www.nimh.nih.gov/health/statistics/suicide.shtml.

Nemecek, Douglas, et al. "Cigna U.S. Loneliness Index." https://www.multivu.com/players/English/8294451-cigna-us-loneliness-survey/docs/IndexReport_1524069371598-173525450.pdf.

Nineham, D. E., ed. *Studies in the Gospels: Essays in Memory of R. H. Lightfoot*. Oxford: Blackwell, 1955.

Parker, Wayne. "Key Statistics about Kids from Divorced Families." https://www.verywellfamily.com/children-of-divorce-in-america-statistics-1270390.

Przywara, Erich. *Analogia Entis*. 2nd ed. Einsiedeln: Johannes, 1962.

————. *Deus Semper Maior: Theologie der Exerzitien*. 3 vols. Freiburg: Herder, 1938.

Robinson, H. W. *Corporate Personality in Ancient Israel*. Philadelphia: Fortress, 1980.

Rousselot, Pierre. *L'Intellectualisme de saint Thomas*. 2nd ed. Paris: Beauchesne, 1924.

Schleiermacher, Friedrich. *The Christian Faith*. Edited by H. Mackintosh and J. Stewart. Edinburgh: T. & T. Clark, 1928.

Schulman, Jerome. *Coping with Tragedy*. Chicago: Follett, 1976.

Swift, Jonathan. *The Writings of Jonathan Swift*. Edited by R. Greenberg and W. Piper. New York: Norton, 1973.

Theological Dictionary of the New Testament. 10 vols. Edited by Gerhard Kittel and Gerhard Friedrich. Translated by Geoffrey W. Bromiley. Grand Rapids: Eerdmans, 1964–76.

Thérèse of Lisieux. *Story of a Soul*. Translated by J. Clarke. Washington, DC: ICS, 1976.

Tolkien, J. R. *The Return of the King*. Boston: Houghton Mifflin, 1955.

————. *The Simarillion*. Edited by C. Tolkien. Norwalk: Easton, 1999.

Wojtyła, Karol. *The Acting Person*. Translated by A. Potocki with A. Tymieniecka. Dordrecht: Reidel, 1979.

————. "The Person: Subject and Community." *Review of Metaphysics* 33.2 (1979) 273–308.

Zaehner, Robert. *Hinduism*. London: Oxford University Press, 1966.

5

The Sacrifice of the New Covenant
in Hebrews

Scott W. Hahn

Just over a half-century ago, F. F. Bruce pronounced the Letter to the Hebrews to be "among the more difficult books of the New Testament." In search of a unifying principle he settled on what he called "inwardness of true religion." According to Bruce, true religion, as presented in Hebrews, is not only non-liturgical. It's anti-liturgical. He said: "True religion or the worship of God is not tied to externalities of any kind." Ronald Williamson, in 1975, took Bruce's assertion and made of it an argument. He argued against the existence of any Eucharistic allusions whatsoever in Hebrews.[1] Their strongest support is that there is no explicit mention in Hebrews of the Eucharistic rite.

I would propose, however, that the Eucharist is implicit throughout the text. As Stephen Fahrig demonstrates in his recent dissertation, "The Context of the Text," Hebrews is best read as a "Eucharistic Homily," originally proclaimed to an assembly of new covenant believers.[2] This is a likely *Sitz im Leben* for Hebrews, which provides the context that would make the text intelligible to its earliest readers. It is also the context that makes the text more comprehensible for readers today. I wish to show how the Eucharist is an important—though implicit—theme in Hebrews.

In his monumental work, *The New Testament and the People of God*, N. T. Wright notes how widespread and central was the Eucharist (and baptism) in the early church: "It is clear, remarkably, that these two basic forms of Christian praxis were equally taken for granted as early as the 50s of the first century. Paul can write of baptism as a given, from which

---

1. See Bruce, *Epistle to the Hebrews*, xi–xii; Williamson, "The Eucharist and the Epistle to the Hebrews."

2. See Fahrig, "The Context of the Text." Also see Swetnam, *Hebrews*.

theological conclusions can be drawn (Rom 6:3–11). He can describe, or allude to, the Eucharist in similar fashion (1 Cor 10:15–22), taking it (as read) that the Corinthian church regularly meets to partake of the Lord's Meal together, and moving on to argue on this basis about what is and is not appropriate."[3] Or in the language of Hebrews, they undergo the "enlightenment" of Christian ablutions, and they "taste the heavenly gift" (Heb 6:4). These, Wright goes on to say, "were not strange actions which some Christians might on odd occasions perform, but ritual acts which were taken for granted, part of that praxis which constituted the early Christian worldview." The worldview Wright evokes is the only worldview that makes Hebrews intelligible. The text presents a consistent and comprehensive vision of a new and eternal covenant *that is essentially cultic.* Yet Wright also observes a rather glaring omission in this cultic worldview: "Among the striking features of early Christian praxis must be reckoned one thing that early Christians did *not* do. Unlike every other religion known in the world up to that point, the Christians offered no animal sacrifices."[4] Such a novel cultic worldview is precisely what one discovers with a Eucharistic reading of the New Covenant in Hebrews, then and now.

Yet the word Eucharist does not appear in Hebrews, nor do analogous terms such as "breaking of the bread." But there is a preponderance of imagery normally associated with early Christian liturgy. First, the assembly is made up of those who have "been enlightened . . . and *tasted the heavenly gift*" (6:4). Second, we read that the congregation is "sanctified through the offering of the body of Jesus Christ once for all" (10:10). Third, the assembly has come to experience the "blood that speaks more graciously than the blood of Abel" (12:24). Fourth, the author confidently asserts that the Christian assembly has "an altar from which those who serve the tent have no right to eat" (13:10). Furthermore, the assembly's festival is shared not only among Christians on earth, but also "innumerable angels in festal gathering" (12:22), and the "spirits of just men made perfect," (12:23) . . . "the great cloud of witnesses" in heaven (12:1). The text describes realized eschatology in a cultic setting—and for primitive Christianity this meant the Eucharist. Hebrews also relies on the Eucharistic typology that would become commonplace in early Christian commentaries, art, and liturgical poetry. The author invokes Abel's offering, Melchizedek's priestly blessing, and God's oath of blessing to Abraham after he offered Isaac. These factors point to the Eucharist as an interpretive key for reading the homily known as Hebrews.

---

3. Wright, *The New Testament and the People of God*, 362.

4. Wright, *The New Testament and the People of God*, 363.

Nevertheless, Bruce and Williamson could argue that the Eucharistic meaning of each of these details is contestable. What still remains uncontested, however, is the overarching *theme* of the Letter to the Hebrews. What is invoked most frequently in the text is the *covenant*—and specifically the *New Covenant*. Yet this too, in itself, is evidence in favor of a Eucharistic reading of Hebrews. The author presents Jesus as mediator of a New Covenant, a "better covenant," established as the former covenant had been, by the ritual sprinkling of blood. As high priest of *this* covenant, Jesus offers his *body and blood* as a once-for-all sacrifice on our behalf, a perpetual self-offering. Its effect is nothing less than "eternal salvation" (5:9), "eternal redemption" (9:12), by "the blood of the eternal covenant" (13:20).

I propose, then, that the Eucharist may be an important yet *implicit* theme of Hebrews, despite the term's absence. In point of fact, references to the *Eucharist* are only found in late first century sources (e.g., Didache, Ignatius). Rather, in the first generation, the NT terms used to denote what is later called the Eucharist, come from the words directly used by Jesus: *the new covenant* (Luke 22:20; 1 Cor 11:25), or the *blood of the covenant* (Matt 26:28; Mark 14:24). Notably, these words lie at the heart of the argument of Hebrews, where they occur in a strikingly disproportionate way. For example, just over half of the occurrences of the word *diatheke* in the NT are found in Hebrews (seventeen of thirty-three). Likewise, four of the six references to *new covenant* in the NT occur in Hebrews (Heb 8:8, 13; 9:15; 12:24). Hebrews is also unique in its focus on the cultic/liturgical aspects of the covenant, both old and new. This focus reinforces the author's emphasis on Christ's superior High Priesthood and New Covenant sacrifice.[5]

This is most obvious in chapters 8–9 of Hebrews,[6] where the author contrasts two covenant orders: the old (Heb 8:3–9:10) and the new (Heb 9:11–28). Both covenant orders have a cultus which includes a high priest (Heb 8:1, 3; 9:7, 11, 25; ἀρχιερεύς) or "celebrant" (Heb 8:2, 6; λειτουργός) who performs ministry (Heb 8:5; 9:1, 6; λατρεία) in a tent-sanctuary (Heb 8:2, 5; 9:2–3, 6, 8, 11, 21; σκηνή), entering into a Holy Place (Heb 8:2; 9:2–3, 12, 24; ἅγια) to

---

5. In ancient Israel, the establishment of covenants and their renewal consisted essentially of a *liturgy*: ritual words and sacrificial actions done in God's presence. This liturgical dimension of covenant-making appears frequently in the OT, where the priests and Levites mediate the covenant on God's behalf (Num 6:22–27). Reflecting on the OT traditions of "covenant," the author of Hebrews, while not forgetting the legal dimension, places the liturgical (or cultic) in the foreground. The mediation of both covenants is primarily cultic, the sacred realm of liturgy, which is precisely what remains in the foreground of the argument of Hebrews.

6. On the cultic background of Heb 9, see Swetnam, "A Suggested Interpretation of Hebrews 9, 15–18," 375; Behm, "διαθήκη," in *TDNT* 2:131–32; Vanhoye, *Old Testament Priests and the New Priest*, 176–77.

offer (Heb 8:3; 9:7, 14, 28; προσφέρω) the blood (Heb 9:7, 12, 14, 18–23, 25; αἷμα) of sacrifices (Heb 8:3–4, 9:9, 23, 26; θυσίαι) which effects purification (Heb 9:13; ἁγιάζω; Heb 9:14, 22–23; καθαρίζω) and redemption (Heb 9:12, 15; λύτρωσις) of worshippers (Heb 8:10, 9:7, 19; λαός; Heb 9:9, 14; λατρεύοντες) who have transgressed cultic law (Heb 8:4; 9:19; νόμος).[7] The mediation of both covenants is primarily cultic, the sacred realm of liturgy.

Outside of the Letter to the Hebrews the word "covenant" is, as I said, little used—and "new covenant" even less. In all of Jesus's sayings, we find just one instance when he uses the word (and the phrase), and he uses it to describe a specific liturgical act. Paul, in his First Letter to the Corinthians, provides the earliest historical record of the event: "In the same way [Jesus] also [took] the cup, after supper, saying, 'This cup is the *new covenant* in my blood. Do this, as often as you drink it, in remembrance of me'" (1 Cor 11:25; cf. Luke 22:20). For Paul (and Luke), Jesus explicitly ratifies what he calls the *New Covenant* by instituting (what others will later call) the *Eucharist*; he also commands the apostles to "do this in remembrance of me." Closely related, but slightly different, Matthew and Mark show Jesus using sacrificial language in their Institution Narratives: "This is the blood of the covenant, which is poured out for many for the forgiveness of sins" (Matt 26:28). With these explicit cultic terms, Jesus initiated the sacrificial offering that he would consummate on Calvary, and continuously offer in heaven—as "a priest forever."

Jesus's death was clearly an essential part of his once-for-all sacrifice, the singular unrepeatable sacrifice of the New Covenant. All Christians in every age agree on this point. But it may be useful for us to ask, how did this consensus come about? What made Jesus's crucifixion a sacrifice? To those formed by millennia of Christian tradition, the idea seems self-evident, but to a first-century Jew it would have seemed unthinkable. Sacrifice was permitted in only one place: the holy city of Jerusalem, inside the holy Temple, upon the sacrificial altar. Yet Jesus was crucified outside the city walls, a good distance from the Temple, with no altar in sight. To even the most careful observer, Jesus's suffering and death would have appeared to be a profane event, another brutal Roman execution. Jesus's devout followers might have judged this death to be an act of martyrdom (like the deaths of the seven brothers recounted in 2 Macc 7), but not a sacrifice. Some years ago, Joseph Ratzinger (the future Pope Benedict XVI) made a similar observation: "How could it ever occur to anyone to interpret the Cross of Jesus in such a way as to see it as actually effecting what had been intended by the cults of the

---

7. See Lane, *Hebrews 9–13*, 235: "The essence of the two covenants is found in their cultic aspects; the total argument is developed in terms of cultus. . . . The interpreter must remain open to the internal logic of the argument from the cultus."

world, especially by that of the Old Testament . . . and had never been truly achieved? What opened up the possibility at all of such a tremendous re-working of this event, of transferring the whole of the Old Testament's theol-ogy of worship and cult to this apparently most profane occurrence?" What made Jesus's death at Calvary a sacrifice was the Eucharist he instituted in the Upper Room—in explicitly sacrificial terms—precisely by ratifying the New Covenant and instituting the Eucharist with his disciples. There he made an offering of "body" and "blood." He declared it to be his "memorial," a term (Gk. *anamnesis*; Heb. *zikkaron*) associated with the Temple's sacrificial liturgy. And he identified his action in terms of prophetic categories, most explicitly the "new covenant" of Jeremiah's oracle. For Ratzinger, this detail of the biblical record is the key to the Church's theology of the Eucharist: "The interpretation of Christ's death on the Cross in terms of the cult . . . represents the inner presupposition of all Eucharistic theology. . . . An event that was in itself profane, the execution of a man by the most cruel and hor-rible method available, is described as a cosmic liturgy, as tearing open the closed-up heavens—as the act by which everything that had hitherto been ultimately intended, which had been sought in vain, by all forms of worship, now in the end actually comes about."[8] In sum, if we think of the Last Sup-per as only a meal, then Calvary is simply an execution. But if, in fact, Jesus instituted the Eucharist as the sacrificial memorial of the New Covenant, then we can see how the sacrifice that he initiated in the Upper Room was consummated at Calvary. At the same time, if what Jesus did in the Upper Room turns his crucifixion into a sacrifice, then we can see how, for the author of Hebrews, Jesus's resurrection and ascension are what transform that same sacrifice into a heavenly liturgy—and an earthly sacrament. From now on, Jesus's body is not only glorified in heaven, but also *communicable* on earth, which is exactly the divine action of the Holy Spirit. For the author of Hebrews, what the OT "gifts and sacrifices," "the food and drink," could never do, that is, "perfect the conscience of the worshipper" (9:9–10), is what our high priest now does—for us on earth—by means of the "gifts and sacri-fices" he offers in heaven (8:3). Indeed, this is the New Covenant "food and drink" we share in the Eucharist: "How much more shall the blood of Christ, through the eternal Spirit . . . purify your conscience . . . to serve the living God" (9:14). It should be noted, perhaps, that Jesus does this only for those whose consciences still need to be purified (us), not for "spirits of just men [already] made perfect" (12:23).

What, then, is Hebrews telling us? Christ's sacrifice does not consist simply *in* his suffering and death on the cross, but in his perfect act of

---

8. Ratzinger, *Pilgrim Fellowship of Faith*, 94–97.

self-offering to God *through* suffering and death. Thus, his suffering and death are over and done, but *not* his priestly self-offering, which continues forever in heaven, precisely in his deified humanity (i.e., that which *was* crucified, resurrected, ascended, but now *is* enthroned in heaven, at the right hand of the Father.) Christ's crucified-glorified humanity thus embodies the new covenant in at least four ways: *First*, his is the body of our heavenly *high priest*. *Second*, his body is our *sanctuary* ("the true tent not made with hands"). *Third*, his body is the *sacrifice* of the new covenant, which constitutes the everlasting liturgy in the heavenly Jerusalem (Heb 12:22–24). *Fourth*, this heavenly liturgy is what the Church on earth enters through the *Eucharist*: "You *have come* . . . to the heavenly Jerusalem . . . and to Jesus, the mediator of a new covenant." Thus, Hebrews echoes the gospels in proclaiming the New Covenant, that is, how Jesus made his passion and death both a perfect sacrifice and an everlasting liturgy. Thus, when we "do *this* in remembrance of him," we share in Jesus's sacrifice even as we renew our covenant with him in the Eucharist (as *sacramentum*; or covenant oath). We enter into his real presence—by the eternal Spirit—to worship alongside the angels and saints in the heavenly liturgy of our risen High Priest-King. It is the Holy Spirit's *divine action* that causes the "real presence" of Christ among us—in the sacrament of the Eucharist—as our *High Priest*, our *Sanctuary*, our *Sacrifice*, and our *Liturgy*. Jesus ordered his disciples to "do this as my memorial" (*anamnesis*), which implies their participation in his priestly sacrifice. Hebrews shows us how *this* is done, after his ascension, by the power of the Holy Spirit: Christ's redemption *accomplished* for us *perfectly*—is now *applied* to us *perfectingly*, as the pilgrim Church on earth.[9]

Bibliography

Bruce, F. F. *Epistle to the Hebrews*. Grand Rapids: Eerdmans, 1990.

Fahrig, Stephen D. "The Context of the Text: Reading Hebrews as a Eucharistic Homily." Ph.D. diss., Boston College, 2014.

Lane, William L. *Hebrews 9–13*. Word Biblical Commentary 47b. Dallas: Word, 1991.

Ratzinger, Joseph. *Pilgrim Fellowship of Faith: The Church as Communion*. San Francisco: Ignatius, 2005.

9. As "a priest forever," his sacrifice is offered "once for all," not as something *terminated*, but precisely as *perpetuated*—in the self-offering of a heavenly high priest ("forever"); i.e., you cannot repeat that which never ends. Christ's sacrifice is also extended—by the Eternal Spirit—to the faithful who partake on earth ("we have an altar" [Heb 13:10]). In showing how Christ ratified the New Covenant in his own body and blood (when he instituted the Eucharist), the author points not only to his (unrepeatable) sacrificial death, but to how his sacrificial self-offering can now be celebrated and re-presented: on earth as it is in heaven.

Swetnam, James. *Hebrews: An Interpretation*. Rome: Gregorian & Biblical, 2016.

————. "A Suggested Interpretation of Hebrews 9, 15–18." *Catholic Biblical Quarterly* 27 (1965) 373–90.

Theological Dictionary of the New Testament. 10 vols. Edited by Gerhard Kittel and Gerhard Friedrich. Translated by Geoffrey W. Bromiley. Grand Rapids: Eerdmans, 1964–76.

Vanhoye, Albert. *Old Testament Priests and the New Priest: According to the New Testament*. Petersham, MA: St. Bede's, 1986.

Williamson, Ronald. "The Eucharist and the Epistle to the Hebrews." *New Testament Studies* 21 (1975) 300–312.

Wright, N. T. *The New Testament and the People of God*. Minneapolis: Fortress, 1992.

IV. Diversified Evangelization

6

Race in the Catholic Imagination

CARY DABNEY

A Survey of Recent United States Bishops' Documents on Racism

OVER THE PAST CENTURY, the number of Catholics around the globe has increased dramatically. From an estimated 291 million in 1910 to over one billion as of 2010, according to the Pew Research Center. Interestingly, over the same period the world's overall population also has risen rapidly. As a result, Catholics have made up a remarkably stable share of all people on earth. In 1910, Catholics comprised about half of all Christians and 17 percent of the world's total population. A century later, Catholics still comprise about half of Christians worldwide and 16 percent of the total global population. However, the geographic distribution of the world's Catholics has vastly changed. In 1910, Europe was home to about two-thirds of all Catholics, and nearly nine-in-ten lived either in Europe or Latin America. By contrast, in 2010, less than a quarter of all Catholics were in Europe, with only 39 percent residing in Latin America.

Rapid growth has occurred in sub-Saharan Africa, which today is home to about 171 million Catholics, up from an estimated one million in 1910. There also has been an increase of Catholics in the Asia-Pacific region, where 131 million Catholics now live, up from fourteen million a century ago. In North America the Catholic population has increased from about fifteen million in 1910 to eight-nine million as of 2010.[1]

It would appear that the diversity the Church is experiencing today is a direct reflection of Saint Paul's words to the Galatians, "There is neither Jew nor Greek, there is neither slave nor free person, there is not male and female; for you are all one in Christ Jesus" (3:28). We are seeing the

---

1. Pew Research Center, "The Global Catholic Population."

emergence of a Christian brotherhood from all corners of the earth. Yet, at the same time, we are seeing a crippled consciousness when it comes to race in the Catholic imagination.

At significant times in the American Church's history, she has written pastoral letters of concern over the sin of racism. In 1958, the United States bishops wrote *Discrimination and Christian Conscience* to condemn the blatant forms of racism found in segregation and the "Jim Crow" laws. Ten years later, in the spring of 1968, the bishops again penned a letter entitled *National Race Crisis* to condemn the scandal of racism and the policies which led to violence that erupted in many major cities across our nation. Then again, in 1979, the bishops wrote *Brothers and Sisters to Us*, a pastoral letter addressing how racism was still affecting so many, highlighting the institutional forms of racial injustice evident in the economic imbalances found in our society. These three documents directly addressed issues concerning the American Catholic Church and race. It demonstrates that during the turbulent sixties and seventies the Church was aware of the persistent evil of racism. However, along with the strong words of condemnation of racism found among its pages, there were shortcomings.[2]

For example, in *Discrimination and Christian Conscience*, though the document asserts in a powerful way that enforced segregation could not be reconciled with the Christian view of the human person, the document made no specific recommendations or proposals for action. Though the document called upon all to act "courageously, and prayerfully," it simultaneously deplored "rash impetuosity" that leads to "ill-timed and ill-considered ventures."[3] This suggests a "quiet conciliation,"[4] with no concrete or bold call to action. The document was a watershed moment in the history of the Catholic Church in the US, but the document had little secular or ecclesial significance.

If we shift our attention ten years later to *The National Race Crisis*, we read within the document, "It is evident that we did not do enough; we have much more to do . . . It became clear that we failed to change the attitudes of many believers."[5] As this quote indicates, the bishops realized that their previous document did not do what had been intended. In addition, the Church found itself amid a nation trying to recover from the long summer of 1967, when racially motivated rioting and civil disturbances rocked many

2. My critique of *Discrimination and Christian Conscience, The National Race Crisis,* and *Brothers and Sisters to Us* has been drawn heavily from a similar critique featured in Bryan Massingale's book *Racial Justice and the Catholic Church.*

3. USSCB, *Discrimination and Christian Conscience,* 205.

4. USSCB, *Discrimination and Christian Conscience,* 201.

5. NCCB, *Statement on National Race Crisis,* 156.

major urban cities. The civil unrest found in these urban centers stoked the fears of racial insurrection in the nation. Within the Church itself, the National Black Catholic Clergy Caucus made their first attempt to speak to the Church from the perspective of the black experience. The black clergy called upon the Church to recognize the increasing alienation and estrangement that was taking place between the black community and the Catholic Church due to the Church's "past complicity with and active support of the prevailing attitudes and institutions of America."[6]

In response to both the civil crisis that the nation faced and the voices among the black Catholic faithful, the document urgently calls for the faithful to act decisively. The document advances the positions taken in the previous document. It contains an explicit acknowledgment of Catholic culpability in the increasing racial crisis. The document states, "Catholics, like the rest of American society, must recognize their responsibility for allowing these conditions to persist."[7] Furthermore, the document takes a much broader view of the problem of racism. It recognizes that racist attitudes and behaviors "exists not only in the hearts of men, but in the fabric of their institutions."[8] Thus, a concern is shown not just for individual race prejudice but for institutional racism as well.

Unlike its predecessor, this document makes several concrete recommendations for action. Bishops called for the "total eradication of any elements of discrimination in our parishes, schools, hospitals, and homes for the aged."[9] In addition, an Urban Task Force was established to direct and coordinate all Catholic efforts in this field on a national level. Dioceses too were urged to establish similar programs on the local level. However, despite these significant advances that *The National Race Crisis* made over the previous letter, it nonetheless did not have the result that was intended, and another ten years later the US bishops found themselves again having to address the issue of racism both among the general populace and within the walls of the Church.

In 1979, *Brothers and Sisters to Us* opens with the following words, "Racism is an evil which endures in our society and in our Church. Despite apparent advances and even significant changes in the last two decades, the reality of racism remains." Despite changes in the nation's laws, the granting of voting rights, and the elimination of enforced segregation, the bishops were forced to conclude that "too often what has happened has been only a

6. Schachern, "Priests Call Church 'Racist,'" 3.

7. NCCB, *Statement on National Race Crisis*, 156.

8. NCCB, *Statement on National Race Crisis*, 157.

9. NCCB, *Statement on National Race Crisis*, 157.

covering over, not a fundamental change." This document once again force-fully and unequivocally condemns racism. As a result of the words of the document, more black men were ordained to the episcopacy, many dio-ceses and religious communities increased their efforts to recruit men and women into the priesthood and into religious life, and efforts were made to encourage liturgical adaptions to include cultural heritage of communities of color among the faithful. However, the publicity given this document was very limited. As a result, the promulgation of this pastoral letter was soon forgotten by all but a few. Ultimately, these three pastoral letters have made little impact on the majority of Catholics in our nation.

Nearly thirty-five years ago, a Catholic organization sponsored a conference entitled "Voices of Justice: The Challenge of Being Catholic and American in the 1980s." One of the keynote speakers, James Cone, issued a "theological challenge" to the Catholic Church. He stated:

> What is it about the Catholic definition of justice that makes many persons of that faith progressive in their attitude toward the poor in Central America but reactionary in their views toward the poor in black America? . . . It is the failure of the Catholic Church to deal effectively with the problem of racism that causes me to question the quality of its commitment to jus-tice. . . . I do not wish to minimize the importance of Catholic contributions to poor people's struggles for justice, but I must point out the ambiguity of the Catholic stand on justice when racism is not addressed forthrightly.[10]

Bryan Massingale, explains Cone's comments. He states, "(Cone's) contention is that there are critical faults and deficits in Catholic reflection on racism. He adduces this from an apparent disparity between Catholic concern regarding issues, such as poverty and the sanctity of life, when compared to the Church's peripheral attention given to the endemic rac-ism of American society."[11]

Cone's reservations concerning the adequacy and effectiveness of American Catholic reflection on racism also has been expressed by offi-cial voices within the American Catholic Church. In 1989, the US Bishops Committee on Black Catholics issued a statement commemorating the tenth anniversary of *Brothers and Sisters to Us*. Surprisingly, this anniversary committee found little worth celebrating. It concluded that:

10. Massingale, "James Cone and Recent Catholic Episcopal Teaching on Racism," 700.

11. Massingale, "James Cone and Recent Catholic Episcopal Teaching on Racism," 702.

The promulgation of the pastoral letter on racism was soon forgotten by all but a few. A survey . . . revealed a pathetic, anemic
response from archdioceses and dioceses around the country.
. . . The pastoral letter on racism had made little or no impact
on the majority of Catholics in the United States. . . . In spite of
all that has been said and written about racism in the last twenty
years, very little—if anything at all—has been done in Catholic
education; such as it was yesterday, it is today.[12]

Two years later, at a symposium celebrating the centennial anniversary
of modern Catholic social teaching, Joseph Francis, an African American
bishop, declared that the lack of attention given *Brothers and Sisters to Us*
made it "the best kept secret in the church in this country." He concluded by
voicing sentiments very much like those expressed by Cone:

Social justice vis-à-vis the eradication of racism in our church
is simply not a priority of social concern commissions, social
concern directors and agencies. While I applaud the concern of
such individuals and groups for the people of Eastern Europe,
China, and Latin America, that same concern is not expressed,
is not incarnated for the victims of racism in this country . . .
The question is, Is the quality of our mercy strained when black
people are concerned?[13]

In 2004, twenty-five years after *Brothers and Sisters to Us*, the US
Catholic Bishops commissioned a study to discern its implementation
and reception.[14] The commission's results paint a disheartening picture of
the Church's relationship with the black community. For example, since
the *Brothers and Sisters to Us* was first promulgated, only 18 percent of
the American bishops have issued statements condemning racism, and
of those very few address systemic racism found in America; rather, they
address personal attitudes of direct racial malice. In addition, the commission notes that many diocesan seminaries and ministry formation
programs are inadequate in terms of their incorporation of the history,
culture, and traditions of the black community. Most disturbing is the
commission's report that white Catholics over the last twenty-five years
"exhibit diminished—rather than increased—support of government

12. United States Bishops Committee on Black Catholics, *For the Love of One Another*, 39, 41.

13. Bishop Joseph Francis, "Revisiting Five Bishops' Pastorals: Justice for All," 659,
cited in Massingale, "James Cone and Recent Catholic Episcopal Teaching on Racism."

14. Massingale, *Racial Justice and the Catholic Church*, 68–70.

policies aimed at curbing racial inequality."[15] These official statistics detail the significant lack of compliance of the Church with its own recommendation contained in *Brothers and Sister to Us*.

Recently, the rise in anti-migrant rhetoric, coupled with the increasing visibility of white supremacist groups and explicit racist behavior, has resulted in a national race crisis that is in some ways similar to the racial tensions experienced in previous eras. For Catholic communities of color, this crisis, and the ensuing dialogues regarding race in America, has created an urgent desire for the Church to deliver a pastoral response. In the fall of 2018, the bishops once again penned a pastoral letter to address racism, *Open Wide Our Hearts: The Enduring Call to Love*. At first glance, the document impressively includes both the Native American and Hispanic experiences, alongside the African American experience. In addition, the bishops admit that the Church's silence in these matters at various points throughout American history was, in a way, giving tacit approval to the practices of racism, and that the Church needs to repent and ask for forgiveness for this lack of response.

However, just as in the previous pastoral letters from the bishops, alongside these high points, we find several shortcomings. The most prevalent disappointment in the document is the inability for the authors to deliver frank language about the systemic racism that exists as part of the reality of Catholics of color *today*. While the document does a fantastic job of detailing the atrocities carried out by the early European settlers against the Native Americans, the inhumane treatment of African Americans during the slave trade and "Jim Crow" era, and the discrimination experienced by Hispanic Americans over the years, the document does not address current systemic racism nor identify how current white Catholics, unconsciously or consciously, participate in the continued oppression of communities of color.

The word "racism" appears more than 50 times in the document; however, when "white" appears in the document, it is only when speaking to historical eras long ago. Furthermore, while the word "sin" is used just under 20 times, always in reference to racism, the terms "privilege" or "supremacy" are not mentioned at all. Stated another way, the document goes to great length to identify that racism is a sin, but equally appears to make effort not to identify the sinner. One of the major failures of *Open Wide Our Hearts* is the missed opportunity to acknowledge the reality that racism, while it *affects* communities of color, is not fundamentally *their* problem; rather, it is a problem for white Catholics. It is obvious to any Catholic that overt acts of

15. Massingale, *Racial Justice and the Catholic Church*, 70.

racism are contrary to the Christian tradition; however, what is not as evident is the unwitting complicity in the very structures that are designed to ensure continued oppression of communities of color and to maintain the dominance of whites in America. Ultimately, what was needed was a strong pastoral statement with a clear message to those in positions of social power and privilege that they must discontinue their blissful silence and change. In a sense, one could say that while racism is America's most persistent sin, it appears that the Church still has a reluctance to demonstrate passion regarding racism. This prompts the question: What is the place of race in the Catholic imagination, particularly here in America?

Most expressions of racism today can be traced directly to our nation's involvement with the transatlantic slave trade during colonial times. Therefore, it would be prudent for us to begin the investigation at that point in history.

The History of Race and the Roman Catholic Church

The issue of slavery is one that historically has been treated with concern by the Catholic Church. After the recognition of Christianity under the Roman Empire, there was a growing sentiment that many kinds of slavery were not compatible with Christian conceptions of charity and justice; some argued against all forms of slavery while others argued the case for slavery subject to certain restrictions. Initially, Church teaching made a distinction between "just" and "unjust" forms of slavery, with unjust slavery being that which enslaves those who have been baptized.

For example, in 1435, Pope Eugene IV authored a papal bull, *Sicut dudum*, addressed to Bishop Ferdinand in the Portuguese colonies of the Canary Islands condemning the enslavement of the indigenous people that had converted to the faith. Eugene IV commanded "all and each of the faithful . . . within the space of fifteen days of the publication of these letters in the place where they live, [be restored] to their earlier liberty" with the threat "of excommunication . . . from which [you] cannot be absolved."[16]

A century later as Europe expanded into the Americas, enslaving the Native Americans of this newly "discovered" land, the Church once again responded to the evilness of slavery. This time it was Pope Paul III with his encyclical *Sublimis Deus*. However, *Sublimis Deus* presents a slightly different understanding of slavery. To begin, Paul III addressed this encyclical to "all faithful Christians to whom this writing may come," thereby not limiting its significance to the clergy alone but universalizing it to all the

16. Pope Eugene IV, *Sicut dudum*, 4.

faithful. Furthermore, Paul III was not concerned about articulating a "just" slavery in juxtaposition to "unjust" slavery. Rather, he asserted that whoever is endowed with *the capability* to receive the faith of Christ and receive his Gospel, baptized or not, should "by no means be deprived of their liberty or the possession of their property." This advancement in the articulation of the Church's position on slavery clearly indicates that the Church did not hesitate to condemn the forced servitude of others.

Such denouncements against the slave trade and the enslavement of human persons helped to create a negative tone within Catholic communities in the colonies of North America. But as the colonies of North America began to expand, the institution of slavery was so entrenched into the fabric of the colonies, that the complete abolition of slavery was not considered realistic among any of the colonies, including the Catholic communities in North America. A contributing factor of this was the pressure that accompanied the distrust that many colonists had of Catholics in their communities. As the revolutionary spirit began to increase, Catholic settlers reminded the revolutionaries of the oppressive crown from which they wished to be emancipated. Therefore, Catholics in early America found themselves needing to reduce their behaviors that seemed contrary to their Protestant neighbors. As a result, Catholic communities among the colonists developed an understanding of slavery like the Protestant colonists; namely, that masters and slaves, though unequal on earth, inhabited the same plane in the eyes of God.

In two black slaveholding states, Maryland and Louisiana, that had a large population of Catholic residents, blacks received public baptisms and had their marriages officially recorded. Furthermore, as opposed to non-Catholic colonies, American Catholics considered baptized slaves in full communion with the Church, and therefore, masters could not kill a slave without facing murder charges. In addition, slaves could not be worked on Sundays or holy feast days, guaranteeing some days of leisure. These protections provided slaves in Catholic territories with a small degree of protection from the harshness of the dehumanizing experience of slavery.

In 1839, Pope Gregory XVI issued *In supremo*, an apostolic letter that condemned the slave trade in the strongest possible terms. By this time, the slave trade and slavery itself was completely abolished in Britain. Both Spain and Portugal continued to operate slave trading and had many enslaved. Gregory XVI had hoped that this apostolic letter might persuade Spain and Portugal to enforce laws against slave trafficking in their domains. In America, Gregory's pronouncement set off a debate within the Catholic community in the United States.

The Catholic population of the United States, which had been thirty-five thousand in 1790, increased to 195,000 by 1820 and then ballooned to about 1.6 million by the time of Gregory's apostolic letter, making Catholicism the country's largest faith tradition. As the Catholic ranks began to swell arguments raged over what Gregory's letter taught about slavery. While some put forward Gregory's letter to make the case that the Church opposed slavery, most American Catholic leaders sought to interpret it in a narrow fashion to minimize its significance regarding slavery in general, particularly in the southern Catholic communities. Many bishops in the South were slave owners. Inevitably, some of them did engage in the buying and selling of slaves. For some of the southern bishops, slavery was not simply an institution that had to be endured; many considered themselves as apologists for slavery.

In the years leading up to the Civil War, many of these bishops fought bitterly in support of the institution of slavery despite the Vatican's continued teachings in opposition to the enslavement of others. Some southern bishops openly embraced slavery and sought to show how it was a force of good. For example, four months after the beginning of the Civil War, Bishop Auguste Marie Martin wrote a pastoral letter to his flock in northern Louisiana entitled, *A Pastoral Letter of the Bishop of Natchitoches on the Occasion of the War of the South for Its Independence.*

In the pastoral letter, when he approached the question of slavery, Martin stated, "The manifest will of God is that in exchange for a freedom of which they were incapable and for a labor of the whole life, we should give to these unfortunate ones . . . their legitimate portion of the truth and the goods of grace, which consoles them in their present miseries."[17] Considered from this point of view, according to Martin, slavery was really not an evil; rather, a "betterment both material and moral for a degraded class."[18] The bishop argued that slavery was an eminently Christian work, the redemption of millions of human lives. Thus, Martin attempted to introduce a theological justification for slavery, it was something noble because it was God's plan for the conversion of the black man, who were dependent on the white race.

This negative attitude towards blacks in the Catholic community was not unique to the South. Even in the North, the sentiment of the Catholic laity, most of whom were recent immigrants, was decidedly anti-black. By and large, the white Catholic community accepted the condition of slavery. In years leading up to and during the Civil War, and even following the emancipation

17. Davis, *History of Black Catholics in the United States*, 51.
18. Davis, *History of Black Catholics in the United States*, 52.

of the black community after the Civil War, there were few white Catholics who really believed that blacks were equal to whites. Just as their Protestant contemporaries, white Catholics carried an assumption of black inferiority. The subordination of blacks in America was an accepted part of the social and cultural landscape for Catholics and non-Catholic alike.

Despite the negative notions that were ever present among the Catholic population concerning black Americans, there was always a remnant of black Catholics that worked diligently to advance the race relations in America. One individual responsible for such efforts among black Catholics was Daniel Rudd. By the end of the nineteenth century, Rudd had made himself known to both clergy and laity as "the leading Catholic representative of the [black] race."[19]

In his newspaper, *American Catholic Tribune*, Rudd wrote, "There is an awakening among some people to the fact that the Catholic Church is not only a warm and true friend to the [black] people, but is absolutely impartial in recognizing them as equals of all."[20] Later, Rudd put the same message more succinctly, when he wrote, "The Catholic Church alone can break the color line. Our people should help her to do it."[21] With this sentiment, Rudd came up with the idea to call together a national congress of African American Catholics. He felt that black Catholics in America did not realize the extent of the Church among them. Being separated and hidden away from each due to vast distances between them, Rudd thought it would be beneficial to the Church and to faithful black Catholics to come together and simply speak and look upon one another.[22]

The first black Catholic lay congress took place in January of 1889. The delegates, numbering over two hundred black Catholics, made appeals to labor organizations, factory owners, and trade unions to admit black men within their ranks. They spoke of children and the need of orphanages, hospitals, and Catholic schools. Subsequent black congress meetings stressed the Church's need to preserve the deposit of faith regarding "the equality of all peoples before God. The meetings consistently reminded the Church of the mission to announce love in place of hate, to raise up the downtrodden, and to proclaim the essential value of all men and women."[23]

These congress meetings of black Catholics demonstrated beyond a doubt that a black Catholic community not only existed, but it was active,

---

19. Davis, *History of Black Catholics in the United States*, 164.

20. Rudd, "Apology Accepted."

21. Rudd, "The Negro."

22. Davis, *History of Black Catholics in the United States*, 171.

23. Davis, *History of Black Catholics in the United States*, 189.

devoted to the tradition, and proud. It also demonstrated that given the opportunity, there was real leadership with the black Catholic community. These attributes, demonstrated by the meetings of the black Catholic congress brought to the forefront the lack of a body of priests who commanded respect on a national scale. The efforts of the black lay leadership, through the work of the black lay congress, was the cornerstone of the faith community of black Catholics and was directly responsible for the push for black clergy to service the black community.

Along with the black lay congress, in 1909, another important movement among black Catholics had begun. In Mobile, Alabama, through the initiative of several Josephite pastors in the South, another organization was created along the same lines as the Knights of Columbus. A national association for black men was established to foster fellowship and bring about a spiritual awareness and interest in the Church's tradition. In 1922, a ladies' auxiliary was instituted within the organization. This organization, the Knights of Peter Claver, became a very important element in the religious life of black Catholics. Many members began to work on issues of civil rights and worked with organizations like the NAACP and the National Urban League.

The efforts of the black laity serving in the black Catholic congress, the Knights of Peter Claver, and others caught the attention of the Roman Curia. Cardinal Gaetano De Lai and Cardinal Willem van Rossum, prefects of the Consistorial Congregation and the Congregation of Propaganda, respectively, communicated with Archbishop Giovanni Bonzano, the Apostolic Delegate to the US, to launch a series of initiatives to provide spiritual welfare for black Catholics and to further the evangelization of black Americans as a whole. Bonzano enlisted the help of Father John Burke of New York. Father Burke organized the Catholic Board for Negro Missions. Burke's primary effort was to stress the need that the Church's missionary efforts should be directed toward raising "[black] sons to the ministry, until finally a complete body of clergy"[24] of black priests was established. Burke believed that once the number of black clergy had grown to sufficient numbers, a black bishop should be consecrated. Burke's work is exceptional because of its fairness. Unlike many Catholics of the early twentieth century, though being white, Burke never spoke about blacks in a condescending and demeaning manner. He made no assumption of black inferiority and no complacent observations about black people's morality. Burke represented a small minority within the Catholic community that pushed for an end to the racist rhetoric within America, especially among the Catholic community.

24. Davis, *History of Black Catholics in the United States*, 201.

The efforts of both the black laity and pioneers like Father Burke helped influence the idea of establishing a seminary for young black men. In November of 1921, the first seminary for black students by members of the Society of the Divine Word was established. The opening of the seminary was accompanied with a letter addressed to all members of the American hierarchy acquainting them with the opening of the seminary. The letter made clear that this seminary had the support and the full blessing of Rome, specifically Pope Benedict XV. This was necessary because not all American bishops were convinced of the wisdom of ordaining black men to the priesthood.

From the end of the nineteenth century to 1965, racial segregation was an official legal policy throughout the American South—better known as the Jim Crow Era. On the issue of race, American Catholics, in general, followed the laws of their respective states by maintaining racial segregation just as their Protestant counterparts. There were some actions taken by local bishops and priests against the practice of racial segregation. For example, in 1951 Archbishop Joseph Rummel of New Orleans asked followers to end segregation in the Church. Rummel, in a pastoral letter, told New Orleans Catholics to end all vestiges of racial separatism within their churches. He worked toward the gradual integration of all Catholic schools, churches, and hospitals. Two years later, Rummel officially declared the end of racial segregation in all New Orleans Catholic institutions in a pastoral letter entitled "Blessed are the Peacemakers." However, these clerical denouncements of segregation were regretfully rare, and certainly were not shared universally among the clerical body.

During the Civil Rights Movement, a response from the Catholic Church in Alabama to the civil rights demonstrations in Birmingham highlights how vast the spectrum was on the issue of segregation within American Catholic communities, the most visible being in a letter addressed to Martin Luther King Jr. In "A Call for Unity," eight white clergymen of Birmingham, Alabama, denounced King's civil rights organization as outsiders seeking to destroy the racial harmony of the city. Though acknowledging the grievances of blacks, and that everyone deserved basic human respect, the authors asked blacks to accept the racial situation for the time being.

One of the authors was Joseph E. Durick, Auxiliary Bishop of Mobile, Alabama. By signing the open letter to the civil rights leader, Durick demonstrated the position of the Alabama Catholic Church leadership during the movement. The state Archbishop, Thomas J. Toole, denied priests the right to participate in demonstrations or speak out against racial segregation. The clergy appeared to uphold human rights in theory, but refused to give legitimacy to protesters, such as King, who broke prevailing state segregation laws.

As a result, most Catholic parishes remained segregated along racial lines during the first half of the 20th century. Within these parishes there tended to be no set standard for segregation inside parishes. Some dioceses created separate parishes for blacks but that was not always the case. In many areas, blacks could attend any Catholic Church. Usually there was some degree of racial separation of the parishioners. In New Orleans, blacks had to sit in the rear pews, and unable to receive communion until every white parishioner had been served. Some parishes also placed screens between the two races.

There were always Catholics who refused to accept segregation. The Southeastern Regional Interracial Commission, founded in 1948 by students of Loyola and Xavier universities, held interracial masses on college campuses. The Commission on Human Rights, organized in 1949, held integrated masses and sent petitions to church officials demanding integration in southern parishes. Nevertheless, the Catholic Church's role during segregation and the Civil Rights Movement was quite ambiguous.

When considering the history of race and the Catholic Church, specifically the black American community and the American Catholic Church, one cannot help but wonder why there was so little social consciousness among everyday Catholics in the United States regarding racism. Despite the bishops' pastoral letters previously mentioned, and in light of the global Church's championing for human dignity and equality during this era, or as Pope Paul VI asserts in *Populorum progressio*, the Church's obligation to address social inequities by "building a human community where men and women can live truly human lives, free from discrimination on account of race, religion or nationality,"[25] why does it appear that the Church in America was incapable of taking any decisive action or have any ability to enunciate clear-cut principles regarding racism?[26] Along with their Protestant brothers and sisters, American Catholics showed, and continue to show, a lack of moral consciousness on the issue of race. Logically, this leads us to conclude that although at times our faith has had influence on racial attitudes—some positive, most negative—the dialogue concerning racism today must run much deeper in the American landscape.

In his letter to the Ephesians, Saint Paul tells us that Jesus is our peace. It is by means of his shed blood and broken body that the dividing walls of enmity have been demolished (Eph 2:14). Today, the Catholic Church in

25. Paul VI, *Populorum progressio*, 47.

26. Phelps, "Communion Ecclesiology and Black Liberation Theology," 675.

America must recognize that Christ wishes to break down the walls created by the evilness of racism, whether this evilness is displayed publicly for all to see or buried deep in the recesses of our hearts. If not, then we are destined for history to continue to repeat itself, and once again the Church will be perceived as a silent observer in the face of racism. And this would result in a Church appearing to be unwilling to play any vital role in the most tragic social sin our nation has had to face. As we enter deeper into the 21st century, how should the Church in America respond to race in a way that accurately reflects the global tradition of the Church?

What Is Racism?

To effectively address the issue of racism, it is essential that we clearly define what actually makes up racist behavior that is contrary to our faith. To state that Christians are to shun and struggle against racism is intuitively obvious. But to know what is meant by "racism" in American society, is another matter. Part of what makes issues regarding race so difficult to address within the Church is that most Catholics lack an adequate understanding of the depth of racism, its extent, and its true nature.

For example, one of the challenges present in addressing racism is that the terminology used to refer to the various issues that revolve around race is fluid, evolving, contested, and never emotionally neutral. Terms such as "people of color," "minority," and even "race" are troublesome terms due to their sometimes varied and ambiguous uses. While these terms make *reference* to skin color, they refer much more to social groups that find themselves without easy access to the political, economic, or social advantages enjoyed by the majority of the population—in most cases those designated as "white" people. In addition, it is important to note that in regard to the use of the term "minority community" or "minorities," it is not consistently employed to mean a "numerical" minority, but rather carries the notion of lacking power, privilege, or value.[27]

All of these considerations are important in an attempt to identify racism. To understand our current era of race relations, the persistence of racial inequality, and the actions that need to be taken to address and combat this evil, we must have a deeper understanding of racism and acknowledge the various ways it manifests itself in our society. One of the obvious manifestations of racism is what can be called "conscious" racism. This form of racism focuses on interpersonal behaviors or deliberate actions, performed by either an individual or the collective effort of a relatively small group

27. Massingale, *Racial Justice and the Catholic Church*, 2.

that intentionally chooses to act in a negative manner towards another of a different race. This form of racism that our society experiences is obviously not a part of God's plan. In our Sacred Scriptures, we read that the Creator lovingly "created man in his image, in the divine image he created him; male and female he created them" (Gen 1:27). The human race is rooted in the loving, creative act of God, who made us and called us to be a family, one human family, made in God's image and likeness. There is no basis to sustain that some are made more in the image of God than others.

Therefore, in whatever form, intolerance of other people because of their race or nationality is the denial of human dignity. One race is not better than another because of the color of their skin or the place of their birth. What makes us equal before God, and what should make us equal in dignity before each other, is that we are all sisters and brothers of one another, because we are all children of the same loving God who brought us into being. Christ Jesus could not have been more direct—if we hope to offer ourselves to God, to live a Christian life in accord with his plan, it cannot be done with disdain or disregard for others in our hearts. Our Lord asserts, "But I say to you, whoever is angry with his brother will be liable to judgment . . . and whoever says, 'You fool,' will be liable to fiery Gehenna" (Matt 5:21–22). The practice of this "conscious" racism denies the basic equality and dignity of all people before God and one another. Although our nation has moved forward in a number of ways against this form of racial discrimination, we are not finished with the work given to us by the Lord to protect and uphold the dignity of each and every person.

In fact, this leads me to move to a more sinister form of racism for which I would like to spend the next few minutes identifying. This manifestation of racism is much more complex, difficult to pinpoint, and, unfortunately, has entangled itself into the very fabric of our nation's social institutions, and in various degrees, crept into some of our beloved Church structures. You see, regardless of how vivid "conscience" racism expresses itself, whether that be blatantly public or concealed in the recesses of one's heart, it does not explain the persistence of the continuation of our nation's infatuation with race within our culture. Despite undeniable changes to civil laws and social policies, there remains an underlying dynamic that remains impervious to civil laws, social equity policies, and equal opportunity mandates.

Fr. Bernard Lonergan provides the following definition of culture: "A culture is simply the set of meanings and values that inform the way of life of a community."[28] Culture, then, denotes a system of meanings

28. Lonergan, *Second Collection*, 232.

and values, communicated in specific forms that conveys and expresses a people's understanding of life. Stated more succinctly, culture is the set of attitudes toward life, beliefs about reality, and assumptions about the world shared by a community. In this sense, culture is more basic and fundamental than society, social institutions, or social policies and customs. To put this another way, culture provides the ideological foundation for social, political, and economic policies.

Understanding culture as the set of meanings and values that inform a people's way of life enables us to get beyond individual racism and better understand its insidious tenacity. In the US, racism functions as a culture, that is, a set of shared beliefs and assumptions that undergirds the economic, social, and political disparities experienced by different racial groups. This set of meanings and values provides the ideological foundation for a racialized society, where society's benefits and burdens are inequitably allotted among the various racial groups. This set of meanings and values not only answers questions about the significance of social patterns, but it also is formative. This racialized culture produces an "unconscious" racism. A society that shapes identity, social consciousness, behavior—and social systems—on the basis of race. Put more simply, because a racialized set of meanings and values permeates all of our socio-cultural products—education, justice systems, health care access, wealth systems, etc.—we learn our cultural "racial code" almost by osmosis. We absorb it tacitly through our everyday process of socialization and learning how to be an "American."

This occurs so much so that this racial coding functions beneath our conscious awareness. This is why even an institution, like the well-meaning Church, can still appear to be indifferent or silent in the presence of systemic racism. Unconscious racism, then, denotes the influence of a cultural lens by which we have been indoctrinated in unintentional and preconscious ways. This unconscious racism, which results in the social or systemic racism that has permeated our nation must also be combated and defeated by the works and actions of the Church.

Developing Passion for Racial Justice

In addition to this unconscious racism that we suffer as a nation, the Church's teaching on race in America has neglected or slighted the voices of the victims and examining the issue from their perspective. The Church's racial justice tradition tends to speak *about* and *for* people of color, but it does not seem to acknowledge minorities' independent thought, action, or leadership. Stated another way, the American Catholic teaching on race often assumes that racism can be overcome by education, dialogue, and moral persuasion alone. This approach fails to take into account that racism is not merely or primarily a sin of ignorance, but one of advantage and privilege.

Most significantly, American Catholic social teaching on race suffers from *a lack of passion*. As a corporate body and as individuals, Catholics espouse a number of beliefs, but not all of these are held passionately. For example, no one can doubt the passion with which the Catholic Church opposes abortion. This position is articulated repeatedly and forcefully. Even in the face of opposition, Catholics hold its view about the sanctity of the life of the unborn fervently. Opposition to abortion is a major public marker; it is intrinsic to a Catholic's identity.

However, despite the bold words the leadership of the Church has penned regarding racism, it is evident that racial justice is not now, nor has ever been, a passionate matter for American Catholics. The past letters and documents on racism have had little impact upon the consciousness and behavior of the majority of American Catholics. Quite simply, standing against racism is just not considered an essential character of Catholic identity.

If we are to change the current lack of passion for issues revolving around racism, we need to have a genuine conversion of the heart, a conversion that will motivate change. In order to do so, the Church must become consistent in its teaching and exhortations against racism. The Church must not only make *a call* to action but *enforce* practices that result in concrete progress in its combat against racism. Church leadership must not simply *suggest* actions within its structure to address racism; rather, it must *demand* reported results that demonstrate a movement toward developing a passion to assist our brothers and sisters of color confront the inequities that they experience not only as American citizens, but as members of the Body of Christ in America. How do we begin to develop this passion?

In addressing the recent racial tensions in our nation, Pope Francis stated, "We cannot tolerate or turn a blind eye to racism and exclusion in any form and yet claim to defend the sacredness of every human life."[29] The Holy Father's statement reveals a clue as to how we should envision our fight against racism; namely, it is a life issue. One of the universal weaknesses of the pastoral documents we have discussed is the lack of emphasis on the connection between racial injustice and pro-life values. For too long, the definition of being pro-life has been connected nearly exclusively to our teachings on abortion. As a result, the disproportionate harm that certain issues plague people of color, including poverty, criminal justice reform, mass incarceration, and access to health care, are seen

29. Francis, "General Audience."

as social justice issues but go unaddressed by pro-life-minded communities of the faithful. However, if we begin to explore the interconnected principals between pro-life values and the many affronts to those values that have resulted in the persistent scourge of racism, we will be able to bridge the gap between racial justice and pro-life values, resulting in the advocacy of racial justice being recognized as an essential character of Catholic identity among all pro-life-minded people.

Conversion is a long road to travel, for the individual, the institution, and even more so for a nation, but in Christ we can find the strength and the grace necessary to make the journey. In Christ, we live in a new reality where the divisions between people that lead to discrimination and hatred can no longer be tolerated. To combat the sin of racism, both "conscious" and "unconscious" racism, we are all in need of ongoing conversion. If racism is confronted by addressing its causes and the injustice it produces, then healing can occur. As a faith community, we must commit ourselves to specific actions with the hope that others in our nation will do likewise in their own lives and communities.

To begin, we must examine our sinfulness—as individuals, as a Church, and as a society. It is only from a place of humility that we can look honestly at past failures, ask for forgiveness, and move towards healing and reconciliation. This requires the Church to acknowledge sinful deeds and thoughts and to ask for forgiveness. As members of the Church, we must humbly acknowledge that there have been many failures in truly living and acting as Christ demands. Acts of racism have been committed by leaders and members of the Church—by bishops, priests, lay faithful, and by her institutions.

The examining of our sinfulness is just the beginning. Efforts of reconciliation and true conversion require even more. In order to work at ending racism, we need to engage the world and encounter others—those who are on the peripheries of our own view. We must invite into dialogue those we ordinarily would not seek out. We must work to form relationships with those we regularly avoid or may never see at all. This demands all of us to go beyond ourselves, to open our minds and hearts to value and respect the experience of those who have been harmed by racism.

"A change of heart cannot occur without strengthening spiritual convictions regarding respect for other races and ethnic groups."[30] For the Church, this must include the formation and practice of its clergy, religious, and lay leadership. Therefore, the Church must enforce our seminaries, deacon formation programs, houses of formation, and our

---

30. Pontifical Commission on Justice and Peace, *Church and Racism*, 25.

education institutions to find new and innovative ways to raise awareness, provide curriculum, and promote adequate incorporation of the history, culture, and traditions of all the people of faith, including our brothers and sisters of color in our nation.

With a renewed emphasis and passion on the sin of racism, we all as a Body of Christ, clergy and lay, can in solidarity confront the roots of racism that have extended into the soil of our society. In our solidarity we can move to contend with the policies and institutional barriers that perpetuate and preserve the inequality—economic and social—that we still see all around us. Pope Francis, in his address before the United States Congress stated, "Even in the developed world, the effects of unjust structures and actions are all too apparent. Our efforts must aim at restoring hope, righting wrongs, maintaining commitments and thus promoting the well-being of individuals and of peoples."[31]

This is not a work we can accomplish alone. Therefore, the Church must join all efforts to repair the breach caused by racism. We must join all Christians and those of other faith traditions in this battle against that which damages the human family. In our nation's past, ecumenical and interreligious cooperation has been pivotal at key moments in our history. That spirit is integral to this fight today and our success will depend very much on such collaboration.

Racism is a sin that has afflicted humanity since the dawn of history, and it will not end overnight. The elimination of racism may seem too great a task for any one of us or even for the whole Church. Yet, nonetheless, the Church must pledge these actions. The Church must remain ever vigilant and aware of instances of both "conscious" and "unconscious" manifestations of racism, and when she identifies these instances, immediately respond by putting into action those things that can lead to a genuine conversion of the heart and recognition of the universal dignity intrinsic to all human life.

Above all, we place our confidence in our Lord, Christ Jesus. In Christ, we are brothers and sisters to one another. With Christ, we stand in the Spirit of justice, love, and peace. Through Christ, we envision the new city of God, not built by human hands, but by the love of God poured out in Christ Jesus. On the journey to that "new heaven and new earth," we make our way with faith in God's grace, with hope in our own determination, with confidence in the workings of the Holy Spirit, and above all with love for each other as children of God.

---

31. Francis, "Address to U.S. Congress."

Bibliography

Davis, Cyprian. *The History of Black Catholics in the United States*. New York: Crossroads, 1990.

Eugene IV, Pope. *Sicut dudum*. http://www.papalencyclicals.net/eugene04/eugene04 sicut.htm.

Francis, Joseph. "Revisiting Five Bishops' Pastorals: Justice for All." *Origins* 20 (1991) 658–59.

Francis, Pope. "Address to U.S. Congress." September 24, 2015. https://www. vatican.va/content/francesco/en/speeches/2015/september/documents/papa-francesco_20150924_usa-us-congress.html.

———. "General Audience." June 3, 2020. https://www.vatican.va/content/francesco/ en/audiences/2020/documents/papa-francesco_20200603_udienza-generale. html.

Lonergan, Bernard. *A Second Collection*. Edited by William F. J. Ryan and Bernard J. Terrell. Philadelphia: Westminster, 1974.

Massingale, Bryan. "James Cone and Recent Catholic Episcopal Teaching on Racism." *Theological Studies* 61.4 (2000), 700–730.

———. *Racial Justice and the Catholic Church*. Maryknoll, NY: Orbis, 2010.

National Conference of Catholic Bishops. *Statement on National Race Crisis*. https:// www.usccb.org/issues-and-action/cultural-diversity/african-american/resources/ upload/Statement-on-National-Race-Crisis-April-25-1968.pdf.

Paul VI, Pope. *Populorum progressio*. https://www.vatican.va/content/paul-vi/en/ encyclicals/documents/hf_p-vi_enc_26031967_populorum.html.

Pew Research Center. "The Global Catholic Population." *Pew Research Center*, February 13, 2013. http://www.pewforum.org/2013/02/13/the-global-catholic-population.

Phelps, Jamie T. "Communion Ecclesiology and Black Liberation Theology." *Theological Studies* 61 (2000) 672–99.

Pontifical Commission on Justice and Peace. *The Church and Racism: Toward a More Fraternal Society*. https://www.humandevelopment.va/content/dam/svilu ppoumano/pubblicazioni-documenti/archivio/diritti-umani/The%20Church%20 against%20Racism%202001-1988.pdf.

Rudd, Danial. "Apology Accepted." *American Catholic Tribune*, June 10, 1887.

———. "The Negro." *American Catholic Tribune*, January 10, 1891.

Schachern, Harold. "Priests Call Church 'Racist.'" *National Catholic Reporter*, April 24, 1968.

United States Bishops Committee on Black Catholics. *For the Love of One Another: A Special Message on the Occasion of the Tenth Anniversary of Brothers and Sisters to Us*. Washington, DC: United States Conference of Catholic Bishops, 1989.

United States Conference of Catholic Bishops (USCCB). *Brothers and Sisters to Us*. https://www.usccb.org/committees/african-american-affairs/brothers-and-sisters -us.

———. *Discrimination and Christian Conscience*. https://www.usccb.org/issues-and-action/cultural-diversity/african-american/resources/upload/Discrimination-Christian-Conscience-Nov-14-1958.pdf.

———. *Pastoral Letters of the United States Catholic Bishops, Vol. I–III*. Washington, DC: United States Conference of Catholic Bishops, 1984.

7

The New Evangelization and
the Pew Dweller

MICHAEL J. McCALLION

Introduction

THIS CHAPTER FOCUSES ON the relationship between new evangelization ministers and ordinary pew-dwelling Catholics. In assessing this relationship, we consider the New Evangelization (NE), sociologically, as an internal ecclesial social movement with Catholic charismatics as some of its most enthusiastic proponents.[1] Pope Benedict XVI and Pope St. John Paul II strongly supported lay ecclesial movements, especially those focused on the New Evangelization (NE) such as Catholic Charismatics. Thus, examining and assessing the relationship between these NE ministers and ordinary Catholics is important with respect to improving NE methods of delivery. Pope Francis has continued that support, perhaps with less enthusiasm, in that he cautions Catholic Charismatic new evangelists to remember that they do not have a franchise on the Holy Spirit.[2] Any new social movement, ecclesial or otherwise, over time will exhibit weaknesses or certain problems as each proclaims its purpose. Cardinal Ratzinger's *Report on the Faith* in 1985 expressed such concerns by claiming that the lay ecclesial movements that had emerged after Vatican II "certainly . . . give rise to some problems. They also entail greater or lesser dangers."[3] For instance, research has shown that a weakness of the Catholic Charismatic Renewal (CCR) new evangelists is their theological emphasis on the individual—having a personal relationship with Jesus—whereas those described as Vatican II ecclesial ministers are

1. See McCallion, "The New Evangelization."
2. See Faggioli, *Catholicism and Citizenship*, chapter 2.
3. See Ratzinger, *The Ratzinger Report*, 43.

more likely to emphasize community.[4] Schuth has found a similar situation among clergy with recently ordained priests emphasizing a more individualistic theology and older priests a more communal theology.[5] Indeed, Pope Francis, using the term "encounter" with the living God and one's neighbor, rather than only having a personal relationship with Jesus, could be understood similarly as emphasizing the communal over the individual. As Wallenfang writes, "Appearing no less than thirty-four times in his recent apostolic exhortation, *Evangelii gaudium*, the word 'encounter' may be one of the best expressions of Francis's ministerial vision for the Church."[6] The word "encounter" then suggests a more communal relationship beyond the "me and Jesus" focus aligned with Protestant individualism.

Analyses of the relative merits of individual versus community orientations has a long history, but only recently, as part of the Catholic NE initiative, has the language of individual versus communal been so clearly articulated and stressed. Although the NE's emphasis on the individual is not the direct focus of this chapter, we note it here because it is relevant to the relationship we are trying to understand between ordinary Catholics and new evangelists. Given this relevance, we argue that new evangelists tend to give the impression that they have a personal relationship with Jesus and that most ordinary Catholics do not, but are in need of one, thus placing a strain on the relationship between professional new evangelists and ordinary pew-dwellers. If we consider the advancement of the personal rather than communal relationship with Jesus to be one of the proximate causes of strain between new evangelists and pew-dwellers, there are more. Some new evangelists are not shy about stating that most ordinary Catholics do not "know" enough about their faith and therefore do not measure up. There is a gate at the last judgement and that gate is narrow when the criteria for entry are having a personal relationship with Jesus and greater knowledge of the faith. These are proximate causes. We assert that the root causes of strain between new evangelists and ordinary Catholics, however, is that new evangelists are unaware or do not acknowledge the Catholic division of spiritual labor. They operate using a deficit model rather than a pastorally sensitive model, and they demonstrate the worst of the shortcomings characteristic of the lay/professional gap. Explanation of these root causes will be the primary focus of this chapter.

Although in many respects the NE is a positive energy infusing the Church overall, this chapter focuses on what we feel to be a weakness in

---

4. See McCallion et al., "Individualism and Community."

5. See Schuth, "Who Pastors."

6. Wallenfang, "Pope Francis and His Phenomenology of *Encuentro*," 57.

new evangelists' missionary efforts. Evangelizing today can be a delicate interactional encounter that occurs in the long shadow of the clerical sex abuse scandal, and therefore critiquing local concrete details of evangelizing efforts and pointing out weaknesses could be the difference between turning someone away or towards the church. Accordingly, Pope Francis's "field hospital" approach to evangelizing is fully endorsed here because of its focus on communities of real people in real local situations and because it insists on listening before preaching. Discussing even the slightest weakness in the implementation of the NE then is important because it could increase awareness and thereby encourage new evangelists to reconsider their relationship to ordinary laity.

Qualitative and Quantitative Data

Conducting research on the transition from the Latin to English Mass (*Novus ordo*) triggered discussions about the Church's division of spiritual labor. This concept is an adaptation of Durkheim's theory of *the social* division of labor as a cause and condition of modern societies. In our usage, it is a description of the differences in spiritual activity between the ordained and the laity and it is a means for positively viewing the laity in their role within the divisions in the Church but *does not* in any way imply that the laity are *passive* in their faith. This view in turn led to discussions about research on the NE concerning the deficit model of Catholicism and the lay/professional attitudinal gap. The former could be described as the "glass is half full" analysis of a pew-dweller at best, or "you-are-not-good-enough," at worst; the latter is the difference in religious thought and practice between the professionally trained and the ordinary pew-dweller. More will be explained below about these concepts but, for now, a brief look at some preliminary data is important because it establishes a base from which broader analyses will be made about the relationship between new evangelists and the laity.

The first step was to conduct interviews of elderly Catholics about their experiences of the transition from the Latin to English Mass after Vatican II. A specific set of questions was formulated and used to provide greater consistency across the remaining interviews. Questions about specific aspects of the Mass were included in the hope these would trigger memories of how the interviewees felt about the changes fifty years ago as well as how they feel today about that transition. The second step, based on the analysis of these interview data, was a short social survey, consisting of four questions, constructed to identify some general feelings about the transition. Fifty survey responses to date have been collected from mostly white American women and men.

To begin, respondents' answers to two survey questions are examined along with interview data. The first question pertained to their experiences as the Mass changed from Latin to English after Vatican II and are shown in Table 1. The second question pertained to the extent to which respondents went along with the changes in the Mass and are shown in Table 2. Overwhelmingly, in the interviews and survey responses the transition was not found particularly disturbing. Table 1 below provides descriptive statistics for the first question about finding the transition disturbing or not, with 55.3 percent responding they felt positive or very positive about the transition to the new Mass of Vatican II with another 42.6 percent feeling neutral about the transition and only one person feeling disturbed by the transition.

Table 1: How I Felt about the Transition

	Frequency	Percent
disturbing	1	2.0
neutral	20	40.0
positive	20	40.0
very positive	9	18.0
TOTAL	50	100.0

This "not finding the transition particularly disturbing" was mentioned repeatedly in the interview data as well. Table 2 below reveals additional similar findings with 100 percent of the respondents going along or supporting the changes in the Mass with a small subset of respondents supporting the changes happily (17 percent) and, once again, the interview data supported these findings.[7]

7. Interestingly, however, most interviewees pined for certain aspects of the Tridentine Mass while still supporting the transition overall. Indeed, a certain nostalgia was clearly evident in their faces—a sadness if you will about something being lost in the transition. When asked what was lost or what they missed in the New Mass several commented about wanting to hear more of the older hymns, others mentioned missing the bells at consecration, a few missed greater use of incense, while others wanted the tabernacle back in the center of the church. This nostalgic sense of loss has been summarized by others as a loss of a sense of reverence.

Table 2: I Went along with Changes to Mass

	Frequency	Percent
I went along with changes	25	50.0
I supported the changes	15	30.0
I supported changes happily	10	20.0
TOTAL	47	100.0

These data mesh nicely with the arguments proposed in this chapter by suggesting first and foremost that they reveal parishioners trust for their pastors about the Mass changes. If this is a fair assessment, then the following question arises, "Why did they trust them?" In answering this question, the concept of the division of spiritual labor can help in that the laity *intuitively understand* and accept this division in that pastors and religious by definition do more spiritual labor than parishioners. We make the assertion that the ordinary laity understand that bishops and pastors are the leaders of the church to assist ordinary Catholics in their journeys to God and, moreover, in doing so, these same laity have come to trust their pastors. Of course, in 2020 this trust is no longer the "pay, pray, and obey" kind that laity embraced before Vatican II. In other words, today, pastors and bishops must truly and sincerely provide spiritual and religious support or ordinary Catholics will simply go somewhere else. Indeed, our research on *de facto* congregationalism showed that in the years following Vatican II 50 percent of the laity in the Detroit Archdiocese do not adhere to the canon laws pertaining to parish boundaries.[8] It is a new Catholic day since Vatican II, emphasizing beyond a doubt that the ordinary Catholic attends his or her parish *voluntarily.*

The second assertion of this chapter is that new evangelists need to keep matters of the laity's role in the division of spiritual labor in mind, because in parishioners' understanding of this basic division, they trust their pastors to do more spiritual labor than they do. It is also important to keep this assertion in mind because the data presented below corroborate the argument that new evangelists are operating out of a deficit model. For example, preaching that ordinary faithful are *sacramentalized but not evangelized*— a ritual incantation of new evangelists—is to maintain they are deficient.[9]

8. See McCallion and Maines, "Representations of Faith."

9. See McCallion, *The New Evangelization.*

Similarly, as the title of the recent conference *Enter through the Narrow Gate* strongly implies, the most virtuous will pass through the gate, the less virtuous, the *deficient*, will not. Implementing the NE in this way with this kind of language will not work in the long run because most will resist such a message while others will simply go somewhere else to hear a different message. In short, new evangelists preaching that laity are insufficiently Catholic will not only not work but it will backfire in the end. New evangelists need to understand the division of spiritual labor, the deficit model of Catholicism, and, we add here, the lay/professional attitudinal gap.

Concepts of Deficit Model, Division of Spiritual Labor, and Lay/Professional Gap

The *deficit* model is the first concept we address and as it is applied to religious participants it has its roots in the era of the Protestant Reformation. Max Weber, a German sociologist, wrote about Calvinists of the Protestant Reformation and argued they developed an inner-worldly asceticism which in turn helped spark tremendous economic productivity—both patterns of behavior proving to themselves their elect status and relieving their salvation status anxiety. These early German Calvinists were the embodiment of Christian discipline, a discipline that not only ushered in the spirit of modern capitalism, but also produced an emphasis on the lone single individual.[10] Basically, Calvinists prayed and worked tirelessly, but were *no* fun. They did not attend parties, drink alcohol, dance, or socialize, much like Dicken's character Scrooge.

Weber's idea that discipline is the engine of most Western forms of subjectivity—in body or mind—is worrying because it focused on intellectuals and elites within Protestantism (Calvin and Luther, for example), not ordinary worshipers on Sunday. This idea of discipline, then, led to what is called an individualistic *earnest* turn in Christianity during and after the Protestant Reformation.[11] If you were *not* earnest, meaning you were not working hard and not going to church, that is, you were not disciplined, not a spiritual athlete, then you were not *good enough or you were deficient*. We use the term spiritual virtuoso to describe a member of the Catholic laity who approaches or nearly approaches the depth and breadth of the spiritual life of

10. See Taylor, *A Secular Age.*

11. Max Weber and Ernst Troeltsch developed the sect/church theory where sects usually start with an earnest spiritual charismatic leader and earnest followers but over time the sect becomes more institutionalized (becomes a church) and the earnestness fades which then leads new earnest spiritual virtuosi to break off (sectarianism) and start a new religious group.

the ordained—most often lay professional ecclesial ministers. This individualistic *earnest* turn was on full display in the content and title of the recent Detroit symposium *Entering through the Narrow Gate*. Another example is the anthropologist Asad whose several writings on religion were inspired *not* from the ordinary laity but from monastic practices—from what the clerical orders did.[12] Within Asad's theory of the development of a Christian self, it is implicitly assumed that the laity followed suit or felt they had to live up to the described monastic ideals, which not only left them feeling guilty but doomed them to failure because of the practicalities of everyday life. The earnest turn may have benefits in the economic sphere, but we propose that it upends an important Catholic structure, the division of spiritual labor, and is therefore counter-productive to new evangelization efforts because new evangelists unwittingly operate out of this model and can leave ordinary Catholics feeling they are insufficiently Catholic.

Again, one of the defining elements of Catholicism, as opposed to many Protestant traditions, is its enshrined *division of spiritual labor* between clergy and laity with clergy expected to be more disciplined and earnest in the spiritual life and the laity less so because of the Church's division of spiritual labor. In its simplest terms, Catholicism is ordered by a priestly caste, an ordained elite who preside at sacramental celebrations, and the laity who participate with the priest. Even though all the baptized are called to holiness, and the celebration of the sacraments cannot happen without the priest and laity participating together, the division of spiritual labor is recognized and acknowledged when the laity ask their pastor to pray for them. The laity are not religiously passive in this regard, it is just that in Catholicism, to be part of the laity is to be part of those who are chosen by God for other tasks/vocations, such as marriage and child rearing. It is in this fundamental division of the visible church into the ordained and the laity that a certain absolution *from* the *intense* performance of spiritual and theological tasks is justified for ordinary Catholics. In Catholicism, the division of spiritual labor distributes the work of piety and religious knowledge onto priests and religious virtuosi full-time, granting ordinary Catholics a partial deferral from such *intense* spiritual labor. In one sense, then, priests let the laity off the spiritual virtuosity hook and necessarily do so because the laity have jobs, families, and kids. Not that the laity are *never* supposed to pray, but given the division of spiritual labor, the laity can justifiably and without guilt play a less intense spiritual role. There is an obvious but important point in all this, especially for Catholicism; far from being an *impossible* religion, Catholicism is, in theory, an infinitely *do-able* religion

12. See Asad, *Genealogies of Religion*.

precisely because it does not exact high levels of spiritual fitness or theological knowledge from ordinary folk—at least not from each individual all of the time—unlike Weber's *earnest* Calvinists.

This ethos is at work in a different way when lay Catholics divide spiritual labor among themselves in terms of gender and generation. Anthropologists have pointed out that among the laity themselves there is a division of spiritual labor with some taking on more spiritual responsibility than others. Consider Sara, a twenty-three-year-old pilgrim in Elaine Peña's study on transnational (Mexico-USA) devotion to the Virgin of Guadalupe.[13] Sara performs a pilgrimage wearing a white T-shirt which her friends and relatives have covered with hand-written petitions for themselves and their loved ones. In such cases one pilgrim's body literally carries the intentions of many other individuals. Now, we may be tempted to describe such folk who write on Sara's T-shirt as less spiritually intense than Sara or not "good enough" because they did not make the pilgrimage. But given the division of spiritual labor ingrained in Catholicism throughout its history, it is understandable that Sara's friends and relatives participated in this way because perhaps that is all they could do at that point in their lives. They have delegated spiritual responsibility to Sara and participate in the pilgrimage vicariously through her.

The lay/professional attitudinal gap, a concept studied in sociology now for over a century, corresponds and therefore accentuates the first two concepts discussed above, but it is important to keep in mind that this concept is more similar to the deficit model concept in revealing that professional new evangelists see the laity negatively and therefore do not grasp the division of spiritual labor idea which defines the role of the laity positively. It corresponds to the deficit model specifically because it is direct in revealing there is a gap between ordinary laity and clergy/spiritual virtuosi in religious thought and practice. So, the deficit model and the lay/professional gap are similar in that both reveal professionals as an elitist group out of touch with the ordinary pew-dweller. Hitchcock, for example, has described this gap as "an elitist middle-class element revolting against the authoritarian hierarchy above, and the ignorant mass below."[14] Wilhelmsen has described the situation as that of "educated prigs who have rejected their own lower-middle class origins."[15] That such a gap is occurring in the Catholic Church therefore should not be surprising. Indeed, Douglas (1970) and Hargrove (1988) have written that an increasingly educated and organizationally-oriented Catholic clergy has contributed to a gulf between themselves and the ordinary

13. See Peña, *Performing Piety.*

14. Hitchcock, *The Decline and Fall of Radical Catholicism*, 107.

15. Wilhelmsen, "Catholicism is Right, So Why Change It?," 12.

pew-dweller, which has been further enhanced with the professionalization of lay spiritual virtuosi—such as new evangelists.[16]

Professionals from many fields tend to unwittingly embrace such attitudes and behavior. Nevertheless, most professionals today resist making quick judgements about ordinary laity, especially their religion, whatever its manifestation. Within the Catholic Church itself, however, negative assessments have arisen anew with professional new evangelists making quick negative judgements of the laity without consideration given to the division of spiritual labor, the deficit model of Catholicism, and the lay/professional attitudinal gap.

Application

The division of spiritual labor, to review, is simply that the Church has made a distinction for centuries between laity and clergy—with the clergy responsible for the bulk of the spiritual labor. The deficit model of Catholicism is when clergy or virtuosi lay Catholics give off the impression that the rest of the ordinary laity are insufficiently Catholic. In the case of the lay/professional gap, professional clergy, new evangelists, and lay spiritual athletes *do not* see or behave in the world the way ordinary pew-dwelling Catholics do. At different times in the Church's history these divisions have been noted with the deficit label used more at some historical moments than others. We claim, however, that one such historical moment is today with the advent of the New Evangelization (1990s). On balance, the NE has been a positive *force in* the Church. However, the initiative's strengths and weaknesses have become clearer over time with one weakness being the overly critical

16. See Douglas, *Natural Symbols*; Hargrove, "Religion, Development, and Changing Paradigms." Given that this phenomenon occurs amongst many types of professionals, it should not be too surprising that even sociologists who have studied this gap have contributed to it in that many have disregarded the material side of religion in their research. McDannell, for instance, in her 1995 book, *Material Christianity: Religion and Popular Culture in America*, claims that American professionals in particular have consistently disregarded the artifacts or material things of religion (although less so since the 1990s) in stating: "I suspect they share the notion with many scholars and theologians that 'real' religion cannot be materialist. It is not surprising that historians and sociologists assume that the American landscape and consumer culture are devoid of religious forms since specialists in religion fail to note the material dimension of explicitly religious culture" (p. 7). Since the Protestant Reformation and the earnest turn, American religionists have privileged the "ear over the eye, hearing over seeing, the word over the image, and the book over the statue" (p. 14). But for many lay Christians, the sensuous and materialist dimensions of religion have remained important. For example, hundreds of Catholics have statues, etc., in their homes and they do not appear to be duped by the material side of faith.

description of the spirituality and practices of ordinary Catholics in the pews on Sunday. Our research reveals these ordinary Catholics doing the best they can, unconsciously embracing the division of spiritual labor, and yet some new evangelists continuing to preach their deficiency—empirical evidence suggesting *not only* that new evangelists are unaware of or not fully understanding their deficit model preaching but also showing their ignorance of the Church's division of spiritual labor.

Indeed, new evangelists who read this chapter will more than likely argue that the division of spiritual labor is exactly the problem—the laity are less active than clergy and therefore need to be evangelized and energized to be more active. Yet research shows that Catholics share their faith or evangelize as much as Protestants, and although their methods differ, it certainly does not mean they are passive spiritually. For example, data in Table 3 below show Catholic laity are especially active in representing or sharing their faith non-verbally: having religious items in their car, yard, at work, and in their homes or in wearing a cross, carrying a Rosary, or wearing a religious item on their clothing or ashes on their forehead on Ash Wednesday.[17]

Table 3: Public Visual Representations of Religious Faith

	Protestant	Catholic
Continues Inactive Display		
Religious items in car	39.6 percent	56.0 percent
Religious items in yard	26.6	45.3
Religious screensaver at work	17.7	21.6
Religious items at work	22.0	32.9
Continuously Active Display		
Wearing cross at work	56.7	61.4
Wearing cross outside work	62.1	67.5
Carry rosary beads	2.6	35.9
Wear religious clothing at work	29.6	29.6
Wear religious clothing outside work	45.4	41.9
Read bible in public	38.9	30.9

17. See McCallion and Maines, "Representations of Faith."

	Protestant	Catholic
Continuously Inactive		
Religious items in living room	68.2	81.3
Religious items in bedroom	73.6	87.9

Although some of these visual representations require only minimal activity (item in car) others require continuous attention (religious item on clothing). Moreover, these ways of sharing Christian faith are common to both Catholics and Protestants, but they tend to be more typical of the manner in which Catholics share their faith. Now, new evangelists operating out of the deficit model might argue that these data prove laity are insufficiently Catholic, but then the new evangelists themselves would have to present their arguments for why these data indicate deficiency.

Given the above, it could be argued that the new evangelists are coming up with their own definition of what it means to be a non-deficit Catholic that we maintain leans heavily on having a personal relationship with Jesus rather than a communal relationship with Jesus—a more holistic Catholic form of relationship. Moreover, these data are just one set of data showing laity are sufficiently Catholic with plenty of other qualitative data showing similar lay active involvement in their faith.[18] Our positive view of the laity is based not only on these data, but also on the fact that we understand and appreciate that the laity, consciously or not, embrace the reality of the division of spiritual labor. That is why we argue that new evangelists need an appreciation of this concept and reality because then, just maybe, they would stop preaching a deficit model of Catholicism to ordinary Catholics.

Again, some new evangelists who might fit the description of virtuoso have articulated and preached a message that ordinary Catholics on Sunday are *not good enough*. From the deficit model and lay/professional gap perspective, one could argue that what some evangelists have brought to NE efforts, ironically, is not "new," but rather a warmed-over quasi-Protestant sensibility originally developed during the Protestant Reformation. Whether or not that is the case, we assert that the division of spiritual labor model is a more accurate and pastorally sensitive mindset to adopt when describing and evaluating ordinary Catholics because this model assumes their goodness and that they are participating the best they can. Of course, we agree that all members of the body of Christ, together, should participate in continuing God's work in bringing about the kingdom. We are all called

18. See Baggett, *Sense of the Faithful*.

to holiness, we are all called to evangelize because of our baptism. It is because of our baptism that we are all given the mission to proclaim the good news, but *how* that mission is done or how it is implemented has always varied throughout the history of the Church with, for the most part, clerics and religious doing the bulk of the spiritual labor.

Conclusion

We assert that those who do less spiritual labor than the spiritual athletes are *not to be considered insufficiently Catholic*. We have emphasized this point throughout yet there is more than a little evidence showing that some new evangelists are not shy in labeling ordinary Catholics *deficient*. But it is important to point out and lend greater legitimacy to the claim—even though many Catholics abide by the pastoral guidance of their pastors while at the same time not operating out of a pre-Vatican II model of "pray, pay, and obey"—that ordinary laity will protest if they don't like something or, more likely than protest, *simply go somewhere else*. Indeed, many have left the Church or become disaffiliated.[19] We are not arguing they left because of the NE, but neither has the NE brought them back. We understand some new evangelists want a smaller and more committed Church, as Pope Benedict once remarked, but disaffiliated Catholics already make-up the second largest denomination in America. More specifically, the Catholic population of the Detroit Archdiocese has declined 15 percent between 2001 and 2015, with infant baptism down 52.7 percent, Catholic marriages down 48.7 percent, and Catholic funerals down 19 percent. Based on these numbers, it appears the NE, which has been the main focus of the Detroit Archdiocese since the late 1990s, is not attracting new members or bringing back disaffiliates. Of course, it could be argued, there would be even more disaffiliates today if it were not for the NE, but we suggest that is not the case because of what we have argued above, that is, the unintended consequences of the new evangelists' lack of appreciation for the division

---

19. Disaffiliation is a complicated issue, and it is often extremely difficult to separate cause from symptom or intended consequence from unintended side-effects. The reasons why the Church is in decline is a related but completely different topic and so we mention it here only in passing. It is clear however that the decline did not begin with Vatican II but much earlier—at least back to the 1940s, so argues Stephen Bullivant in his 2019 book *Mass Exodus: Catholic Disaffiliation in Britain and America since Vatican II* as well as others. Indeed, causal explanations are difficult to make and it is why a figure as towering as Max Weber wrote about 'elective affinities' in explaining the rise of Western capitalism. See also Taylor, *A Secular Age*.

of spiritual labor, preaching a deficit model, and being unaware of the attitudinal gap between laity and professionals.

Laity know when they are being slighted even in the most minute verbal and non-verbal ways, and if such is detected they will simply go somewhere else. As mentioned above, we believe evangelization is a delicate and fragile interactional encounter in a modern social context of individualism, voluntarism, and the sex abuse crisis, and so a pastoral field hospital approach to evangelizing is imperative. The ordinary parishioner must be treated with respect, with understanding, and given the benefit of the doubt that they are doing the best they can in their faith. So, we suggest to new evangelists that they do some self-evaluation and soul-searching on their own. If they find that the lay/professional gap is operative in their ministry or that they may be preaching a deficit model of Catholicism, then they should try to understand and acknowledge the laity's role in the Church's division of spiritual labor and view it positively. In doing this, new evangelists are more likely to orient their ministry more positively toward the laity. Finally, new evangelists' language of having a personal relationship with Jesus needs to be balanced with a language of having a communal relationship with Jesus in order for ordinary Catholics to understand evangelization as "Catholic," not just something Protestants do. Many Catholics have said in response to questions about the new evangelization that it sounds Protestant and that we Catholics don't do that.[20] This may be a matter of education, but it could also be that by proclaiming a personal relationship with Jesus new evangelists are, perhaps unknowingly, re-defining what it means to be Catholic as applied to the laity and many of the laity, and some church professionals we might add, take issue with that re-definition. Yet, we believe, this re-defining is partially what new evangelists do when they preach a deficit model of Catholicism to ordinary Catholics which shows new evangelists are the latest example of the lay/professional gap as well as professionals who do not understand the laity's role in the division of spiritual labor, all of which, in the end, reveals their elitism—an elitism Pope Francis has warned against.

Although new evangelizers have blessed the Church, weaknesses in their missionary efforts are evident, primarily and most disturbingly the direct or indirect communication that "you are not good enough" which we tried to refute by discussing the concepts of the division of spiritual labor, the deficit model of Catholicism, and the lay/professional attitudinal gap. Specifically, these concepts provided a lens through which to understand the weaknesses involved in the relationship between ordinary Catholics and New Evangelization leaders. Utilizing the concept of the

---

20. See McCallion, *The New Evangelization.*

division of spiritual labor, ordinary laity are understood positively in their relationship to the Church, whereas utilizing the concepts of the deficit model and the lay/professional gap, NE leaders are negatively understood in their relationship to ordinary Catholics. Consequently, new evangelists, in our estimation, need to be more pastoral in their evangelizing efforts. "Pastoral" is broadly understood, we realize, but in this case, it means "don't beat up on the pew-dweller" and give them the benefit of the doubt that they are doing the best they can.

Bibliography

Asad, Talal. *Genealogies of Religion: Discipline and Reasons of Power in Christianity and Islam*. Baltimore: Johns Hopkins University Press, 1993.

Baggett, Jerome. *Sense of the Faithful: How American Catholics Live Their Faith*. Oxford: Oxford University Press, 2009.

Bullivant, Stephen. *Mass Exodus: Catholic Disaffiliation in Britain and America since Vatican II*. New York: Oxford University Press, 2019.

Douglas, Mary. *Natural Symbols: Explorations in Cosmology*. New York: Vintage, 1970.

Faggioli, Massimo. *Catholicism and Citizenship: Political Cultures of the Church in the Twenty-First Century*. Collegeville, MN: Liturgical, 2017.

Hargrove, Barbara. "Religion, Development, and Changing Paradigms." *Sociological Analysis* 49 (1988) 33–48.

Hitchcock, James. *The Decline and Fall of Radical Catholicism*. New York: Herder and Herder, 1971.

Maines, David R., and Michael J. McCallion. "Evidence of and Speculation on Catholic *de facto* Congregationalism." *Review of Religious Research* 46 (2004) 92–101.

Mannion, Francis M. "Agendas for Liturgical Reform." *America* 175 (1996) 9–16.

McCallion, Michael J. "The New Evangelization in the Archdiocese of Detroit as an Intra-Ecclesial Social Movement." *Church Life: A Journal for the New Evangelization* 2.4 (2014) 23–40.

———. *The New Evangelization in the Roman Catholic Archdiocese of Detroit, Michigan: A Sociological Report*. Lewiston, NY: Mellen, 2015.

McCallion, Michael J., and David R. Maines. "Representations of Faith and the Catholic New Evangelization." *New Theology Review* 22 (2009) 58–69.

McCallion, Michael J., et al. "Individualism and Community as Contested Rhetorics in the Catholic New Evangelization Movement." *Review of Religious Research* 54 (2012) 291–310.

McDannell, Colleen. *Material Christianity: Religion and Popular Culture in America*. New Haven: Yale University Press, 1995.

Peña, E. A. *Performing Piety: Making Space Sacred with the Virgin of Guadalupe*. Berkeley: University of California Press, 2011.

Ratzinger, Joseph. *The Ratzinger Report: An Exclusive Interview on the State of the Catholic Church*. Translated by Salvator Attanasio and Graham Harrison. San Francisco: Ignatius, 1985.

Schuth, Katarina. "Who Pastors: The Priest, the Context, and the Ministry." In *The Future of Catholicism in America*, edited by Patricia O'Connell Killen and Mark Silk, 153–85. New York: Columbia University Press, 2019.

Taylor, Charles. *A Secular Age*. Cambridge, MA: Belknap, 2007.

Wallenfang, Donald. "Pope Francis and His Phenomenology of *Encuentro*." In *Pope Francis and the Event of Encounter*, edited by John C. Cavadini and Donald Wallenfang, 57–71. Eugene, OR: Pickwick, 2017.

Weber, Max. *The Protestant Ethic and the Spirit of Capitalism*. Translated by P. Baehr and G. C. Wells. New York: Penguin, 2002.

Wilhelmsen, Frederick. "Catholicism is Right, So Why Change It?" *Saturday Evening Post*, July, 1967.

V. Sanctified Evangelization

8

Cor Quietum

Saint Augustine and Saint Teresa of Ávila
on the New Evangelization[1]

Donald Wallenfang, Ocds

> Late have I loved you, beauty so old and so new: late have I
> loved you. . . . You called and cried out loud and shattered my
> deafness. You were radiant and resplendent, you put to flight
> my blindness. You were fragrant, and I drew in my breath and
> now pant after you. I tasted you, and I feel but hunger and
> thirst for you. You touched me, and I am set on fire to attain
> the peace which is yours.
>
> —Saint Augustine, *Confessions*, X.xxvii.38

ONE OF THE DISTINCTIVE features of Christian evangelization today is the
peculiar historical milieu in which it finds itself: postmodernity. In order
for evangelization to be most effective in its method of communicating
the Gospel of Jesus Christ, the evangelist must be a student of culture by
reading the signs of the times and maneuvering accordingly.[2] As a study

1. I would like to thank Dr. Matthew Gerlach and the Institute for Lay Ministry at Sacred Heart Major Seminary for inviting me to give the talk "Gathering Up
the Fragments: Pastoral Ministry in a Postmodern World," featured as the 2020 Lay
Ecclesial Minister Speaker Series keynote presentation: https://www.youtube.com/
watch?v=NEuktznRyR8&t=1858s. Most of this essay was developed in preparation
for that event. In addition, I would like to thank Fr. Nathan Cromly, CSJ, the Community of Saint John, and the Saint John Institute of Denver, Colorado, for inviting
me to lead a seminar on pastoral leadership in November of 2020, where this essay
first was shared. In particular, I thank seminar participants Pablo "Paco" Francisco
Patag, Claire Schmitmeyer, Stephen Tony, and Jeffrey Yanuck for their many insights
that helped to sharpen the essay further, as well as their warm reception of its content
and spirit. *Aude Christo Magna!*

2. See Cavadini and Wallenfang, *Pope Francis and the Event of Encounter*, xv–xix.

in culture and evangelical adaptation, this essay aims at four goals: (1) to define some of the basic traits of postmodernism; (2) to recommend Saint Augustine's form of *confessio*, and Jean-Luc Marion's phenomenological uptake of it, as a necessary pathway of the New Evangelization; (3) to show how Saint Teresa of Ávila's contemplative itinerary of the prayer of recollection is instrumental for gathering up the isolated fragments of postmodern lives; and (4) to suggest a new model of pastoral outreach called "montage ministry." By proceeding along these four steps, the know-how of the New Evangelization will be brought into sharper relief vis-à-vis the fragmented world toward which it is directed.

I. Naming the Present

David Tracy (1939–) asserts that "we live in an age that cannot name itself," and that "there is no longer *a* center with margins. There are many centers."[3] This polycentric reality, known as "postmodernity," is as elusive as it is disorienting. Just as there is no "due north," there is no "due east" (*orientem, subsolanus*). What we encounter today is an assortment of fragments that individually and altogether attest to the saturating whole from which they were shattered and scattered. So many fragments of apparent dissociated meaning. Again, according to Tracy, fragments are "the spiritual situation of our times."[4] Jean-François Lyotard (1924–98), in his 1979 essay "The Postmodern Condition: A Report on Knowledge," identifies several characteristics of postmodernity that are essential for us to remember: (1) skepticism toward metanarratives, (2) computerization of society, (3) commodification of knowledge, and (4) spiritual and relational fragmentation.[5] Let us consider each of these marks in turn. First, in the wake of two World Wars and countless social and cultural revolutions (for instance, the Scientific Revolution, the Protestant Reformation, the Industrial Revolution, the French and American Revolutions, the Sexual Revolution, and today's Technological Revolution), postmodernism is incredibly skeptical of metanarratives. Metanarratives are those grand stories that pretentiously claim to be omniscient and completely comprehensive, but, in actuality, these stories are embarrassingly partial and myopic. Similar to Albert Einstein's theory of relativity, just as massive objects cause a distortion within the spacetime

3. Tracy, *On Naming the Present*, 3–4.

4. Tracy, "Fragments: The Spiritual Situation of Our Times," in Caputo and Scanlon, *God, the Gift, and Postmodernity*, 170–84. Also, see Myatt, *Theological Plunderphonics*, 251–54.

5. Lyotard, "The Postmodern Condition: A Report on Knowledge," in McNeill and Feldman, *Continental Philosophy*, 391–405.

continuum, individual and communal narratives cause a distortion within the totality we call history. For postmodernism, there is no single narrative that includes all persons, places and events within its storyline. Each narrative is entirely contingent on its own "web-spinner" or "world-spinner" (Nietzsche), as well as its own "sociology of knowledge" (Mannheim) or "symbolic order" (Chauvet) in which the narrator is ensconced.[6] Each narrative is relative to its narrator and relative to other heterogeneous narratives that tell different stories in varied tempos and keys. Anyone who claims a metanarrative in the polyphonic hall of postmodernity is roundly mocked, even by the honest incredulity of a guilty conscience.

Second, the postmodern era has witnessed a computerization of society. In daily living, we have become more accustomed to facing pixels rather than persons. We have begun to communicate more through text than voice. The world has become digitalized and virtualized with so many avatars of personal possibility punctuated by hashtags and emojis instead of the three-dimensional contours of human bodies in attentive and affective proximity to one another. In an expanding world of artificial intelligence (AI), robots have exceeded human beings along the perceived ontological spectrum of value. Even money has become virtualized and reduced to numbers on glowing screens instead of tangible objects of trade. We would much rather do business with a faceless Amazon than have to face a person and wait for him or her to fulfill the transaction and return our change. Empathy has been swapped for entropy, exceedance has been exchanged for expedience, solicitude has been dickered for (selfish) solitude, and the saddest part is that I am not exaggerating. As I write this essay, the Coronavirus global pandemic has crowned this computerization of society all the more. A world in which looking people in the eye and sincerely shaking hands was growing dim has now become a midnight sea of sociopathic silhouettes.

Third, postmodernism includes a commodification of knowledge. Postmodernity is where time is money, matter is all that matters, and knowledge is considered worthless unless it can turn a monetary profit. Nowhere is this reductionism of knowledge more evident today than in the domain of higher education. As Lyotard predicts, postmodernity will experience the metamorphosis of universities into trade institutes. In the United States, for instance, fields of the liberal arts and humanities are teetering on the brink of extinction. Because of market demands and deluded minds, core curricula are being slashed and amputated at an astounding rate. Even church sponsored institutions are not immune from this curriculum atrophy.

6. See Nietzsche, *Human, All Too Human*; Nietzsche, *Twilight of the Idols*; Mannheim, *Ideology and Utopia*; Chauvet, *Sacraments*; Chauvet, *Symbol and Sacrament*.

Subject areas such as literature, arts, music, history, languages, grammar, logic, rhetoric, cultural studies, astronomy, philosophy and theology receive lip service at best and complete forgetfulness at worst. Secondary education has devolved into a truncated curriculum comprised of natural science, technology, engineering, and mathematics (STEM), without any reference to the greater whole that is the liberal arts. When the humanities fields are removed from education, so too is the human removed from our self-understanding. In a worldview reduced to STEM, it seems that one would be better off a robot than a human being. According to this maimed and acephalous worldview, knowledge has been pulverized into information and algorithms. There is no time allowed for asking why questions in a polytechnic world of pre-programmed informatics.

Fourth, postmodernism signifies the global experience of spiritual and relational fragmentation. If there is one word that could sum up the meaning of postmodernism, it just might be fragmentation. The fragmentation of metanarratives. The fragmentation of personhood and community. The fragmentation of knowledge. The fragmentation of the body and the soul. We can speak of a spiritual fragmentation inasmuch as two new spiritual situations have arrived on the scene: a militant intellectual atheism and a perplexing religious pluralism. Concerning the first situation, in the name of (natural) science, and the methodological atheism and religious indifference its method entails, the God-question has become eclipsed, and, thereby, opposed. This is an instance where "ignorance is bliss" and forgetfulness of God ushers in an amoral and unaccountable atomized world of isolated autonomous individual beings. Every person has become a law unto himself or herself. Spirit is regarded as an empty concept. Things religious have value to the degree that they seem to promote the well-being of the body. Human relationships, too, are treated in utilitarian fashion. Persons are used as means to impersonal ends. The nuclear family, as well as the extended family, have been fragmented to the point of nonrecognition. What is the meaning of "family" now anyway? Even basic sexual identity has been fragmented in multiple directions to the extent that the stable ontological categories of male and female, boy and girl, man and woman, husband and wife, father and mother, have been deconstructed to the level of pure fluidity. With postmodernism comes the dawn of the fragment as the final frontier of meaning.

Concrete examples of Lyotard's four features of postmodernism abound: the average number of hours per day people spend staring at an electronic screen (seven-plus hours typically for teenagers and adults); a radical decline in attendance of weekly worship in community; trending STEM education curricula across public and private sectors of education; the gradual elimination of humanities majors in institutions of higher education; the rapid increase of online learning at all levels of education; the replacement of face-to-face and phone conversation with instant messaging; and the proliferation of social media and virtual socializing. Over the past few years, I have observed some of my daughter's Snapchat exchanges with friends. We would be riding together in the car, and she would take these random pictures of a corner of her head, the roof of the car, or any fragment of an image, and then send this to a friend as a way to let him or her know what she was up to. I would ask her, "Ellen, why do you and your friends send these random and fragmentary pictures to one another? Why not send a full profile picture or some other scenic shot?" Ellen would answer, "Oh, Dad, this is just the way you have to send things on Snapchat!" Since I studied phenomenology, I probed the meaning of this phenomenon through a silent descriptive analysis. I could not help but connect the dots between the Snapchat phenomenon and postmodernism: fragmentation. I was witnessing my own teenage children communicate with friends through the form of fragments: fragmented images, fragmented texts, fragmented video clips, fragmented storylines. TikTok is another recent social media app through which users post up to fifteen-second-long videos . . . fragmentary videos. And the same goes for Instagram, Twitter, Facebook, and countless other social media platforms: fragmentary communication, fragmentary existence. Fragmentariness is the defining trademark of postmodern culture.

In addition to these general attributes of postmodernism, one last trend should be mentioned: identity shifting. The expanse of the virtual world has permitted us to express and reinvent our virtual selves without limit. I can create a new avatar of myself in some online venue in a matter of minutes. I also can erase an old avatar of myself in a matter of minutes. We are able to project legion identities in the virtual world through caricature formats, gaming figures, social media profiles, and picture and video outlets. It often seems that we live more of our lives within virtual worlds than actual ones. We are now perpetually arrested in the virtual imaginative zone of the temptation of temptation, and there seems to be no way out.[7] Moreover, new virtual phenomena are emerging such as digital photo and video manipulation and deepfakes. Through encoding techniques, morphing and superimposing images is possible. It is like the children's game in which you can change out different outfits or faces on a generally stable figure. However, in the case of deepfakes, the images of real persons are being swapped in and out, superimposed on other persons' body images, without consent.

7. See Wallenfang, "Virtual Counterfeit of the Infinite: Emmanuel Levinas and the Temptation of Temptation," in Lewellen and Frederick, *The HTML of Cruciform Love*, 132–50.

In this phenomenon, digital chimeras are being created that doubly confuse the real world with the virtual one. Here is an instance where digital fragments are being mixed and matched to generate new social spaces of being that desacramentalize the bodies and the souls of actual persons.

So, what to make of this world of fragments aside from admitting its inevitability within postmodernity? Let us turn our attention to the 1920 monoprint of Swiss-German artist Paul Klee (1879–1940), entitled *Angelus Novus*.[8] I suggest that this piece of art will help us to interpret the situation of the fragment in the most hopeful way possible.

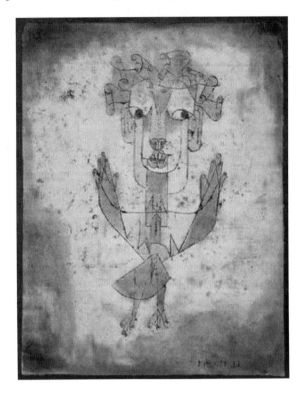

Angelus Novus **by Paul Klee, 1920.**

Walter Benjamin (1892–1940), in his 1940 essay "Theses on the Philosophy of History," proffers the following interpretation of Klee's work:

> A Klee painting named *Angelus Novus* shows an angel looking as though he is about to move away from something he is

8. It is meaningful to note that this Klee image was repainted in the year 2000 by Detroit-born artist Ken Aptekar.

fixedly contemplating. His eyes are staring, his mouth is open, his wings are spread. This is how one pictures the angel of history. His face is turned toward the past. Where we perceive a chain of events, he sees one single catastrophe which keeps piling wreckage upon wreckage and hurls it in front of his feet. The angel would like to stay, awaken the dead, and make whole what has been smashed. But a storm is blowing from Paradise; it has got caught in his wings with such violence that the angel can no longer close them. The storm irresistibly propels him into the future to which his back is turned, while the pile of debris before him grows skyward. This storm is what we call progress.[9]

Klee's artwork and Benjamin's interpretation of it are worth our time to ponder. This piece very well may be a hermeneutical key for navigating the cultural debris called postmodernity. *Angelus Novus.* "The New Angel." The new angel is fixedly contemplating on something. Contemplation—a sure solution to fragmentation. A gathering up of the fragments precisely through contemplative prayer. Eyes are staring, patiently gazing on what begs for redemption. Mouth is open in wonder and awe, yet speechless before the power of God at work in the wreckage. "I am the LORD your God, who brought you up from the land of Egypt. Open wide your mouth that I may fill it" (Ps 81:11). Wings are spread so as to hover aloft for an aerial view of the fragments. A coherent and meaningful mosaic appears from this vantage point. The face of the angel is turned toward the past—the very place where all of the fragments have accumulated. A chain of events is perceived that is tethered to a single catastrophe—the death of God?—wherein the wreckage of fragments gains momentum and is hurled at the shoeless, discalced bare feet of the contemplative. Vulnerable contemplation. Empathetic contemplation. Riskful contemplation. The intentionality of the contemplative angel is to linger, to stay before the tragic and traumatic in order to raise the dead and retrieve the fragments and return them to the whole from which they were fractured. Nevertheless, a storm rages from Eden and escorts the angel violently, with back turned, into the unknown future, all the while continuing to contemplate the swelling pile of fragments in need of harvesting, constellation and recollection. Altogether, the paradigm of this storm is what is called progress, whether in the name of a hidden utopian vision that never seems to come, or in the name of gluttonous fragmentation that accumulates without integration or synthesis.

What else can we notice about the artistic portrayal of this angel that speaks of a responsible response to postmodern fragmentation? The hair

---

9. Benjamin, "Theses on the Philosophy of History," in *Illuminations*, 249.

is disheveled and chaotic, stirred up by the divine Wind that furnishes the potency of metamorphosis and restoration. Perhaps the violent movement of the Wind, and the angel's reception of it, announces "the terrible speed of God's mercy" (Flannery O'Connor). Similar to biblical prophetic figures such as Moses, Miriam, Esther, Elijah, Mary of Nazareth, and John the Baptizer, this nappy hair signifies divine intoxication and the steadfastness of the prophet's will in the face of adversity. The angel's hair even assumes the form of miniature scrolls that register the tiny scrolls of Torah nestled within the tefillin of devout Jewish worshippers. Wind-swept hair like the wind-swept desert wilderness where prophets and hermits live only at the hand of the Lord. We notice an over-sized head in disproportion to a smaller body, along with dilated pupils and enlarged, straining ears turned toward whatever sounds and voices could be heard from the echoes of catastrophe. Further, we observe a deeper reddish hue at the center of the angel's body, marked with the shape of a cross. It must be that the angel contemplates from the spiritual core of its being, animated by the Sacred Heart of Jesus who shed his Blood for the redemption of humanity—paschal Blood that would reverberate throughout the vaults of heaven. Angels seem to find their abode in the fragments of the past that push into the present. The Jewish concept of *tikkun olam* ("repairing a broken world") dominates the posture of the angel, issuing the messianic confidence that all of these disparate fragments can be pieced back together inasmuch as every instant of time is the strait gate (*Detroit* meaning "strait") through which the Messiah may enter. And, for Christian belief, this is true in a redoubled way to the extent that every instant of time is full of the ever-present event of resurrection.

In light of Klee's painting, and Benjamin's interpretation of it, we are better positioned to elucidate the meaning of the fragment within post-modernity. Fragments are problematic because they tend to confuse the part for the whole (ideology); they imply ruptured relationships and dis-organized thinking; they are experienced always with a painful yearning of reintegration; they never cease to testify to the catastrophe that caused their alienation from the whole; they witness to violence, tragedy and trauma—to all those "frag-events" (Tracy) that puncture and tear apart the whole; they cast a sense of ambiguity over history and its interpre-tation; they disrupt the coherence, intelligibility and meaningfulness of being by calling into question every metaphysical presupposition; they attest to the ineluctable force of deconstruction and the inability to go back in time and prevent it; they accompany and reinforce the isolation of individuals and the anxiety experienced alongside the powerlessness to desegregate perfectly what has been separated, secluded, quarantined, immured and incarcerated; they throw doubt against every metanarrative and testimony to the whole; they proliferate to the degree of vertigo and absolute disorientation; they corroborate the caducity of the mind and its incompetence to synthesize parts and direct them to a greater whole; they etiolate and enervate the mind's capacity for assimilating sustained intellectual arguments; and, worst of all, they extinguish any living flame of hope of transformation within the soul.[10] As Pope Francis puts it, "We find that the locus of this reconciliation of differences is within ourselves, in our own lives, ever threatened as they are by fragmentation and breakdown. If hearts are shattered in thousands of pieces, it is not easy to create authentic peace in society."[11] The problem with fragmentation is that, if left unreconciled, it robs us of our peace and fraternity.

Yet, might we point to any positive qualities of fragments? Fragments, indeed, are the existential situation of our times. We can do none other than face them head-on. If we deny them and persist in our insular ignorant metanarratives, turning a blind eye to the untamable pluralism of the world, living only within the echo-chamber of the self's almighty thoughts, then we betray our covenant with truth that refuses to be reduced to the possession of a lone individual according to the hegemonic homogeneity of his hobbit-hole experiences. Fragments, first of all, bear a positive meaning insofar as they are bits of truth. In our age, we cannot pursue the truth apart from the patient procedure of gathering up the fragments and reorienting them toward the mosaic whole from which they were broken apart originally. Fragments themselves witness to the incompleteness of the self, the syncategorematic status of the self's story, and the partial and unfinished singularity of the self's knowledge. Altogether, the radical insufficiency of

10. Cf. Louis Wirth's Preface to Mannheim, *Ideology and Utopia*, xxiii: "The world has been splintered into countless fragments of atomized individuals and groups. . . . When the bases of unified collective action begin to weaken, the social structure tends to break and to produce a condition which Emile Durkheim has termed *anomie*, by which he means a situation which might be described as a sort of social emptiness or void."

11. Francis, *Evangelii gaudium*, 229. Cf. Francis, *Frattelli tutti*, 7, 191: "As I was writing this letter, the Covid-19 pandemic unexpectedly erupted, exposing our false securities. Aside from the different ways that various countries responded to the crisis, their inability to work together became quite evident. For all our hyper-connectivity, we witnessed a fragmentation that made it more difficult to resolve problems that affect us all. Anyone who thinks that the only lesson to be learned was the need to improve what we were already doing, or to refine existing systems and regulations, is denying reality. . . . Even as forms of fanaticism, closedmindedness and social and cultural fragmentation proliferate in present-day society, a good politician will take the first step and insist that different voices be heard. Disagreements may well give rise to conflicts, but uniformity proves stifling and leads to cultural decay. May we not be content with being enclosed in one fragment of reality."

the self! Fragments serve to remind us of our desperate deficiencies. At the same time, fragments are the gateway to the whole. Hans Urs von Balthasar (1905–88), for instance, introduces the concept of *das Ganze im Fragment* ("the whole in the fragment"). According to this idea, the only way we can access the whole is through the fragment, and the only way the whole manifests and proclaims itself to us is through the fragment. This is the very paradox of the Christian mystery. The whole of divinity is revealed in and through the proximity of particular presence. "The fragment—in its perpetual incompletion—is perpetually conversational," "an incompletion that is itself a mode of fulfillment."[12] Because fragments are incomplete unto themselves, they redirect attention to those other complementary fragments that they themselves are not. In order for this cross-referencing to occur, individual fragments must turn outward in dialogue with other non-identical fragments. Conversation between fragments lights up a revelation of the whole that is greater than the sum of its fragmentary parts. In this dialogical and dialectical progression, fragments function as the condition of possibility for their communal restoration. There is something incredibly beautiful about the mosaic recollection of fragments, just like what we encounter in a stained-glass window, or those mosaic tile works of art in so many places of worship around the globe.

The fragment comes to us as a double-edged sword that can be redeemed only by the delightfully trenchant double-edged sword of the divine Logos: "Indeed, the word of God is living and effective, sharper than any two-edged sword, penetrating even between soul and spirit, joints and marrow, and able to discern reflections and thoughts of the heart. No creature is concealed before him, but everything is naked and exposed to the eyes of him to whom we must render an account" (Heb 4:12–13). It is this accountability to the divine Testator that secures the centripetal intermingling and cross-inculturation of divided miscellaneous fragments. Only the renunciation of sin that fragments the whole divisively—a renunciation of renunciation—can reunite all of the fragments that have become hostile and strangers to one another. Could it be that the relation between the Tower of Babel and Pentecost holds the elusive code to unmask and revive this irascible rabble of fragments? Whereas "the LORD scattered them over all the earth" and confused the language of the people at Babel (Gen 11:1–9), the outpouring of God the Holy Spirit in Jerusalem (Acts 2:1–13) fulfills the promise spoken through the prophet Jeremiah: "I myself will gather the remnant of my flock from all the lands to which I have banished them and bring them back to their folds; there they shall be fruitful and multiply"

---

12. Myatt, *Theological Plunderphonics*, 238.

(23:3).[13] The multilingual event of Pentecost counteracts the monolingual failure of Babel. Whereas the ziggurat of Babel concluded with the miserable idol of the self, exalted in some ethereal heaven, the apostles of Pentecost, in contrast, proclaim not themselves but Jesus Christ as Lord by inverting the Tower of Babel and manifesting the touchdown of heaven on earth. And, as Saint Peter reassures us, "Repent and be baptized, every one of you, in the name of Jesus Christ for the forgiveness of your sins; and you will receive the gift of the Holy Spirit. For the promise is made to you and to your children and to all those far off, whomever the Lord our God will call" (Acts 2:38–39). And who does the Lord our God call, if not "whoever has ears to hear"?[14] The chaos of Babel is reordered and reintegrated by the cosmos of Pentecost. Jerusalem, the place of Pentecost, is rightly called "the city of peace" because it is precisely where the fragmented pieces are tended and mended—for it is the house of the fishermen's bend. The Gordian knot of sin is undone by the Fisherman's knot of grace.

Fragments are potent. Each one is charged with the ambiguity of questioning and the polarity and ambivalence of its negative and positive meanings. Fragments carry a negative meaning as to their disorientation, woundedness, incompleteness and disunity. Fragments conduct a positive meaning by disrupting all those pretensions of totality that confuse the part for the whole, and yet fragments in themselves witness to the saturating whole from which they were strewn and toward which they yearn to return. Fragments are expressed as synecdoches through which the part and the whole signify one another according to their inherent unity, such as in the phrases "the world is treating me well" (the whole is signifying the part) or "I asked for her hand in marriage" (the part is signifying the whole). "The focus of the fragment lies in its nature as *essentially* incomplete, an incompletion

---

13. Cf. Deut 30:1–4: "When all these things, the blessing and the curse which I have set before you, come upon you, and you take them to heart in any of the nations where the LORD, your God, has dispersed you, and return to the LORD, your God, obeying his voice, according to all that I am commanding you today, you and your children, with your whole heart and your whole being, the LORD, your God, will restore your fortunes and will have compassion on you; he will again gather you from all the peoples where the LORD, your God, has scattered you. Though you have been dispersed to the farthest corner of the heavens, even from there will the LORD, your God, gather you; even from there will he bring you back." Neh 1:9; Pss 106:47; 107:2–3; 147:2; Isa 11:11–12; 27:12; 54:7; 56:8; Jer 29:14; 31:10; 32:37; Ezek 11:17; 20:34; 39:27–28; Hos 8:10; Mic 2:12; Zeph 3:20; and Matt 23:27: "Jerusalem, Jerusalem, you who kill the prophets and stone those sent to you, how many times I yearned to gather your children together, as a hen gathers her young under her wings, but you were unwilling!"

14. See Matt 11:15; 13:9, 43; Mark 4:9, 23; Luke 8:8; 14:35; Rev 2:7, 11, 17, 29; 3:6, 13, 22. Cf. Rom 10:17: "Thus faith comes from what is heard, and what is heard comes through the word of Christ."

that is itself a mode of fulfillment. The fragment—in its perpetual incomple-tion—is perpetually conversational."[15] In order to be reunified and probed of their individual and communal meanings, fragments must be put in conversation with one another. Because fragments provoke conversation, they themselves convey a sense of fulfillment every time they begin a new conversation. Even more, fragments help to recuperate "the tradition of the oppressed" that so often goes lost within the historical metanarratives of the oppressive victors.[16] Narratival fragments assist in letting the stories of persons from the underside of history be heard.

What are some examples of fragments? Specifically, fragments can be a variety of things: human souls and distended "parts" of souls; images of human bodies and parts of bodies; partial ideas; disconnected memories; individual recollections; works of art; sound bites; text bites; events; dreams; testimonies; symbols; metaphors; sacred objects; secular objects; cultural artifacts; archeological findings; specimens of natural science; song clips; movie clips; videos; pieces of anything. Fragments tend to connote random-ness, but, at the same time, they yield the promise of participation in a more comprehensive constellation of meaning of which each fragment is only a single point lighting up with implicit reference to others. Similar to how Martin Heidegger (1889–1976) reflected on Vincent van Gogh's painting *A Pair of Shoes* to demonstrate how a solitary image of a pair of worn-out peasant's shoes discloses an entire world of meaning in relation to the life of the peasant, the fragment, like the artistic rendition of the peasant's shoes, reveals a depth of meaning and context in which the fragment is decisively enmeshed.[17] Fragments are packed with the potency of apocalyptic revela-tion, and, for this reason, they both haunt us and fill us with hope.

Now having taken stock of the fragmentary cultural situation of the present, we press on to investigate the possibilities of gathering together and reuniting the fragments through the Pentecostal power of evangelization. Again, as David Tracy suggests, where there are fragments, there also are filaments, like those of "a noiseless patient spider," that carry the potential to "catch somewhere, O my soul."[18] The following section of this essay will recommend three lineaments of Saint Augustine's theology that will act as filaments to gather up the fragments of human souls in relation to God:

15. Myatt, *Theological Plunderphonics*, 238.

16. See Myatt, *Theological Plunderphonics*, 214, for reference to this concept of Wal-ter Benjamin, "*Die Tradition der Unterdrückten*."

17. See Heidegger's essay, "The Origin of the Work of Art," in Heidegger, *Poetry, Language, Thought*, 15–86.

18. See the epigraph of Walt Whitman's poem in Tracy, *Filaments*.

confession of sin, confession of praise, and the contemplative gaze. Let us begin by reflecting on the perennial "restless heart" and proceed from there.

II. Saint Augustine on the Art of Confession

Tu excitas, ut laudare te delectet, quia fecisti nos ad te et inquietum est cor nostrum, donec requiescat in te.

You stir man to take pleasure in praising you, because you have made us for yourself, and our heart is restless until it rests in you.

—Saint Augustine, *Confessions*, I.i.1

Inquietum est cor nostrum—disquieted is our heart. This is exactly how we should describe the cardiological malaise of the postmodern condition. Disquieted hearts in a foreign land. For we have been inexorably exiled from ourselves, from our God, and from one another. We yearn for a return—a reprisal—a reunification of hearts gathered around the Sacred Heart of Jesus. Only the Sacred Heart of the God-man could cure the congenital heart failure of this postmodern scene. It is not more solitude and isolation apart from each other that we need to grant us peace, but what we need is more communion, participation, fellowship, fraternity (κοινωνία). Yet how would we achieve this communion of persons if we are left unreconciled with one another and with God? It would remain impossible without reconciliation. And what is the route of reconciliation? None other than confession of sin and confession of praise. The time of conversion is the time of confession. This is what Saint Augustine teaches us in his *Confessions*.

Jean-Luc Marion (1946–) reminds us that "for Saint Augustine *confessio* is twofold, confession of sins and confession of praise."[19] If a person desires reconciliation, to "launch forth filament, filament, filament, out of itself, ever unreeling them, ever tirelessly speeding them . . . in measureless oceans of space," then one must confess his or her personal sins, as well as the praise to God that is due.[20] Quoting and commenting on the *Confessions* of Saint Augustine, Marion argues along with him that "'confession joins us to Christ. For confession itself, namely the first "thought," already performs in us the rest of thought. . . .The first "thought" possesses the confession.' Here confession (and in the sense of *confessio*) appears as first thought, *prima cogitatio*. The first thought . . . thinks insofar as it confesses."[21] Why does confession appear as the first thought, as *prima cogitatio*? It is because

19. Marion, *In the Self's Place*, 13.
20. Again, see the epigraph of Walt Whitman's poem in Tracy, *Filaments*.
21. Marion, *In the Self's Place*, 13.

confession is the most necessary thought and the first-person narrative is the most immediate, transparent and ready thought. For what first thought do I think that does not immediately reverberate with what my heart feels? I can pretend to bracket all of my most valiant longings, hurts, disappointments, discontents, joys, sorrows, hopes, fears and passions, but this attempt to bracket all of that only confirms its urgency all the more. *Cogito, ergo sum*? Rather, *Confessio, ergo sum*. I confess, therefore I am. Thought is expressed in speech, and, without speech, thought lacks clarity and definition. Verbal concrete confession opens the cognitive space of clarity necessary for gathering up the fragments of broken lives.

Interpersonal mending happens to the measure that the hidden and overt acts of violent fragmentation are owned and announced, only then to be disowned and renounced. Confession and renunciation of sin is indispensable for reconciling oppositional fragments of being. For Saint Augustine, it was necessary to face his demons by confessing his sinful prodigality in Book II of the *Confessions*—the Book that has come to be known as his "Book of Shadows." Without owning up to one's personal sins, and without ceasing to project blame on everyone else for their guilty faults, no reconciliation is possible. In contrast to confession, fragmented ideologies blame someone else for all of the problems at hand. What perpetuates the walls of division between the fragments that we are, and the fragments of our broken lives, is the obstinate refusal to confess. By confessing our sins, we admit that there is a problem and we identify what is in need of healing. I am the one responsible for the fragmentation of my people and my culture! This I must confess with assurance, for it is true. Because of my moral dereliction, the fragmentation continues. I need only to review the course of my life over the past few weeks to discover the certitude of this statement. So, what to do now? Confess once again.

However, it is not only the confession of sins that brings everything back together. If we stop short at the confession of sins alone, we may only become more infuriated with one another! Do not my sins infuriate you? Do not your sins infuriate me? How could I be so stupid? How could you be so ignorant? In addition to "confessing our sins to one another and praying for one another, that we may be healed" (Jas 5:16), we must praise the Lord, our God, together to seal the process of reconciliation. Why is this so? It is because one of our most grotesque collective sins is our failure to give praise where praise is due. This is the worst deprivation of justice and the most heinous amnesia of creaturely purpose. *Quia fecisti nos ad te*. Because you have made us for yourself, O Lord. This we have forgotten, and, to the extent that we have forgotten our ultimate purpose, we remain fragmented. If the fragments are to be gathered together by the filaments, will this not be something new? "See, I am doing something new! Now it springs forth, do you not perceive it? In the wilderness I make a way, in the wasteland, rivers, wild beasts honor me, jackals and ostriches, for I put water in the wilderness and rivers in the wasteland for my chosen people to drink. The people whom I formed for myself, that they might declare my praise" (Isa 43:19–21).[22] If jackals and ostriches can praise the Lord, why can't I? For this I was created: to praise his holy Name. "So what is to be done? I will pray with the spirit, but I will also pray with the mind. I will sing praise with the spirit, but I will also praise with the mind" (1 Cor 14:15), for *tu excitas, ut laudare te delectet*—you rouse us to delight in praising you! Once again, confession is the *prima cogitatio* both as confession of sin and as confession of praise. Through this dual confession of sin and praise, I tell my story of being saved by the Savior.

And herein we find the medicine for postmodernism, namely, in-person community. Both confession and praise cannot be performed by isolated persons, but only by persons in present and proximate communion with one another. In Saint Augustine's *Confessions*, "the praise is extended from the ego to the community of readers, or at least of those who accept the call to praise. It is carried out in a church."[23] Moreover, "that praise can constitute a place, the place for the hermeneutic of the *Confessions*, should not be surprising. (It is) a city, of which one becomes a citizen only by carrying out, in truly believing it, this very praise, which consists only in saying this—that God certainly is worthy of praise."[24] Church and city. This is the place of praise, where Church and city are united in a complementary symphony of praise. Since praise has a twofold dynamism, both interior and exterior, it must breathe with the two lungs of Church (interiority) and city (exteriority). Praise circulates like blood in our veins. As one homeless man on the streets of Chicago assured me before, "The praise goes up, and the blessings come down!" Praise circulates according to the circadian rhythm of to and from, of contraction and expansion. This is the harmonious meter of the heart—systolic and diastolic pulsation, centrifugal and centripetal cadence. Praise is at once ethically bound and contemplatively oriented. According to the logic of Christian confession, an intentionality of praise prevails over and against all that would disturb the soul daily. Praise, therefore, is able to reel in the postmodern distention of fragments into the sheltering Barque of

22. Cf. King David's song of praise in 1 Chr 16:8–36.

23. Marion, *In the Self's Place*, 15.

24. Marion, *In the Self's Place*, 15.

the Church—an unsinkable Ship with both anchor and sail.[25] *Tunditur non submergitur*—the Boat of Saint Peter is "tossed about but not submerged."

Once caught in the net of the Church by the filaments of faith, the healed soul is catapulted into the city to invite so many other fragments of fear to "taste and see that the LORD is good; blessed is the stalwart one who takes refuge in him. Fear the LORD, you his holy ones; nothing is lacking to those who fear him" (Ps 34:9–10). And this is the paradox, that for the one who fears the LORD, all other illusive fears are abated. "Why are you terrified, O you of little faith?" (Matt 8:26). The Church gives calm to the city that never sleeps because she introduces the Master who is fast asleep in the stern of the Boat. If contemplation accompanies our busyness, even busyness is enveloped in rest. "My Father is always working, and so am I" (John 5:17). Saint Augustine's *Confessions* lead us to a place of communal encounter where confession of sin and confession of praise form the bookends of conversion by mending back together a fragmented and distended existence. The more sin is confessed and renounced, the more contemplation and praise are addressed and pronounced. The fragmentary babble of Babel is exchanged for the fiery holocaust of Pentecost.

Pope Francis observes how "it is curious that God's revelation tells us that the fullness of humanity and of history is realized in a city. We need to look at our cities with a contemplative gaze, a gaze of faith which sees God dwelling in their homes, in their streets and squares."[26] Through a contemplative gaze of praise, the fragments of life are validated in themselves and reorganized in relation to a greater redemptive whole. Effective pastoral ministry in postmodern culture must begin with a contemplative gaze, able "to see God in all things."[27] By noticing God's presence active in every corner of the city, the contemplative pastoral minister collaborates with this divine activity. "When people see things with the help of your Spirit, it is you who are seeing them."[28] It is incredible to realize that God delights to gaze upon

---

25. For more on the distention of the soul, see Saint Augustine's *Confessions*, Book XI.

26. Francis, *Evangelii gaudium*, 71. Cf. Rev 21:9–11: "One of the seven angels who held the seven bowls filled with the seven last plagues came and said to me, 'Come here. I will show you the bride, the wife of the Lamb.' He took me in spirit to a great, high mountain and showed me the holy city Jerusalem coming down out of heaven from God. It gleamed with the splendor of God. Its radiance was like that of a precious stone, like jasper, clear as crystal."

27. Ignatius, *Spiritual Exercises and Selected Works*, 459.

28. Augustine, *Confessions*, XIII.xxxi.46. Cf. Luke 12:6–7: "Are not five sparrows sold for two small coins? Yet not one of them has escaped the notice (*enópion*) of God. Even the hairs of your head have all been counted. Do not be afraid. You are worth more than many sparrows"; Wallenfang, *Phenomenology*, 34: "Notice is the key that unlocks access to givenness. The Greek word *enópion* encompasses the sense of

his world through our own eyes, and thereby to transform it. By willing the good of the other, the good of the other just might come about. This is the power of God at work in and through us. In writing to encourage the disenchanted and fatigued deacon, Deogratias, toward a rejuvenated catechetical ministry, Saint Augustine urges him on by exhorting, "If our understanding finds its delight within, in the brightest of secret places, let it also delight in the following insight into the ways of love: the more love goes down in a spirit of service into the ranks of the lowliest people, the more surely it rediscovers the quiet that is within when its good conscience testifies that it seeks nothing of those to whom it goes down but their eternal salvation."[29] And that is assuredly what is meant by the disinterested passionate love manifest and taught to us by Christ Jesus. This is a love that refuses to use people as a means to some mean impersonal end, but rather regards every human being as an ultimately dignified purpose in himself or herself.[30]

Finally, Saint Augustine concludes his *Confessions* by contemplating the eternal Sabbath rest of the blessed known as heaven: "As for ourselves, we see the things you have made because they are. But they are because you see them. . . . Of your gift we have some good works, though not everlasting. After them we hope to rest in your great sanctification . . . the peace of quietness, the peace of the sabbath, a peace with no evening."[31] When we look out at the world with a contemplative gaze, God is seeing the world through us and recreating it. When I look upon the abandoned run-down building with a contemplative gaze, I lend a visual sacramental conduit for the Holy Spirit to be channeled in that place. The contemplative gaze itself is redemptive because it is oriented around the Orient (*Subsolanus*) that is the kingdom of God and not around any nation of this world. The contemplative

presence—being present to, with or for another. To say that God takes notice is to say that God is present to what is happening and to the soul who is undergoing some trial or joy. The meaning of notice is to face that which is being noticed—to be met with the otherness of the face of the other. Because God notices, it gives. With the notice of God comes the creation of a creature. In other words, God notices creatures into existence. What phenomenology notices about the notice of God is not so much being, but the act of noticing itself. The phenomenon of noticing is what is noticed by phenomenology. Notice triumphs over the natural attitude that was too busy to be enraptured by the beauty, goodness and truth of givenness. Ignorance of divine notice is enslavement to the natural attitude."

29. Augustine, *De catechizandis rudibus*, 10.15, as translated and quoted in Canning, "Teaching and Learning," 6.

30. Cf. Vigneron, *Unleash the Gospel*, Marker 2.1: "Evangelizing aims to lead others to life-changing encounters with Jesus, with the result that he becomes the Lord of one's life. An encounter is a person-centered form of contemplation; it is two people being present to each other with no utilitarian purpose."

31. Augustine, *Confessions*, XIII.xxxviii.53; XIII.xxxv.50.

gaze is always a personal life-giving gaze. It bears within itself transcendence, all the while approaching the world with concentrated immanence. The Augustinian Pope Benedict XVI puts it this way: "Seeing with the eyes of Christ, I can give to others much more than their outward necessities; I can give them the look of love which they crave."[32] This, again, is the divine potency of the contemplative gaze: Christ looks out at the world through my own eyes. Through my eyes—through my entire body—the uncreated love of Jesus Christ gives birth to a world redeemed, just as blood and water gushed forth from his pierced side to give birth to the sacrament of salvation that is the Catholic Church.[33] "But we hold this treasure in earthen vessels, that the surpassing power may be of God and not from us . . . as we look not to what is seen but to what is unseen; for what is seen is transitory, but what is unseen is eternal" (2 Cor 4:7, 18). If the gaze of Christ is seeing the world through my own contemplative gaze, this implies that my gaze looks beyond what is seen through what is seen, all the way to behold what is not yet seen and eternal, uniting all that is seen to the hidden life of the Most Holy Trinity as a sacramental chiasm.[34] The contemplative gaze brings about the intertwining between the sacred and the profane according to the saturating dehiscence of the world.[35] The *requiem aeternam*—the eternal rest of heaven—breaks through the mundane monotony of supply and demand by virtue of the contemplative gaze. As the final cause of confession, the *requiem aeternam* reorients souls toward their divinely intended destiny

32. Benedict XVI, *Deus caritas est*, 18.

33. See Vatican II, *Lumen gentium*, 48: "Christ, having been lifted up from the earth has drawn all to Himself. Rising from the dead He sent His life-giving Spirit upon His disciples and through Him has established His Body which is the Church as the universal sacrament of salvation. Sitting at the right hand of the Father, He is continually active in the world that He might lead men to the Church and through it join them to Himself and that He might make them partakers of His glorious life by nourishing them with His own Body and Blood. Therefore the promised restoration which we are awaiting has already begun in Christ, is carried forward in the mission of the Holy Spirit and through Him continues in the Church in which we learn the meaning of our terrestrial life through our faith, while we perform with hope in the future the work committed to us in this world by the Father, and thus work out our salvation."

34. See Merleau-Ponty, *The Visible and the Invisible*, chapter 4, entitled "The Intertwining–The Chiasm"; Merleau-Ponty, *Phenomenology of Perception*, xiv: "In order to see the world and grasp it as paradoxical, we must break with our familiar acceptance of it and, also, from the fact that from this break we can learn nothing but the unmotivated upsurge of the world."

35. The word "dehiscence" is derived from the Latin verb, *dehiscere*, which means "to part, divide, gape, yawn; to develop a crack; to split open and reveal," in a word, "to burst open."

and supplies the necessary unmotivated Motivation for sustaining so many unpredictable adventures in ministry.

Before unpacking the notion of "montage ministry" for the last section of this essay, it is necessary for us to consider the meaning of contemplative prayer from a Carmelite perspective by turning our attention to the life and work of Saint Teresa of Ávila. In particular, her concept of the prayer of recollection will help us to understand more clearly the process of gathering up the fragments of postmodernity beginning with the act of contemplation. But before examining the prayer of recollection, let us transition to the end of the scene where Jesus miraculously feeds a large crowd of people from only five barley loaves and two fish.

III. Saint Teresa of Ávila on the Prayer of Recollection

> When they had had their fill, he said to his disciples, "Gather (*Synagágete*) the fragments left over (*perisseúo klásmata*), so that nothing will be wasted (*apóllymi*)." So they collected (*synágo*) them, and filled twelve wicker baskets with fragments (*klásmata*) from the five barley loaves that had been more than they could eat. . . . Since Jesus knew that they were going to come and carry him off to make him king, he withdrew (*anágo*) again to the mountain alone (*mónos*).
>
> —John 6:12–13, 15

There is no shortfall in the company of Jesus. As God in the flesh, Jesus "grants the increase" (1 Cor 3:7). This narrative of the feeding of a large crowd of people is a paradigmatic case wherein Jesus surprises his unsuspecting witnesses with plenty. The end of the story is the most interesting part because, just when the climax was felt to have taken place already, we are met with a redoubled gathering of the abandoned scraps that surpasses in wonder even the miraculous multiplication of food. Alleviating hunger is one thing, gathering up abandoned and fragmented souls is another. While Jesus came to do both, the accent seems to be on the latter. In this passage recounting the gathering up of food fragments, we are being taught much more than the laws of conservation. We are witnessing the very power of God "to seek and to save what was lost (*apololós*)" (Luke 19:10).

The first thing to notice about this final fragment of the narrative is that Jesus commands his disciples to gather the fragments of food left over so that nothing would be wasted. The Greek verb *synágo* can mean several things: "to gather, assemble, call together, welcome, receive a stranger as a guest, catch fish, come together."[36] Having the same root as the Greek word for synagogue (*synagogé*), *synágo* communicates the mission of Jesus: "And this is the will of the one who sent me, that I should not lose anything of what he gave me, but that I should raise it on the last day" (John 6:39).[37] Just as the Blessed Virgin Mary "kept (*syntereó*) all these things, reflecting (*symbállo*) on them in her heart" (Luke 2:19), Jesus desires that all of the fragments (*klásmata*) be collected (*synágo*) to prevent anything from being lost (*apóllymi*). Both Mary and Jesus synthesize, sympathize, symbolize and evangelize in order to stabilize, catalyze, mobilize, harmonize, galvanize and fraternize what otherwise would have become jeopardized, compromised, and eventually sterilized and amortized. Again, the symbolism is all too apparent. We are not dealing here merely with breadcrumbs. What Jesus desires above all is for fragmented souls to be gathered back together and united with his own. Eventually by stretching his wounded body across the cross of wood, reaching across the chasma of enmity between us and God, Jesus prevents the entropic cataclasm of the universe by gathering (*synágo*) all of the fragments (*klásmata*) to himself.[38] The abundance (*perisseúo*) of food fragments remaining after everyone had their fill, signifies the abundance of mercy and healing Jesus came to bring: "Now to him who is able to accomplish far more (*hyperperisseúo*) than all we ask or imagine, by the power at work within us, to him be glory in the church and in Christ Jesus to all generations, forever and ever. Amen" (Eph 3:20–21). With Jesus is abundance, and, moreover, superabundance.[39] With Jesus, there is always more than enough.

Jesus refuses to abandon the abandoned by himself becoming the abandoned.[40] Jesus prevents anyone from being destroyed, killed or lost

36. Cf. Matt 4:18–20: "As he was walking by the Sea of Galilee, he saw two brothers, Simon who is called Peter, and his brother Andrew, casting a net into the sea; they were fishermen. He said to them, 'Come after me, and I will make you fishers of men.' At once they left their nets and followed him."

37. Cf. John 10:28–29; 17:12; 18:9.

38. Cf. Ezek 34:11–16.

39. See Wallenfang, *Phenomenology*, 86–99. For two typological scenes of abundance, see Ruth 2:14: "At mealtime Boaz said to (Ruth), 'Come here and have something to eat; dip your bread in the sauce.' Then as she sat near the harvesters, he handed her some roasted grain and she ate her fill and had some left over"; 1 Kgs 17:14–16: "'For the LORD, the God of Israel, says: The jar of flour shall not go empty, nor the jug of oil run dry, until the day when the LORD sends rain upon the earth.' She left and did as Elijah had said. She had enough to eat for a long time—he and she and her household. The jar of flour did not go empty, nor the jug of oil run dry, according to the word of the LORD spoken through Elijah."

40. Cf. Matt 27:45–46: "From noon onward, darkness came over the whole land until three in the afternoon. And about three o'clock Jesus cried out in a loud voice,

(*apóllymi*) by himself losing his own life: "Whoever finds his life will lose (*apóllymi*) it, and whoever loses (*apóllymi*) his life for my sake will find it" (Matthew 10:39). Jesus resists being made king of a world of blasé ideological uniformity, and instead patiently awaits his coronation of the King of the fragments and diversified delinquents made whole, precisely in and through their beautiful otherness and diversity. Jesus overcomes the negative solitude of anthropological alienation by withdrawing (*anágo*) alone (*mónos*) to the anagogical monastic mountain of contemplation, through which even more fragments are gathered. Jesus redeems the fragments by becoming a fragment: "The Lord, in the culmination of the mystery of the Incarnation, chose to reach our intimate depths through a fragment of matter."[41] This mystery of Incarnation is perpetuated sacramentally through the Eucharistic liturgy and is pondered reverently through contemplation. The *Catechism of the Catholic Church* synthesizes these elements eloquently: "Entering into contemplative prayer is like entering into the Eucharistic liturgy: we 'gather up' the heart, recollect our whole being under the prompting of the Holy Spirit, abide in the dwelling place of the Lord which we are, awaken our faith in order to enter into the presence of him who awaits us. We let our masks fall and turn our hearts back to the Lord who loves us, so as to hand ourselves over to him as an offering to be purified and transformed."[42] The contemplation of the Blessed Virgin Mary and her Christ-child are models for us. Their humility punctures our pride and enables our pretentious masks to fall in confessing both sin and praise. Our hearts are gathered up, and our whole beings are recollected, as we become living kaleidoscopes of the world being redeemed. From its Greek roots—*kalós* ("good, honorable, beautiful, precious"), *eidos* ("form"), *skopós* ("watcher")—kaleidoscope signifies "a watcher of beautiful forms." This is the very definition of the contemplative. And the most beautiful form is the unformed Form of divinity. Contemplative prayer aims at gathering up the fragments by gazing upon beautiful forms and giving glory to God.

Among the saints, some were given the gift of contemplation, soaring to mystical heights of divine communion on this side of eternity. Saint Teresa of Ávila was one of them. She has much to teach us about the itinerary of contemplative prayer.[43] For our purposes, we want to focus on

---

'*Eli, Eli, lema sabachthani?*' which means, 'My God, my God, why have you abandoned me?'"; Ps 22.

41. Francis, *Laudato si'*, 236.

42. *Catechism of the Catholic Church*, 2711.

43. For a very brief summary of the five distinct stages of prayer as described by Saint Teresa of Ávila, especially in relation to the phenomenological concept of givenness (*Gegebenheit*), see Wallenfang, *Phenomenology*, 25–29, and Wallenfang and

the middle stage of prayer that begins contemplation proper, namely, the prayer of recollection. Following the shallow-entry types of prayer, specifically vocal prayer and mental prayer (meditation), the prayer of recollection commences the stilling of the soul's typically frenetic operations and entry into the depth of what Saint John of the Cross calls the dark night of the spirit. At this stage of prayer, sin and all attachments to sin have been subdued and the soul is set free to ascend Mount Carmel by the strength that only the Lord supplies.

It is important to understand that contemplative prayer is the high-hanging fruit reached only after the long, arduous and disciplined practice of vocal prayer and mental prayer that cultivate habits of virtue in the soul. Contemplative prayer is both reward and responsibility. Above all, it is a gift given directly by God and in the Lord's timing. In most cases, however, it takes years (if not decades) for a person to experience the higher stages of contemplative prayer after having lived faithfully and consistently within the Church's culture of vocal prayer and mental prayer. If a mountaineer embarks on climbing one of the most challenging mountains in the world, for example, Mount Everest or K2, he must do so much research and training in order to climb the mountain in a safe and manageable way. He cannot climb such a mountain alone but must be accompanied by expert guides who have climbed the mountain before. He must climb the mountain not as a lone climber but with a community of climbers, each one trusting the others. Every climber must begin his ascent at the base of the mountain and pass through many base camps or checkpoints on the way up. Certain conditions must be present to proceed up the face of the mountain at each stage, and it will take somewhere around two months to climb Mount Everest or K2. Most climbers need to use oxygen tanks in the high altitudes where it can be difficult to breathe. Once reaching the summit, climbers cannot stay for very long, but must descend the mountain carefully since the descent often is more dangerous than the ascent. Mountaineering is a good analogy for the spiritual life and for realizing the relationship of contemplative prayer to vocal prayer and mental prayer. Before becoming acclimatized to contemplative prayer, one must have become well acclimatized to vocal prayer and mental prayer. There is no other way, just as there is no other way to the summit of the mountain other than those well-established routes that best avoid avalanche and insurmountable formations of rock. With this analogy now made, let us return to a discussion of the prayer of recollection.

Saint Teresa of Jesus's most precise definition of the prayer of recollection is found in *The Way of Perfection*: "This prayer is called 'recollection,'

Wallenfang, *Shoeless: Carmelite Spirituality in a Disquieted World.*

because the soul collects its faculties together and enters within itself to be with its God."[44] The Spanish noun *recogimiento* is derived from the verbs *coger* ("to gather, get, touch, grasp, catch, hook, take, lift, grab, nab, land, accept") and *recoger* ("to collect, pick up, gather, reap, harvest, glean, scoop up, bring in, rake in, lift, scavenge"). The prayer of recollection is about gathering up the soul that has been scattered, diverted and spread so thin across so many appetites, affections and distractions from the *unum necessarium*, "the one thing necessary."[45] The prayer of recollection describes the process of gathering up the fragments of the soul that have been scattered about over the course of earthly temporality. There are two phases to the prayer of recollection: (1) the active phase, and (2) the passive phase. This distinction between active and passive is essential to understand the written works of both Saints Teresa of Jesus and John of the Cross. The first stage of contemplative prayer is active recollection. This stage surpasses that of all mental prayer as it involves a real putting to sleep of the lower and higher faculties of the soul. The soul is personally and actively involved in freely surrendering all of its powers to divine control and mastery. Here the soul utters its final and lasting *fiat*—let it be done unto me!—before the face of divine gift. The soul relinquishes command of itself and yields absolutely to the sway of the Most Holy Trinity. Thereby the soul is stilled and hushed. All appetites and affections are quieted. All attachments are perfectly detached and disengaged. The soul is set free to contemplate God and God alone. Because completely

44. Teresa of Ávila, *Way of Perfection*, 28.4 (351, Spanish edition; 141, English edition): "*Llámase recogimiento, porque recoge el alma todas las potencias y se entra dentro de sí con Dios.*" The Spanish word *potencias* also could be translated as "powers" of the soul as well as "potencies" of the soul. Specifically, the faculties of the soul include the lower sense faculties and its affective or emotional states as moved by the passions (joy, hope, fear, sorrow), and the higher faculties that include the intellect, the memory, and the will. Cf. Teresa of Ávila, *Way of Perfection*, 35.1 (387, Spanish edition; 174, English edition): "*Heme alargado tanto en esto—aunque había hablado en la oración del recogimiento de lo mucho que importa este entrarnos a solas con Dios—por ser cosa tan importante.*" ("Because this matter is so important I have greatly enlarged upon it, even though in discussing the prayer of recollection I spoke of the significance of entering within ourselves to be alone with God.") It is necessary to combine these two passages of Saint Teresa to synthesize her definition of the prayer of recollection as one in which "the soul collects its faculties together and enters within itself to be alone with its God."

45. See Luke 10:42: "There is need of only one thing. Mary has chosen the better part and it will not be taken from her." And once again, see *Catechism of the Catholic Church*, 2711: "*Entering into contemplative prayer* is like entering into the Eucharistic liturgy: we 'gather up' the heart, recollect our whole being under the prompting of the Holy Spirit, abide in the dwelling place of the Lord which we are, awaken our faith in order to enter into the presence of him who awaits us. We let our masks fall and turn our hearts back to the Lord who loves us, so as to hand ourselves over to him as an offering to be purified and transformed."

recollected back together and re-membered, the soul is positioned to make its final ascent to the summit of Mount Carmel by letting itself be lifted by God as an infant in her mother's arms (see Ps 131). During the passive phase of the prayer of recollection, God is found to be doing everything in the soul and there is nothing left for the soul to do by its own powers, save for remaining open, dilated and porous for the divine operations alone. This pure passivity marks the character of the two final stages of contemplative prayer: the prayer of quiet and the prayer of union.

What does the prayer of recollection have to do with gathering the memories of life in relation to the complete gathering up of the soul? Here we meet with yet another paradox of faith. Though the Carmelite Doctors do not go into great detail in response to this question, *The Story of a Soul* of Saint Thérèse of Lisieux is instructive. Of the three manuscripts that make up this work, the first and third are comprised of a recollection, or gathering up, of her life memories. This is a necessary kataphatic task before the apophatic holocaust (redemption rather than annihilation) of memories can take place. During the active phase of the prayer of recollection, memories from one's life may be gathered up for their greatest purpose in giving themselves as reasons to give thanks to God. When I actively gather up my life before the Lord, both through the examination of conscience and simply recalling "what marvels the Lord worked for us" (Ps 126:3), I gather it all up not as an end in itself (nor individual memories as ends in themselves), but as an offering to place into the hands of Jesus in turn to offer to the Father: "And it happened that, while he was with them at table, he took bread, said the blessing, broke it, and gave it to them. With that their eyes were opened and they recognized him" (Luke 24:30–31). In offering the recollected and remembered memories of our lives as an evening oblation to Jesus the Great Physician, everything assumes the potential to be healed, and everything bears the potential to be part of the Father's plan to gather all of creation back into his bosom of fatherly care. This procedure is empowered by the anamnetic Eucharistic liturgy of the Church in which we remember the saving works of God throughout the time of creation. The alleged idolatry and paralysis of memories is overcome insofar as these assorted memories of life are intermingled (just like the intermingling of the Eucharistic Body and Blood of Christ) with the memory of Jesus's paschal mystery as the apogee of salvation history.

The prayer of recollection is really the target prayer for one serious about contemplative prayer. It is the beginning of contemplation and where the Wind of the Holy Spirit increases its velocity, so to speak. The prayer of recollection capitalizes on the self-exerting stages of purification and illumination that have preceded and prepared the way for contemplation. I say that the prayer of recollection is "the target prayer" for the soul because it is quite difficult to reach in itself. It certainly is not a given in the daily life of prayer. It presupposes that a soul is in no way stuck in the mire of sin, even venial sins in thought or of omission. It presupposes that a soul is perfectly detached from all things of the world and that all unruly affections are in a maximal comatose state. It presupposes that even the higher faculties of the soul—the intellect, the memory, and the will—have become entirely recollected and are not given over to activities other than being totally immersed in this prayer. The prayer of recollection presupposes so much, and one cannot assume that this prayer is happening regularly, especially if all that it presupposes is not in place. All the same, divine grace makes it possible and desires that every soul makes progress toward this degree of prayer. While the prayer of recollection begins with its active phase—the soul working to gather up all of its powers fully in the direction of divinity—the passive phase of recollection begins the radical passivity of the soul that will characterize the subsequent prayer of quiet and prayer of union. With this transition to the passive stages of contemplative prayer, the Carmelite saints attest that vocal prayer and mental prayer can become more laborious and less productive at this time. Once the soul is swooning in the silent love of her divine Bridegroom, the stacking up of words can seem like a hindrance to being enraptured in the saturation of "the Love that had no beginning" (Jessica Powers).

The prayer of recollection, as described by Saint Teresa of Ávila, is the concentrated spiritual channel through which personal fragments are gathered back together. Recollection draws in the distended soul of the one praying and then, by way of substitution, acts as a proxy for sinners by extending those "filaments, filaments, filaments" of spirit that escort other distended souls to the foot of the throne of grace. No person is left outside of the net of grace since "every person is immensely holy and deserves our love. . . . We achieve fulfillment when we break down walls and our heart is filled with faces and names!"[46] There is a spiritual and sacramental power in prayer to metamorphose the world, to rearrange souls, and to gather back together what had been scattered and spread so thin. The prayer of recollection is imperative for the process of gathering up the fragments of postmodernity. So much contemplation, so much evangelization. And yet, this is not all. In addition to the prayer of recollection, ministries must be calibrated according to this effective reach of recollection. It is now time to proceed to our final section of this essay, introducing the original concept of "montage ministry" that is built upon all that has been said so far. I will

46. Francis, *Evangelii gaudium*, 274.

show the basic components of montage ministry and so empower pastoral leaders toward a fulfillment of the New Evangelization.

IV. Montage Ministry as Motown Evangelization

> How beautiful upon the mountains are the feet of the one bringing good news, announcing peace, bearing good news, announcing salvation, saying to Zion, "Your God is King!"

—Isa 52:7

The word "montage" is pregnant with meaning: "to mount, increase, soar, climb, rise, intensify, elevate." It even conveys the idea of testimony, as in "mounting the witness stand." Montage has to do with a mountain and the proclamation of good news from this mountaintop. Its summit is salvation and its crags are the kingdom of God. It is Mount Carmel where a soul finds its rest in the living God. This is the mountain toward which all Christian ministry should be directed. If ministry is not aimed here, if it is not concerned with ascending this mountain, then it is bankrupt and barren. Within the cultural milieu of postmodernity, this mountain is difficult to see, but it is there, concealed by the fragmentary haze of strung out souls. Pastoral servant leaders must understand themselves as guides, loving souls up this mountain. As Blessed Pier Giorgio Frassati was keen to say, *Verso l'alto!*—"To the top!"

Let us consider the primary aspects of montage ministry in turn. Once again, the concept "montage" expresses not only the image of a mountain, but also signifies an artistic composition that is created by combining heterogeneous fragmentary elements. Montage is an agglomeration of fragments, the uniting together of fragments to form an extraordinary unforeseen whole. It is the only way of ministry in the postmodern era. The good news is that the picture formed through montage could not be seen otherwise than by assembling the diverse fragments in close and constellate proximity to one another. "The re-presentation of the fragment in montage is thus experienced as a kind of mirror energizing cultures toward new possibilities for redemption."[47] Here we notice that the fragment, while having some meaning on its own, gathers so much more meaning when related to the greater whole in whose service it always has lived as a sign. Fragments are fraught with the potential to reform and renew cultures when they are assembled together in montage to form an organic whole.

---

47. Myatt, *Theological Plunderphonics*, 212.

Montage ministry has its model in the liturgical and sacramental assembly of the Church. Persons coming together and becoming present to one another around the altar of the Lord where he, too, becomes present in the midst of the gathered assembly. In the fraction rite of the Eucharistic liturgy, for instance, "the breaking of the bread" carries much theological significance: "Christ's gesture of breaking bread at the Last Supper, which gave the entire Eucharistic Action its name in apostolic times, signifies that the many faithful are made one body (1 Cor 10:17) by receiving Communion from the one Bread of Life which is Christ, who died and rose for the salvation of the world. The fraction or breaking of bread is begun after the sign of peace and is carried out with proper reverence, though it should not be unnecessarily prolonged, nor should it be accorded undue importance. . . . The priest breaks the Bread and puts a piece of the host into the chalice to signify the unity of the Body and Blood of the Lord in the work of salvation, namely, of the living and glorious Body of Jesus Christ."[48] How instructive is this rite of fraction for us to understand the soteriological process of fragment redemption! Jesus fragments his own flesh in order to generate the redemptive process of defragmentation. The rite of fraction occurs directly following the sign of peace and is accompanied by the singing or recitation of the *Agnus Dei*: "Lamb of God, you take away the sins of the world, have mercy on us . . . grant us peace." Jesus becomes fragmented Eucharist (though each fragment is the whole Christ—Body, Blood, Soul, and Divinity), so that all who partake of these whole Eucharistic fragments might be defragmented and made one: "Because the loaf of bread is one, we, though many, are one body, for we all partake of the one loaf" (1 Cor 10:17). A fragment (though whole) of the Sacred Body of the Lord is immersed in the chalice of his Precious Blood by way of intinction to signify, once again, the unity of the Body and Blood of Christ—the Blood of Christ as the final Filament that gathers up the whole—in procuring salvation for fragmented souls. A veritable montage of persons is gathered up through the liturgy of the Eucharist through the mutual and reciprocal loving abandonment of Christ the Bridegroom and his Church the Bride, one-for-the-other. So, in this sense, montage ministry is nothing new, but seeks to retrieve this in-person gathering that has become all too fragmented and missing in our time. Based on what has been presented thus far in this essay, let us decipher montage ministry in light of culture, confession, and contemplation.

---

48. Congregation for Divine Worship and the Discipline of the Sacraments, *General Instruction of the Roman Missal*, 83.

A. Montage Ministry as the Ongoing Study of Culture

Because montage ministry must navigate the turbulent waters of postmodernity, it has no choice but to study the changing climates of culture without ceasing. Montage ministers must be persistent students of culture. Without familiarity with the varied terrain of culture, ministers remain ignorant of the inroads that are necessary to reach souls in their fragmented isolation from one another. Montage ministers need the courage to migrate to the fringes of fragmentation in order to rescue all those souls drowning in depression, loneliness, anxiety, fear, and the legion neuroses that plague body, soul and community. Pope Francis recalls the fearlessness of Jesus, the Good Shepherd, the Master of the margins, the Friend of the fringes: "Unafraid of the fringes, he himself became a fringe. So if we dare to go to the fringes, we will find him there; indeed, he is already there. Jesus is already there, in the hearts of our brothers and sisters, in their wounded flesh, in their troubles and in their profound desolation. He is already there."[49] Students of culture live in solidarity with marginalized persons who exercise a prophetic magnetism in the Church. Such persons living at the margins of society—the disabled, the poor, the children, the unpopular, the forgotten, the despised, the uncanny pariahs—disorient the self-sufficient status quo so that all becomes reoriented to Christ. Montage ministers not only pay attention to such persons on the fringes of the fold but invite and empower them to take on meaningful leadership roles within ministry. When margins are brought to the middle, metamorphosis materializes.

Students of culture take seriously Jesus's appointment of them as "fishers of people." Savvy fishers know where the fish are and move the boat to where they are. Just as you cannot catch fish from a distance, you cannot lead people into the Church from far away. You must move to where they are so that you can draw them in to where they are not. You must meet people on their own turf in order to invite them to experience a new surf (baptismal existence). Effective fishers of people are not afraid to move all the way to the fringes of society and to be present there, listening and adapting to the real needs of people. "Put out into deep water and lower your nets for a catch" (Luke 5:4). Oftentimes, ministry game-changers happen simply by way of a daring flip-flop: "'Cast the net over the right side of the boat and you will find something.' So they cast it, and were not able to pull it in because of the number of fish" (John 21:6). Masterful fishers of people also know the right tackle to use to catch people in the net of grace. "Filaments, filaments, filaments." Proficient fishers of people have a deep bag of filaments that function to fasten on to the fragments in the "deep waters" of postmodernity, hauling

49. Francis, *Gaudete et exsultate*, 135.

in "a great number of fish," so numerous that "their nets were tearing" and the boats "were in danger of sinking" (Luke 5:1–11). With so many filaments that are able to reach into culture and rescue weary souls, maybe as many as "one hundred fifty-three large fish" (John 21:11) will be caught as "fishermen will stand along the river's shore from En-gedi to En-eglaim . . . a place for drying nets, and it will abound with as many kinds of fish as the Great Sea" (Ezek 47:10). For the Church is destined to be a unified diversity of souls "from every nation, race, people, and tongue" (Rev 7:9).

Students of culture take time to notice. Like Saint Paul in Athens, how "he debated in the synagogue with the Jews and with the worshipers, and daily in the public square with whoever happened to be there" (Acts 17:17), persistent students of culture go to where the people are and engage them in dialogue. Because Saint Paul took ample time to look, listen and learn, he discerned the perfect inroad through which to proclaim the Gospel of Jesus Christ: "You Athenians, I see that in every respect you are very religious. For as I walked around looking carefully at your shrines, I even discovered an altar inscribed, 'To an Unknown God.' What therefore you unknowingly worship, I proclaim to you" (Acts 17:22–23). In a similar way, students of culture must take careful note of those cultural paragons that lend themselves to segue toward the kerygmatic summons to conversion and communion. Serene in the fray, montage ministry evangelists will recognize those avenues of inculturation that facilitate encounter with the living Christ.

B. Montage Ministry as an Atmosphere of Confession and Testimony

There is no tool more persuasive than personal testimony for the accomplishment of montage ministry. As Archbishop Allen Vigneron writes in his 2017 pastoral letter, *Unleash the Gospel*, that "personal testimony has an indispensable role in evangelization. Testimony has a unique power to touch hearts, since it is almost impossible to ignore the witness of someone who has encountered Jesus personally and whose life has been transformed by him."[50] Montage ministry involves a kaleidoscope of testimonies—that of the evangelist and all those of the evangelized. Montage ministry is a mosaic convergence of living testimony about all that went wrong, as well as all those possibilities of what could go right. Montage ministry creates an atmosphere of testimony in which all are invited to share their stories of victory and defeat. The Gospel of Jesus Christ is meant to be personalized since it is, in its essence, a dynamic encounter between persons, human and divine. The bull's-eye of montage ministry is the intermingling of the

50. Vigneron, *Unleash the Gospel*, Marker 2.3.

stories of bleeding and fragmented individuals with the story of a bleeding yet resurrected Lord and Savior, Jesus Christ. It is this intermingling of personal life narratives that is the very crux of salvation.

For this purpose, montage ministry calls the entire gamut of stories to mount the witness stand. Montage ministry is intent on carving out regular space for people to give their testimonies, telling what wonders the Lord worked for them. Pastoral ministry in a montage style weaves together three types of storytelling in order to invite conversion of one into the other. The first kind of storytelling is the invitation of a wounded and lost sheep to tell his or her story in a confidential setting to the pastoral minister(s) who listen without judgment or advice. This is the first moment of liberation. When a person is able to share his or her story with another person who is simply there to listen and not propose to fix anything on the spot, a space is opened for trust, empathy and hearts ripe for deepened conversion, both that of the storyteller and that of the pastoral minister. It is best for this first story to be told in a comfortable and non-sterile environment. Creating an environment of warm hospitality is a requisite task for montage ministry, without which people would be much less willing to make themselves vulnerable and bear their hearts that are in dire need of healing. The second moment of liberation is when these same storytellers (whose stories may or may not include reference to Jesus and his intervention in their lives) listen to the testimony of someone whose life has been disentangled, changed and rearranged by the saving touch of the Lord. This is the second kind of storytelling that lets the stories of the broken and the healed intermingle to channel the message and medicine of healing to those who remain in need of it. Those who have experienced the healing touch of Christ accompany those who are looking for it. And finally, the third type of storytelling is that of the Eucharistic liturgy wherein the story of salvation in Christ is not only told but performed. Eucharistic liturgy is the ultimate atmosphere of testimony in which wounded souls are able to touch the hem of the sacrificial Lamb's garment, only to find that he is reaching out to embrace them with a love ever old, ever new.[51]

Perhaps there is no greater filament than testimony for entwining the fleece of faith. Testimony lets people know that what is taking place in ministry is real. It involves real life, real people, real stories. This is one of the defining features of Christianity that sets it apart from all of the other great religious traditions around the world: for Christianity, salvation is a historical process and the Savior has a real face and a real name. Because it is a historical incarnate process (and not an ahistorical disincarnate one),

---

51. See Mark 5:25–34.

Christianity is therefore replete with stories of personal salvation that intermingle with the personal story and personal history of the Savior, Jesus of Nazareth. Through confession of sin and confession of praise, lost souls become found and distended fragmentary lives are made new within the communion of disciples that is the Church. "What we have seen and heard we proclaim now to you, so that you too may have fellowship with us; for our fellowship is with the Father and with his Son, Jesus Christ" (1 John 1:3).

C. Montage Ministry as a Chamber of Contemplation

Further than being a studio of culture and an atmosphere of confession and testimony, montage ministry is constructed out of a quiet and hidden chamber of contemplation. This is to say that the prayer of recollection sets the pattern for the concrete work of gathering together the shifting and wandering fragments of postmodernity. Montage ministers must abide with Christ the Vine, serene in the storms of violence, chaos and nihilism that incessantly threaten to rob the Church of her missionary purpose. Montage ministers must be contemplatives as far as possible inasmuch as "the devout Christian of the future will either be a 'mystic,' one who has experienced 'something,' or he will cease to be anything at all."[52] So much contemplation, so much evangelization. This is because evangelization needs fuel, and the fuel for evangelization is God the Holy Spirit animating the mystical Body of the Church. The way the fuel of God the Holy Spirit is channeled into the veins of evangelization is through word and sacrament, and their sustained reverberation in the spiritual chamber of contemplation. It is true that the missionary efforts of the Church are supported by the concealed contemplative prayer of the cloistered communities of religious brothers and sisters devoted to this apostolate. At the same time, all those active montage ministers must engage in at least a preliminary contemplative prayer of recollection as much as possible so as to let the fuel of God the Holy Spirit invade their own hearts and ministerial activities. Contemplation should be a recurring phase within the overall process of evangelization—contemplation not only for the sake of evangelization, but for its own sake as well.

What might this preliminary prayer of recollection look like for the faithful montage minister? Just like it is good for an engine to take time to warm up in the cold before running at its highest capacity, the montage minister needs to approach the prayer of recollection by taking time "to warm up" through vocal prayer and the prayer of meditation (or mental

---

52. Rahner, "Christian Living Formerly and Today," in *Theological Investigations VII*, 15.

prayer). These prayers come in many forms, with the most central form being Eucharistic liturgy. Other practical forms include the Liturgy of the Hours, the Rosary, the Chaplet of Divine Mercy, *lectio divina*, prayers found in the Manual of Indulgences, novenas, the Ignatian spiritual exercises, the Salesian meditations in the *Introduction to the Devout Life*, prayers of minor exorcism, deliverance and blessing authorized by the magisterium of the Church, and so many more. Adoration of the Blessed Sacrament is a prime place both for the prayer of meditation and the prayer of recollection. The beginnings of contemplation in the active prayer of recollection will involve a stilling of the senses, and, as much as possible, a quieting of the intellect, memory and will of the soul. Let us recall Saint Teresa of Ávila's shorthand definition of the prayer of recollection: "This prayer is called 'recollection,' because the soul collects its powers together and enters within itself to be alone with its God." Can you, the montage minister, do this? Can you collect your faculties together and enter into the expansive interior of your soul to be alone with your God? If your answer is yes, then you are able to approach this pregnant prayer of recollection.

Evangelization without contemplation is like dough without leaven or heat. "Again Jesus said, 'To what shall I compare the kingdom of God? It is like yeast that a woman took and mixed in with three measures of wheat flour until the whole batch of dough was leavened'" (Luke 13:20–21). Contemplation is the leaven and heat that makes the whole batch of dough rise. Because it permeates the entire mixture of fragments by its spiritual agility, contemplation unites, fortifies and elevates. Without the centripetal force of contemplative interiority, the centrifugal propulsion of evangelical exteriority is limp and lifeless. If montage ministers are not contemplative from the inside out, they will fail to find the fish and to cast their filaments in the right places with apostolic zeal. Contemplative souls count on the Lord to make a way out of no way. Contemplative souls see possibility where most see only devastation. Contemplative souls love with the Love that reaches to the fringes to find Christ waiting for them there. Contemplative souls stretch across the impossible since the specious line we draw between possibility and impossibility suggests the possibility that this line too can be crossed. The breathing flame of hope is never extinguished in the souls of contemplative evangelists because they remember that "only for the sake of the hopeless have we been given hope."[53] For virtue to be actual virtue, it must be given away for the sake of the other. Montage ministry exists for the

---

53. A quote from Walter Benjamin's essay "Goethe's *Elective Affinities*," as referenced in Myatt, *Theological Plunderphonics*, 209–10.

sake of the other, and contemplation is the adhesive that binds the self to the other in relentless responsibility and affirming affection.

And, so, we have come to the end of this protracted essay dedicated to the topic of a contemplative New Evangelization in the postmodern era. Beginning with Saint Augustine's notion of the *cor inquietum* ("the disquieted heart"), we proposed a course toward the *cor quietum* ("the quieted heart") that rests in the Lord of glory. By considering the central characteristics of postmodernism, and by investigating sources for a solution to the postmodern malady, we arrived at some practical steps for conducting a montage ministry in a sea of distended and disunited fishy fragments. To become compleat anglers of fragmentary souls, "filaments, filaments, filaments" must be learned and applied. Without such evangelical filaments, fragments will drift forever across the wide and weary sea of relativism, nihilism and anxious terrorism. Montage ministry—that patient process of gathering up the fragments to form a reunified mosaic of persons—may be our only hope in a disoriented land where the sun seems to have set long ago. To conclude, I "give thanks to God in advance" along with Blessed Solanus Casey, that Motown saint who reminds us "to keep our eyes fixed on Jesus, the leader and perfecter of faith" (Heb 12:2), so that we might be reoriented to the *Subsolanus* that transcends even the heliocentrism of creation.

> No longer shall the sun be your light by day, nor shall the brightness of the moon give you light by night; rather, the LORD will be your light forever, your God will be your glory. No longer will your sun set, or your moon wane; for the LORD will be your light forever, and the days of your grieving will be over. Your people will all be just; for all time they will possess the land; they are the shoot that I planted, the work of my hands, that I might be glorified. The least one shall become a clan, the smallest, a mighty nation; I, the LORD, will swiftly accomplish these things when the time comes.

—Isa 60:19–22

Bibliography

Augustine of Hippo. *Confessions.* Translated by Henry Chadwick. New York: Oxford University Press, 1998.

Benedict XVI, Pope. *Deus caritas est.* https://www.vatican.va/content/benedict-xvi/en/encyclicals/documents/hf_ben-xvi_enc_20051225_deus-caritas-est.html.

Benjamin, Walter. *Illuminations.* Translated by Harry Zohn. New York: Schocken, 1969.

Canning, Raymond. "Teaching and Learning: An Augustinian Perspective." *Australian eJournal of Theology* 3 (2004) 1–10.

Caputo, John D., and Michael J. Scanlon, eds. *God, the Gift, and Postmodernity.* Bloomington: Indiana University Press, 1999.

Catechism of the Catholic Church. https://www.vatican.va/archive/ENG0015/_INDEX. HTM.

Cavadini, John C., and Donald Wallenfang, eds. *Pope Francis and the Event of Encounter.* Eugene, OR: Pickwick, 2018.

Chauvet, Louis-Marie. *The Sacraments: The Word of God at the Mercy of the Body.* Translated by Madeleine Beaumont. Collegeville, MN: Liturgical, 2001.

———. *Symbol and Sacrament: A Sacramental Interpretation of Christian Existence.* Translated by Patrick Madigan and Madeleine Beaumont. Collegeville, MN: Liturgical, 1995.

Congregation for Divine Worship and the Discipline of the Sacraments. *General Instruction of the Roman Missal.* http://www.vatican.va/roman_curia/congregat ions/ccdds/documents/rc_con_ccdds_doc_20030317_ordinamento-messale_ en.html#III._THE_INDIVIDUAL_PARTS_OF_THE_MASS.

Francis, Pope. *Evangelii gaudium.* http://www.vatican.va/content/francesco/en/apost_ exhortations/documents/papa-francesco_esortazione-ap_20131124_evangelii- gaudium.html#_ftnref183.

———. *Frattelli tutti.* http://www.vatican.va/content/francesco/en/encyclicals/docum ents/papa-francesco_20201003_enciclica-fratelli-tutti.html.

———. *Gaudete et exsultate.* http://www.vatican.va/content/francesco/en/apost_exhort ations/documents/papa-francesco_esortazione-ap_20180319_gaudete-et- exsultate.html.

———. *Laudato si'.* http://www.vatican.va/content/francesco/en/encyclicals/documents/ papa-francesco_20150524_enciclica-laudato-si.html.

Heidegger, Martin. *Poetry, Language, Thought.* Translated by Albert Hofstadter. New York: HarperCollins, 1971.

Ignatius of Loyola. *Spiritual Exercises and Selected Works.* Edited by George E. Ganss. New York: Paulist, 1991.

Lewellen, Eric, and John Frederick, eds. *The HTML of Cruciform Love: Toward a Theology of the Internet.* Eugene, OR: Pickwick, 2019.

Mannheim, Karl. *Ideology and Utopia: An Introduction to the Sociology of Knowledge.* Translated by Louis Wirth and Edward Shils. New York: Harcourt, Brace, and World, 1936.

Marion, Jean-Luc. *In the Self's Place: The Approach of Saint Augustine.* Translated by Jeffrey L. Kosky. Stanford: Stanford University Press, 2012.

McNeill, William, and Karen S. Feldman, eds. *Continental Philosophy: An Anthology.* Malden, MA: Blackwell, 1998.

Merleau-Ponty, Maurice. *Phenomenology of Perception.* Translated by Colin Smith. London: Routledge, 1981.

———. *The Visible and the Invisible.* Edited by Claude Lefort. Translated by Alphonso Lingis. Evanston, IL: Northwestern University Press, 1968.

Myatt, William. *Theological Plunderphonics: Public Theology and "the Fragment."* PhD diss., Loyola University Chicago, 2012. https://ecommons.luc.edu/luc_diss/424/.

Nietzsche, Friedrich. *Human, All Too Human.* Translated by Gary Handwerk. Stanford: Stanford University Press, 2000.

————. *Twilight of the Idols, Or, How to Philosophize with a Hammer.* Translated by Duncan Large. New York: Oxford University Press, 1998.

Rahner, Karl. *Theological Investigations VII.* Translated by David Bourke. New York: Herder and Herder, 1971.

Teresa of Ávila. *The Collected Works of Saint Teresa of Ávila.* Translated by Kieran Kavanaugh and Otilio Rodriguez. 3 vols. Washington, DC: ICS 1980.

Tracy, David. *Filaments: Theological Profiles: Selected Essays, Volume 2.* Chicago: University of Chicago Press, 2020.

————. *Fragments: The Existential Situation of Our Time: Selected Essays, Volume 1.* Chicago: University of Chicago Press, 2020.

————. *On Naming the Present: God, Hermeneutics, and Church.* Maryknoll, NY: Orbis, 1994.

Vatican II. *Lumen gentium.* https://www.vatican.va/archive/hist_councils/ii_vatican_council/documents/vat-ii_const_19641121_lumen-gentium_en.html.

Vigneron, Allen H. *Unleash the Gospel.* https://www.unleashthegospel.org/the-letter/

Wallenfang, Donald. *Phenomenology: A Basic Introduction in the Light of Jesus Christ.* Eugene, OR: Cascade, 2019.

Wallenfang, Donald and Megan Wallenfang. *Shoeless: Carmelite Spirituality in a Disquieted World.* Eugene, OR: Wipf and Stock, 2021.

9

Mary and the New Evangelization

Robert Fastiggi

Introduction

What is the role of the Blessed Virgin Mary in the new evangelization? In order to answer this question, we need first to understand what is meant by the new evangelization. In his 2010 apostolic letter, *Ubicumque et semper*, establishing the Pontifical Council for Promoting the New Evangelization, Pope Benedict XVI emphasized the mandate given to the Church to evangelize:

> It is the duty of the Church to proclaim always and everywhere the Gospel of Jesus Christ. He, the first and supreme evangelizer, commanded the Apostles on the day of his Ascension to the Father: "Go therefore and make disciples of all nations, baptizing them in the name of the Father and of the Son and of the Holy Spirit, teaching them to observe all that I have commanded you" (Mt 28:19–20).[1]

Through the course of this letter, the Holy Father describes the new evangelization as making the fullness of the Gospel known to people of today, especially in areas that had been once largely Christian but now have given way to secularism, atheism, and religious indifference. The new evangelization, therefore, involves an effort to awaken and renew the faith in areas of the world where people live as if God does not matter.

What role, then, does the Blessed Virgin Mary play in the new evangelization? The answer to this question is found in the role played by the Mother of God in the Gospel itself, which is the revelation of God's plan of salvation. According to St. Thomas Aquinas, God, in his omnipotence, could have redeemed the human race in many ways, but He chose to redeem us by

1. Benedict XVI, *Ubicumque et semper*.

164

becoming man in the womb of the Blessed Virgin Mary.[2] God saw the Incarnation as the most fitting or appropriate means for redeeming the human race.[3] Because God chose to redeem the human race by becoming man, He needed a Mother in order to assume a human nature and become like us in all things but sin (cf. Heb 4:15). The Church teaches that "God ineffable . . . from the beginning and before the ages, chose and ordained a mother for his only begotten Son, from whom he would become incarnate and be born in the blessed fullness of time."[4] The Blessed Virgin Mary, therefore, was "predestined from eternity by that decree of divine providence which determined the incarnation of the Word to be the Mother of God."[5] The Blessed Virgin was in this way "above all others and in a singular way the generous associate and humble handmaid of the Lord."[6]

In preaching the Gospel, we must always be aware of the essential role the Blessed Virgin played and still plays in God's plan of salvation. Mary's role in the new evangelization, therefore, is not incidental but central because her role in the economy of salvation is central. This is not to say that God had any absolute need of the Blessed Virgin Mary. St. Louis de Montfort (1673–1716) makes this clear in *True Devotion to the Blessed Virgin*:

> With the whole Church I acknowledge that Mary, being a mere creature fashioned by the hands of God is, compared to his infinite majesty, less than an atom, or rather is simply nothing, since he alone can say, "I am he who is." Consequently, this great Lord, who is ever independent and self-sufficient, never had and does not now have any absolute need of the Blessed Virgin for the accomplishment of his will and the manifestation of his glory. To do all things he has only to will them.
>
> However, I declare that, considering things as they are, because God has decided to begin and accomplish his greatest works through the Blessed Virgin ever since he created her, we can safely believe that he will not change his plan in the time to come, for he is God and therefore does not change in his thoughts or his way of acting.[7]

---

2. Aquinas, *Summa Theologiae*, III.1.2.

3. Aquinas, *Summa Theologiae*, III.1.2.

4. Pope Pius IX, *Ineffabilis Deus*, as cited in Denzinger and Hünermann [D-H], *Enchiridion symbolorum*, 2800.

5. Vatican II, *Lumen gentium*, 61.

6. Vatican II, *Lumen gentium*, 61.

7. De Montfort, *True Devotion to the Blessed Virgin*, 6.

St. Louis de Montfort shows that, although God had no absolute need of the Blessed Virgin Mary, she was essential to the works He chose to accomplish through her.

In this essay, I will explain the importance of the Blessed Virgin Mary in the new evangelization by exploring the following themes: (I) the indissoluble bond between Mary and Jesus; (II) Mary's role as the one who represents Israel, the Church, and the human race when she says yes to being the Mother of the Word Incarnate; (III) the papal witness to Mary and the new evangelization; and (IV) the ways in which the Blessed Virgin Mary is at the heart of the new evangelization as spiritual Mother and the Mother of the Church.

I. The Indissoluble Bond between Mary and Jesus

In a homily given on April 24, 1970, at the Marian shrine of Our Lady of Bonaria in Cagliari, Sardinia, Pope Paul VI remarked. "If we wish to be Christian, we must also be Marian; that is we must recognize the essential, vital, providential bond that unites Our Lady with Jesus and opens to us the way that leads us to him."[8] The bond that unites Mary to her divine Son is indissoluble. Vatican II refers several times to this indissoluble bond. In *Lumen gentium*, 53, we read:

> The Virgin Mary, who at the message of the angel received the Word of God in her heart and in her body and gave Life to the world, is acknowledged and honored as being truly the Mother of God and Mother of the Redeemer. Redeemed by reason of the merits of her Son and united to Him by a close and indissoluble tie (*arcto et indissolubili vincolo*), she is endowed with the high office and dignity of being the Mother of the Son of God, by which account she is also the beloved daughter of the Father and the temple of the Holy Spirit. Because of this gift of sublime grace she far surpasses all creatures, both in heaven and on earth.

The bond between Jesus and Mary is also affirmed in the Second Vatican Council's *Sacrosanctum concilium*:

> In celebrating this annual cycle of Christ's mysteries, holy Church honors with especial love the Blessed Mary, Mother of God, who is joined by an inseparable bond (*indissolubili nexu*)

---

8. Paul VI, *Acta apostolicae sedis*, 300–301. The original Italian reads: "Se vogliamo essere cristiani, dobbiamo essere mariani, cioè dobbiamo riconoscere il rapporto essenziale, vitale, provvidenziale che unisce la Madonna a Gesù, e che apre a noi la via che a Lui ci conduce."

to the saving work of her Son. In her the Church holds up and admires the most excellent fruit of the redemption, and joyfully contemplates, as in a faultless image that which she herself desires and hopes wholly to be.[9]

In his January 1, 2015 homily for the Solemnity of Mary, Mother of God, Pope Francis made it clear that we cannot understand Jesus without his Mother:

The Blessed Virgin is the woman of faith who made room for God in her heart and in her plans; she is the believer capable of perceiving in the gift of her Son the coming of that "fullness of time" (*Gal* 4:4) in which God, by choosing the humble path of human existence, entered personally into the history of salvation. That is why Jesus cannot be understood without his Mother.[10]

We must always keep in mind this "providential bond" which links our Lord Jesus to his Mother. St. Paul, in Gal 4:4–5 writes that, "when the fullness of time had come, God sent his Son, born of woman, born under the law, to ransom those under the law, so we might receive adoption."[11] This means that a woman named Mary, the Mother of the Incarnate Word of God, is at the very center of salvation history. St. John Paul II affirms the central role of the Blessed Virgin Mary in salvation history in *Mulieris dignitatem*:

The sending of this Son, one in substance with the Father, as a man "born of woman," constitutes the culminating and *definitive point of God's self-revelation to humanity*. . . . A woman is to be found at the *center of this salvific event*. The self-revelation of God, who is the inscrutable unity of the Trinity, is outlined *in the annunciation at Nazareth*.[12]

Jesus and Mary are united by an inseparable bond because God became flesh in her. St. Louis de Montfort (1673–1716) exclaims: "Lord, you are always with Mary, and Mary is always with you."[13] St. Teresa of Calcutta put it even more simply: "Without Mary, there is no Jesus."[14] The evangelizing mission of the Church cannot be separated from the Blessed Virgin Mary because she is at the very center of salvation history grounded in the Incarnation.

9. Vatican II, *Sacrosanctum concilium*, 103.

10. Francis, "Homily for the Solemnity of Mary."

11. All translations from Scripture are from the *New American Bible* (1991).

12. John Paul II, *Mulieris dignitatem*, 3.

13. De Montfort, *True Devotion to the Blessed Virgin*, 63.

14. Teresa of Calcutta, *Where There Is Love*, 37.

II. Mary Represents Israel, the Church, and the
Human Race, Saying Yes to the Word Made Flesh

Pope Leo XIII, in his encyclical letter of September 22, 1891, *Octobri mense*, writes:

> The Eternal Son of God, about to take upon Him our nature for the saving and ennobling of man, and about to consummate thus a mystical union (*mysticum . . . conubium*) between Himself and all mankind, did not accomplish His design without adding there the free consent of the elect Mother, who represented in some sort all human kind, according to the illustrious and just opinion of St. Thomas, who says that the Annunciation was effected with the consent of the Virgin standing in the place of humanity.[15]

The actual text of St. Thomas Aquinas uses the term "*quoddam spirituale matrimonium*" to express the union between the Son of God and human nature, but the reference to the Blessed Virgin Mary in Leo XIII's encyclical is directly from the text of the *Summa Theologiae*: "Through the Annunciation the consent of the Virgin, in the place of all human nature (*loco totius humanae naturae*) was awaited." This passage from St. Thomas—cited in Leo XIII's encyclical—shows that the Incarnation is a type of mystical union or marriage between God and the human race. The Incarnation, as we know, is the "new and everlasting covenant" between God and the human race. This covenant can be understood in light of the Church as the Bride of Christ who joins with Christ, the Bridegroom. Mary assumes the role of the Bride. She is Israel saying yes to the coming of the Messiah. She is the Church saying yes to the coming of the Word made Flesh. She is the New Eve saying yes to entrance of the new Adam into human history. In the Gospel of St. Luke 1:38, Mary responds to the invitation to be the Mother of the Son of God by saying: "Behold I am the handmaiden of the Lord. May it be done to me according to your word." In her yes to the invitation of the angel, Mary played an active role in the history of salvation. Vatican II, in *Lumen gentium*, puts it this way:

> Thus Mary, a daughter of Adam, consenting to the divine Word, became the mother of Jesus, the one and only Mediator. Embracing God's salvific will with a full heart and impeded by no sin, she devoted herself totally as a handmaid of the Lord to the person and work of her Son, under Him and with Him, by the grace of almighty God, serving the mystery of redemption.

---

15. D-H 3274; cf. Aquinas, *Summa Theologiae*, III.30.1.

Rightly therefore the holy Fathers see her as used by God not merely in a passive way, but as freely cooperating in the work of human salvation through faith and obedience. For, as St. Irenaeus says, she "being obedient, became the cause of salvation for herself and for the whole human race." Hence not a few of the early Fathers gladly assert in their preaching, "The knot of Eve's disobedience was untied by Mary's obedience; what the virgin Eve bound through her unbelief, the Virgin Mary loosened by her faith." Comparing Mary with Eve, they call her "the Mother of the living," and still more often they say: "death through Eve, life through Mary."[16]

Mary's active role in the history of salvation did not end with her saying yes to the invitation of the angel to be the Mother of the Word Incarnate. She continues to play an active role in the evangelizing mission of the Church with her maternal presence. This is beautifully expressed in *Lumen gentium*, once again:

This maternity of Mary in the order of grace began with the consent which she gave in faith at the Annunciation and which she sustained without wavering beneath the cross, and lasts until the eternal fulfillment of all the elect. Taken up to heaven she did not lay aside this salvific duty, but by her constant intercession continued to bring us the gifts of eternal salvation. By her maternal charity, she cares for the brethren of her Son, who still journey on earth surrounded by dangers and difficulties, until they are led into the happiness of their true home.[17]

Mary provides an example of true discipleship by her complete surrender to the will of God. Her "fiat" provides a model for all Christians who must say "yes" to the invitation of Christ to enter into their hearts. But the Virgin Mary is more than a model. She is the Mother of the Church, and, as Mother, she intercedes and guides the faithful in the work of the new evangelization. The Virgin Mary accompanies the Church in preaching the Good News. Recourse to her maternal presence and love will greatly enrich the new evangelization.

16. Vatican II, *Lumen gentium*, 56.
17. Vatican II, *Lumen gentium*, 62.

III. Papal Witness to Mary and the New Evangelization

Since Vatican II, the popes have affirmed the Blessed Virgin Mary's role in evangelization and the new evangelization. St. Paul VI, in his 1975 apostolic exhortation, *Evangelii nuntiandi*, presents Mary as the star of evangelization:

> May the light of the Holy Year, which has shone in the local Churches and in Rome for millions of consciences reconciled with God, continue to shine in the same way after the Jubilee through a program of pastoral action with evangelization as its basic feature, for these years which mark the eve of a new century, the eve also of the third millennium of Christianity.
>
> This is the desire that we rejoice to entrust to the hands and the heart of the Immaculate Blessed Virgin Mary, on this day which is especially consecrated to her and which is also the tenth anniversary of the close of the Second Vatican Council. On the morning of Pentecost she watched over with her prayer the beginning of evangelization prompted by the Holy Spirit: may she be the Star of the evangelization ever renewed which the Church, docile to her Lord's command, must promote and accomplish, especially in these times which are difficult but full of hope![18]

We might wonder what it means to say Mary is "the Star of the evangelization every renewed within the Church." A scriptural foundation is found in Matt 2:1–12, which tells of the star that leads the Magi to the child, Jesus.[19] Just as the star led the Magi to Christ, so Mary leads us to her divine Son. In his 2001 apostolic letter, *Novo millennio ineunte*, St. John Paul II speaks of Mary as "the Star of the New Evangelization" who will accompany the Church in her journey into the new millennium:

> On this journey we are accompanied by the Blessed Virgin Mary to whom, a few months ago, in the presence of a great number of Bishops assembled in Rome from all parts of the world, I entrusted the Third Millennium. During this year I have often invoked her as the "Star of the New Evangelization." Now I point to Mary once again as the radiant dawn and sure guide for our steps. Once more, echoing the words of Jesus himself and giving voice to the filial affection of the whole Church, I say to her: "Woman, behold your children" (cf. *Jn* 19:26).[20]

---

18. Paul VI, *Evangelii nuntiandi*, 81–82.

19. See Phillips, *Mary, Star of the New Evangelization*, 5.

20. Pope John Paul II, *Novo millennio ineunte*, 58.

Mary as the star of the new evangelization also recalls the title, *stella maris*, or "star of the sea." This title has been linked to St. Jerome, but many now believe he actually meant "*stilla maris*" or "drop of the sea."[21] St. Bernard of Clairvaux (d. 1153) linked the title "star of the sea" to Mary's virginity because "just as a star emits its rays without being corrupted, so the Virgin gave birth without any injury [to her virginity]."[22] St. Bernard, though, also understood Mary, the star of the sea, as "the distinguished and bright shining star, necessarily lifted up above this great broad sea, gleaming with merits, giving light by her example."[23]

In his apostolic constitution, *Ecclesia in America* (Jan. 22, 1999), St. John Paul II points to Our Lady of Guadalupe as "the Star of the first and the new evangelization":

> The appearance of Mary to the native Juan Diego on the hill of Tepeyac in 1531 had a decisive effect on evangelization. Its influence greatly overflows the boundaries of Mexico, spreading to the whole Continent. America, which historically has been, and still is, a melting-pot of peoples, has recognized in the *mestiza* face of the Virgin of Tepeyac, "in Blessed Mary of Guadalupe, an impressive example of a perfectly inculturated evangelization." Consequently, not only in Central and South America, but in North America as well, the Virgin of Guadalupe is venerated as Queen of all America.
>
> With the passage of time, pastors and faithful alike have grown increasingly conscious of the role of the Virgin Mary in the evangelization of America. In the prayer composed for the Special Assembly for America of the Synod of Bishops, Holy Mary of Guadalupe is invoked as "Patroness of all America and Star of the first and new evangelization"[24]

Here we see that John Paul II recognizes Our Lady of Guadalupe as playing a preeminent role in the evangelization of the Americas and in the ongoing work of the new evangelization. The approved apparitions of the Blessed Virgin—especially Guadalupe, Lourdes, and Fatima—testify to Mary's active role in the life of the Church as spiritual Mother.

21. See Gillespie, "The Role of the Blessed Virgin Mary," 176.

22. Bernard of Clairvaux, *Super missus est* 2, 17; PL 183, 70–71, as cited in Gambero, *Mary in the Middle Ages*, 139.

23. Bernard of Clairvaux, *Super missus est* 2, 17.

24. John Paul II, *Ecclesia in America*, 11.

Mary is also a guide for the Church. Benedict XVI, in his 2011 homily for a Mass for the new evangelization, points to Mary as the model and guide of the new evangelization:

> May the Virgin Mary, who was not afraid to answer "yes" to the Word of the Lord and, after conceiving in her womb, set out full of joy and hope, always be your model and your guide. Learn from the Mother of the Lord and our Mother to be humble and at the same time courageous, simple and prudent; meek and strong, not with the strength of the world but with the strength of the truth. Amen.[25]

Pope Francis likewise recognizes the Blessed Virgin Mary as "the star of new evangelization."[26] In his 2013 apostolic exhortation, *Evangelii gaudium*, he delineates the Marian style of evangelization:

> We ask the Mother of the living Gospel to intercede that this invitation to a new phase of evangelization will be accepted by the entire ecclesial community. Mary is the woman of faith, who lives and advances in faith and "her exceptional pilgrimage of faith represents a constant point of reference for the Church." Mary let herself be guided by the Holy Spirit on a journey of faith towards a destiny of service and fruitfulness. Today we look to her and ask her to help us proclaim the message of salvation to all and to enable new disciples to become evangelizers in turn.... There is a Marian "style" to the Church's work of evangelization. Whenever we look to Mary, we come to believe once again in the revolutionary nature of love and tenderness. In her we see that humility and tenderness are not virtues of the weak but of the strong. Contemplating Mary, we realize that she who praised God for "bringing down the mighty from their thrones" and "sending the rich away empty" (*Lk* 1:52–53) is also the one who brings a homely warmth to our pursuit of justice. She is also the one who carefully keeps "all these things, pondering them in her heart" (*Lk* 2:19).... This interplay of justice and tenderness, of contemplation and concern for others, is what makes the ecclesial community look to Mary as a model of evangelization. We implore her maternal intercession that the Church may become a home for many peoples, a mother for all peoples, and that the way may be opened to the birth of a new world.[27]

25. Benedict XVI, "Homily for the Mass for the New Evangelization."
26. Francis, *Evangelii gaudium*, 287–88.
27. Francis, *Evangelii gaudium*, 287–88.

This passage sums up the importance of Mary for the new evangelization. She provides a model of faith and holiness for us to follow. She embodies a style of evangelization exemplified by humility, tenderness, and concern for others. She highlights the importance of docility to the Holy Spirit, and she is the Mother who helps the Church become a home for all peoples.

IV. The Ways in Which the Blessed Virgin Mary Is at the Heart of the New Evangelization:

A. Mary Is Our Model of Holiness.

Pope Benedict XVI has noted the importance of holiness for the new evangelization. In his 2012 address on the internal forum, he made it clear that "the new evangelization draws its lifeblood from the holiness of the children of the Church."[28] In May 2013, the Mariological Society of America held a conference on the theme of "Mary and the New Evangelization." At this conference, Patricia Sullivan pointed to Hans Urs von Balthasar's conviction that Mary and the saints are "guides in responding to Christ's redemptive work."[29] The holiness of Mary and the saints makes Christian love credible, and they are the "guiding stars" of the work of the new evangelization.[30]

B. Marian Devotion Leads Us Closer to Jesus.

If the goal of the new evangelization is to awaken the love of Christ in human hearts, there is no better way to do this than through Marian devotion. In *True Devotion to the Blessed Virgin*, St. Louis de Montfort writes:

> If then we are establishing sound devotion to our Blessed Lady, it is only in order to establish devotion to our Lord more perfectly, by providing a smooth but certain way of reaching Jesus Christ. If devotion to our Lady distracted us from our Lord, we would have to reject it as an illusion of the devil. But this is far from being the case. As I have already shown and will show again later on, this devotion is necessary, simply and

---

28. Benedict XVI, "Address on the Internal Forum," at a conference organized by the Apostolic Penitentiary.

29. Sullivan, "Mary as Missionary," 59.

30. See Sullivan, "Mary as Missionary," 83–84.

solely because it is a way of reaching Jesus perfectly, loving him tenderly, and serving him faithfully.[31]

The Church knows from experience that an authentic devotion to the Blessed Virgin Mary leads to a deeper knowledge and love of Jesus Christ. The Catholic faithful are encouraged to develop a true love and devotion to the Virgin Mary. As Vatican II teaches, the more the Mother is honored the more her divine Son "is rightly known, loved, and glorified and that all his commands are observed."[32]

C. Marian Popular Piety and Art Foster the New Evangelization.

The life of the Church is enriched by many Marian devotions such as the Rosary, Marian prayers, and pilgrimages. The devotion to Mary expressed in art, music, and liturgy nourishes the faith of the Church. Popular piety plays a special role in awakening and sustaining the life of Christian faith. In his 2003 exhortation, *Ecclesia in Europa*, St. John Paul II writes:

> Special consideration also needs to be given to *popular piety*. Widely diffused in different areas of Europe through confraternities, pilgrimages and processions to numerous shrines, it enriches the unfolding of the liturgical year and inspires traditions and customs in families and in society. All these forms of popular piety should be carefully evaluated through a pastoral effort of promotion and renewal aimed at helping them to accent those elements which authentically express the wisdom of the People of God. An example of such devotions is surely the Holy Rosary. In this Year dedicated to the Rosary, I once more heartily recommend its recitation, for "the Rosary, reclaimed in its full meaning, goes to the very heart of Christian life; it offers a familiar yet fruitful spiritual and educational opportunity for personal contemplation, the formation of the People of God, and the new evangelization."[33]

In its 2002 *Directory on Popular Piety and the Liturgy*, the Congregation for Divine Worship and Discipline of the Sacraments draws attention to the importance of popular devotion to the Virgin Mary in the life of the Church:

---

31. De Montfort, *True Devotion to the Blessed Virgin*, 28.

32. Vatican II, *Lumen gentium*, 66.

33. John Paul II, *Ecclesia in Europa*, 79.

Popular devotion to the Blessed Virgin Mary is an important and universal ecclesial phenomenon. Its expressions are multifarious and its motivation very profound, deriving as it does from the People of God's faith in, and love for, Christ, the Redeemer of mankind, and from an awareness of the salvific mission that God entrusted to Mary of Nazareth, because of which she is mother not only of Our Lord and Savior Jesus Christ, but also of mankind in the order of grace.[34]

Authentic and Church-approved popular devotions to the Blessed Virgin Mary have nourished the faith of Catholics over the centuries. When these devotions are dismissed or distorted the life of faith suffers.

D. Mary Intercedes for Us in Our Battle against the Devil.

Satan is the enemy of the new evangelization, and many exorcists testify to the hatred of demons to the name of Mary. St. Louis de Montfort drives home this point: "Thus the most fearful enemy that God has set up against the devil is Mary, his holy Mother."[35] Pius IX, in his 1854 bull, *Ineffabilis Deus*, notes that Mary's Immaculate Conception enables her to "have the most complete triumph over the ancient serpent."[36] Pius XII, in his 1950 apostolic constitution, *Munificentissimus Deus*, explains that Mary, the New Eve, "although subject to the New Adam is most intimately associated with him in that struggle against the infernal foe which, as foretold in the *protoevangelium* [*Gen 3:15*], would finally result in the most complete victory over the sin and death that are always mentioned together in the writings of the Apostle to the Gentiles [*Rom 5* and 6; *1 Cor* 15:21–26, 54–57]."[37] As the New Eve, the Blessed Virgin is intimately associated with her divine Son in overcoming the wickedness and snares of the Devil. The Italian exorcist, Fr. Gabriele Amorth (1925–2016), once reported that a demon told him: "I am more afraid when you say the Madonna's name, because I am more humiliated by being beaten by a simple creature, than by Him."[38] The protection of the Blessed Virgin Mary—whether by consecration or simple devotion—is a great help in the new evangelization because the Devil constantly seeks to resist the spread of the Gospel.

---

34. Congregation for Divine Worship and Discipline of the Sacraments, *Directory on Popular Piety and the Liturgy*, 183.

35. De Montfort, *True Devotion to the Blessed Virgin*, 52.

36. D-H, 2801.

37. D-H, 3901.

38. See Koslowski, "This Is Why the Devil Hates the Blessed Virgin Mary."

E. Mary as Mother of the Church.

The title "Mother of the Church" has roots in the Fathers of the Church. St. Augustine (354–430) sees Mary as "the mother of the members of Christ . . . having cooperated by charity so the faithful might be born in the Church, who are members of that Head."[39] St. Leo the Great (c. 400–461) states that "Christ's generation is the origin of the Christian people; and Christ's birth as head is also the birth of his Mystical Body."[40] In the Middle Ages, St. Anselm (1033–1109) speaks of Mary as "the Mother of justification and the justified; the Mother of reconciliation and the reconciled; the Mother of salvation and of the saved."[41] Pope Benedict XIV, in his 1748 apostolic letter, *Gloriosae Dominae*, states that Mary on Calvary is "in the proper sense Mother of the Church, a gift the Church received from the lips of her dying Bridegroom."[42] Pope Leo XIII, in his 1895 encyclical, *Adiutricem*, extols Mary as "the Mother of the Church, the Teacher and Queen of the Apostles."[43] In his 1964 address at Vatican II, St. Paul VI notes that "as soon as Christ took on a human nature in Mary's virginal womb, He united to himself, as its head, his Mystical Body, which is the Church. Mary, therefore, as the Mother of Christ, must be regarded as the Mother of all the faithful and pastors, which means the Church."[44] St. John Paul II, in his General Audience of September 17, 1997, observes: "On Calvary, Mary united herself to the sacrifice of her Son and made her own maternal contribution to the work of salvation, which took the form of labor pains, the birth of the new humanity." He goes on to say that "in addressing the words 'Woman, behold your son' to Mary, the Crucified One proclaims her motherhood not only in relation to the Apostle John but also to every disciple."[45] Cardinal Robert Sarah, in the 2018 Decree on the Memorial of the Blessed Virgin Mary, Mother of the Church, writes:

> This celebration will help us to remember that growth in the Christian life must be anchored to the Mystery of the Cross, to the oblation of Christ in the Eucharistic Banquet and to the

---

39. Augustine, *De Sancta Virginitate*, 6; PL 40, 399, as cited in Vatican II, *Lumen gentium*, 53.

40. Leo the Great, *Sermon* 26, 6; PL 54, 213B, on the Nativity of the Lord.

41. Anselm, *Oratio* 52; PL 158, 956B–957A.

42. Benedict XIV, *Gloriosae Dominae* (1748), in *Bullarium Romanum* ser. 2, vol. 2, no. 61, 428.

43. Leo XIII, *Adiutricem*, 6.

44. Paul VI, "Address at the Conclusion of the Third Session of Vatican II." See *AAS* 56 (1964) 1015.

45. John Paul II, "General Audience," of September 17, 1997.

Mother of the Redeemer and Mother of the Redeemed, the Virgin who makes her offering to God.[46]

If Mary is the Mother of the Church, she must also be the Mother of the Church's mission in the new evangelization.

F. Mary Is Our Powerful Intercessor and Mediatrix of Grace.

The Catholic faithful know the power of the Blessed Virgin Mary as a heavenly intercessor and Mediatrix of grace. Again, in his 1895 encyclical, *Adiutricem*, Pope Leo XIII writes:

> The power thus put into her hands is all but unlimited. How unerringly right, then, are Christian souls when they turn to Mary for help as though impelled by an instinct of nature, confidently sharing with her their future hopes and past achievements, their sorrows and joys, commending themselves like children to the care of a bountiful mother. How rightly, too, has every nation and every liturgy without exception acclaimed her great renown, which has grown greater with the voice of each succeeding century. Among her many other titles we find her hailed as "our Lady, our Mediatrix," "the Reparatrix of the whole world," "the Dispenser of all heavenly gifts."[47]

Vatican II, in *Lumen gentium*, also speaks of Mary's maternity in the order of grace:

> Predestined from eternity by that decree of divine providence which determined the incarnation of the Word to be the Mother of God, the Blessed Virgin was on this earth the virgin Mother of the Redeemer, and above all others and in a singular way the generous associate and humble handmaid of the Lord. She conceived, brought forth and nourished Christ. She presented Him to the Father in the temple, and was united with Him by compassion as He died on the Cross. In this singular way she cooperated by her obedience, faith, hope and burning charity in the work of the Savior in giving back supernatural life to souls. Wherefore she is our mother in the order of grace.
>
> This maternity of Mary in the order of grace began with the consent which she gave in faith at the Annunciation and which

---

46. Sarah, "Decree on the Celebration of the Blessed Virgin Mary."
47. Leo XIII, *Adiutricem*, 8.

she sustained without wavering beneath the cross, and lasts until the eternal fulfillment of all the elect.[48]

Beginning with Pope Benedict XIV (r. 1740–58), popes have affirmed
Mary as the Mediatrix of all grace. Since the late 19th century there have
also been various movements petitioning the Church to dogmatically define
Mary's universal mediation of grace.[49] Although these movements have not
been successful in procuring a dogmatic definition, Mary's universal mediation of grace has been affirmed by popes in their ordinary magisterium.
Benedict XVI, for example, in his 2007 homily for the Canonization Mass
of Fr. Antonio de Sant'Ana Galvão, OFM in São Paulo, Brazil, testified to the
Blessed Virgin's universal mediation of grace by these words:

> Frei Galvão prophetically affirmed the truth of the *Immaculate
> Conception*. She, the *Tota Pulchra*, the Virgin Most Pure, who
> conceived in her womb the Redeemer of mankind and was pre-
> served from all stain of original sin, wishes to be the definitive
> seal of our encounter with God our Savior. There is no fruit of
> grace in the history of salvation that does not have as its neces-
> sary instrument the mediation of Our Lady.[50]

Because Mary is the Mother of the Church and the Mediatrix of grace,
Catholics involved in the work of the new evangelization should have ongoing reliance on her prayers and intercession.

Conclusion

There has been an unfortunate tendency in some Catholic circles to minimize the importance of the Blessed Virgin in the life of the faith and the
work of the new evangelization. This is often due to a misreading of the
documents of Vatican II and a Marian minimalism motivated by a mis-
guided ecumenism. Fr. James Phalan, CSC, believes the papal call for a
new evangelization is linked to a reawakening of Marian devotion. This
reawakening is extremely important because the Church must be united
in prayer with Mary if the new evangelization is to bear fruit. As Fr. Phalan
writes: "The Church needs Mary to be who she has always been if the New

---

48. Vatican II, *Lumen gentium*, 62.

49. See Dodd, *The Virgin Mary*.

50. Benedict XVI, "Homily for the Canonization Mass of Fr. Antonio de Sant'Ana
Galvão, OFM," in São Paulo, Brazil.

Evangelization is to lead to the Springtime of Christianity, the New Pentecost that continues to be part of its fundamental vision."[51]

The Blessed Virgin Mary is central to the Gospel because she is at the very heart of salvation history. As Pope Francis has said, "We cannot understand Jesus apart from his Mother."[52] Pope Francis also has stated that Mary is more important than the Apostles because "the Church is feminine. She is Church, she is bride; she is mother."[53] The mission of the new evangelization cannot be separated from the Mother of the Church. We must always keep in mind the words of St. Paul VI: "If we wish to be Christian, we must also be Marian."[54]

Bibliography

Aquinas, Thomas. *Summa Theologiae*. https://www.corpusthomisticum.org/sth0000. html.

———. *Summa Theologica*. Translated by the Fathers of the English Dominican Province. 5 vols. Notre Dame: Ave Maria, 1981.

Benedict XIV, Pope. *Bullarium: In quo continentur constitutiones, epistolae, aliaque edita ab initio pontificatus usque ad annum MDCCXLVI*. Ser. 2, Vol. 2. Mechlin: Hanicq, 1826.

Benedict XVI, Pope. "Address on the Internal Forum." http://www.vatican.va/content/ benedict-xvi/en/speeches/2012/march/documents/hf_ben-xvi_spe_20120309_ penitenzieria-apostolica.html.

———. "Homily for the Mass for the New Evangelization." http://www.vatican. va/content/benedict-xvi/en/homilies/2011/documents/hf_ben-xvi_ hom_20111016_nuova-evang.html.

———. "Homily for the Canonization Mass of Fr. Antonio de Sant'Ana Galvão, OFM." http://www.vatican.va/content/benedict-xvi/it/homilies/2007/documents/hf_ ben-xvi_hom_20070511_canonization-brazil.html.

———. *Ubicumque et semper*. http://www.vatican.va/content/benedict-xvi/en/apost_ letters/documents/hf_ben-xvi_apl_20100921_ubicumque-et-semper.html.

Congregation for Divine Worship and Discipline of the Sacraments. *Directory on Popular Piety and the Liturgy*. http://www.vatican.va/roman_curia/congregations/ ccdds/documents/rc_con_ccdds_doc_20020513_vers-direttorio_en.html.

De Montfort, Louis-Marie. *True Devotion to the Blessed Virgin*. Translated by the Monfort Fathers. Bay Shore, NY: Monfort, 1996.

Denzinger, Heinrich, and Peter Hünermann, eds. *Enchiridion symbolorum: A Compendium of Creeds, Definitions, and Declarations of the Catholic Church*. 43rd ed. San Francisco: Ignatius, 2012.

51. Phalan, "Mission, Evangelization, and the Blessed Virgin Mary Today," 11.

52. Francis, "Homily for the Solemnity of Mary."

53. Francis, "Press Conference."

54. Paul VI, "Homily at the Marian Shrine of Our Lady of Bonaria." See *AAS* 62 (1970) 300–301.

Dodd, Gloria Falcão. *The Virgin Mary: Mediatrix of All Grace: History and Theology of the Movement for a Dogmatic Definition from 1896 to 1964*. New Bedford, MA: Academy of the Immaculate, 2012.

Francis, Pope. *Evangelii gaudium*. http://www.vatican.va/content/francesco/en/apost_exhortations/documents/papa-francesco_esortazione-ap_20131124_evangelii-gaudium.html.

———. "Homily for the Solemnity of Mary, Mother of God and the World Day of Peace." http://w2.vatican.va/content/francesco/en/homilies/2015/documents/papa-francesco_20150101_omelia-giornata-mondiale-pace.html.

———. "Press Conference during the Return Flight from Brazil." http://www.vatican.va/content/francesco/en/speeches/2013/july/documents/papa-francesco_20130728_gmg-conferenza-stampa.html.

Gambero, Luigi. *Mary in the Middle Ages: The Blessed Virgin Mary in the Thought of Medieval Latin Theologians*. Translated by Thomas Buffer. San Francisco: Ignatius, 2005.

Gillespie, Christopher. "The Role of the Blessed Virgin Mary in the New Evangelization in the Writings of Blessed John Paul II." *Marian Studies* LXIV (2013) 171–97.

John Paul II, Pope. *Ecclesia in America*. http://www.vatican.va/content/john-paul-ii/en/apost_exhortations/documents/hf_jp-ii_exh_22011999_ecclesia-in-america.html.

———. *Ecclesia in Europa*. http://www.vatican.va/content/john-paul-ii/en/apost_exhortations/documents/hf_jp-ii_exh_20030628_ecclesia-in-europa.html.

———. "General Audience." http://www.vatican.va/content/john-paul-ii/en/audiences/1997/documents/hf_jp-ii_aud_17091997.html.

———. *Mulieris dignitatem*. http://www.vatican.va/content/john-paul-ii/en/apost_letters/1988/documents/hf_jp-ii_apl_19880815_mulieris-dignitatem.html.

———. *Novo millennio ineunte*. http://www.vatican.va/content/john-paul-ii/en/apost_letters/2001/documents/hf_jp-ii_apl_20010106_novo-millennio-ineunte.html.

Koslowski, Philip. "This Is Why the Devil Hates the Blessed Virgin Mary." https://aleteia.org/2018/05/07/this-is-why-the-devil-hates-the-virgin-mary/.

Leo XIII, Pope. *Adiutricem*. http://www.vatican.va/content/leo-xiii/en/encyclicals/documents/hf_l-xiii_enc_05091895_adiutricem.html.

Migne, J.-P., ed. *Patrologia Latina*. 217 vols. Paris, 1844–64.

Paul VI, Pope. *Acta apostolicae sedis*. Vol. 62. https://www.vatican.va/archive/aas/documents/AAS-62-1970-ocr.pdf.

———. "Address at the Conclusion of the Third Session of Vatican II." http://www.vatican.va/content/paul-vi/it/speeches/1964/documents/hf_p-vi_spe_19641121_conclusions-iii-sessions.html.

———. *Evangelii nuntiandi*. http://www.vatican.va/content/paul-vi/en/apost_exhortations/documents/hf_p-vi_exh_19751208_evangelii-nuntiandi.html.

———. "Homily at the Marian Shrine of Our Lady of Bonaria." http://www.vatican.va/content/paul-vi/it/homilies/1970/documents/hf_p-vi_hom_19700424.html.

Phalan, James. "Mission, Evangelization, and the Blessed Virgin Mary Today." *Marian Studies* LXIV (2013) 1–13.

Phillips, Jacob. *Mary, Star of the New Evangelization*. Mahway, NJ: Paulist, 2018.

Pius IX, Pope. *Ineffabilis Deus*. https://www.papalencyclicals.net/pius09/p9ineff.htm.

Sarah, Robert. "Decree on the Celebration of the Blessed Virgin Mary, Mother of the Church in the General Roman Calendar." https://press.vatican.va/content/salastampa/it/bollettino/pubblico/2018/03/03/0168/00350.html#ingD.

Sullivan, Patricia. "Mary as Missionary: Balthasar's Mariology as a Resource for Engaging the Faithful in the New Evangelization." *Marian Studies* LXIV (2013) 59–84.

Teresa of Calcutta. *Where There Is Love, There Is God*. Edited by Brian Kolodiejchuk. New York: Doubleday, 2010.

Vatican II. *Lumen gentium*. http://www.vatican.va/archive/hist_councils/ii_vatican_council/documents/vat-ii_const_19641121_lumen-gentium_en.html.

———. *Sacrosanctum concilium*. https://www.vatican.va/archive/hist_councils/ii_vatican_council/documents/vat-ii_const_19631204_sacrosanctum-concilium_en.html.

10

Symposium Panel Presentation

Scott W. Hahn, Mary Healy, Ralph Martin, \
and Michael J. McCallion

Dr. Mary Healy: It's hard to sum up the insights that come forth from such a rich time of discussion and reflection together. I'll just say a few things about the main talks and the breakout session I attended just now, led by Fr. Peter Ryan.

Dr. Cavadini spoke about the apologetics of love and the fact that while apologetics has an important role in disambiguating the Catholic faith from its distortions and degradations—wiping the dirt off the icon—it's the icon itself that is the goal, the face of Christ. It's his love that is the most grand and the most appealing: his Person. Apologetics needs to lead to an encounter with his Person. Dr. Cavadini also talked about a renewed pedagogy of the basics, which is really another way of saying that the kerygma is what is needed for the New Evangelization. Bishop Flores spoke about the "Eucharistic interruption" and he spoke about the poverty of Christ. We can even think of the poverty of Christ in terms of the Eucharist—that he comes to us in the humble, simple forms of bread and wine. Dr. Hahn talked about the incredibly rich Eucharistic imagery and symbolism in the Letter to the Hebrews, and how the Eucharist is the perpetual making present of and our participation in the new covenant in Christ.

The breakout session by Fr. Peter Ryan was very compelling. He spoke about two primary problems that undermine and inhibit evangelization. First, the failure to communicate the marvelous appeal of heaven. And second, giving people the impression that we don't need to strive for heaven because we're all going there anyway. He gave a little account of an experience he had as a sixth grader, when he learned in his catechism class that heaven would be a perpetual gazing on God, the beatific vision. As he imagined forever gazing at God, it actually imbued him with sadness because it seemed boring. His mother reassured him and, later, studying St. Thomas Aquinas reassured him. But then he began to realize that we actually make a mistake if we reduce the glory of heaven to the beatific vision, because Scripture reveals that it's so much more than that. There's so much biblical imagery of what we will be doing in heaven: it will include human companionship, it will include the bodily resurrection, the renewal of all creation, the new heavens and earth, as well as the vision of God. But because we will remain fully human, it will include human goods like singing, dancing, music, sports, exploring the new heavens and the new earth.

One of the most prominent biblical images for heaven is that of eating and drinking—a great wedding banquet to surpass all banquets. And that, of course, ties back into the Eucharistic liturgy. So, one of the ways we can help communicate the marvelous appeal of heaven is by celebrating the Eucharistic liturgy in a way that brings people into an experience of the foretaste—even though we can only see it in a glass dimly—of that unimaginable gift that will be ours, if we choose to follow Christ, if we are His disciples, and that's what we're inviting people into.

Dr. Michael McCallion: My thoughts derive basically from Dr. Cavadini's talk, Bishop Flores, and a bit from Fr. Cassidy. Specifically, I think the apologetics of encounter, and in my mind went sociological, so it's more of a sociological take. It's about lapsed Catholics. Those who are the opposite of religious virtuosi Catholics, and even those we refer to as ordinary pew-dwelling Catholics. God loves us means he loves all of us, and we need to respond in love with charity as Bishop Flores noted. In my own little sociological search circle, certain studies recently have been about lapsed Catholics, and I think they're worth further consideration when we think about the New Evangelization.

For example, perhaps for some lapsed Catholics, as these studies show, does not always mean secularism is creeping into their veins. Consider Max Weber's Calvinists, whose restless inner worldly asceticism and economic productivity would prove their status among the elect. Those early German capitalists were the embodiment of Christian discipline—a discipline that, we are told, not only ushered in the spirit of modern capitalism, but also produced, in Weber's words, unprecedented inner loneliness of the single individual. Bishop Flores referred to this a bit and this continues today. The idea that discipline, whether in the form of techniques of the self or knowledge, is both the spark and engine of most Western forms of subjectivity, is worrying. It worries me because it writes the lapsed and the indifferent out of Christian history. Take the anthropologist Talal Asad's inspiration, that came not from the laity but from monastic practices from what the clerical orders did, within his theory of the development of a Christian self. It is implicitly assumed that the laity followed suit and were forced to live in an endless cycle of aspiration to monastic ideals, even though they were doomed by the practicalities of ordinary life to failure. But as medieval historians point out, much of the priest–lay interface was economic and social: a matter of ties, rents and meeting in the streets.

So, one of the defining elements of Catholicism, I think, as opposed to many Protestant and nonconformist Christian traditions, is its enshrined division of labor between clergy and laity. In its simplest terms, Catholicism is ordered by a priestly caste and ordained elite who preside over the sacraments and a caste of followers who worship, participate in and receive those sacraments. In Catholicism, to be a layman is to be part of that great multitude, who, although not appointed—not appointed by Jesus—for a more intense ministry, are chosen for other tasks such as marriage and sexual reproduction. It is in this fundamental division of the visible Church into the ordained and the laity that a certain absolution from the performance of spiritual and theological tasks is somewhat justified. For example, in their analytical foray into Orthodox religious worlds and their particularities, Bandak and Boylston have described this form of organization as a community of deferral. In Orthodox, Catholic, and other heavily institutional forms of Christianity, they argue, the division of spiritual labor between priests, lay, and other religious virtuosi distributes the burden of piety and religious knowledge, such that this deferral or distribution affords some individuals a more passive role in religious practice. Rather than striving for correctness, subjects may orient themselves towards a lack of incorrectness without sacrificing their claim to Christian identity.

There is an obvious but important point in all this, and we see it particularly and historically in relation to Catholicism. Far from being an impossible religion, Catholicism is, in theory, an infinitely doable religion precisely because it does not exact high levels of reflexive certainty from each individual, or at least from each individual all of the time. We see this ethos of deferral at work, in a different way, when lay Catholics divide spiritual labor among themselves, often along axes of gender and generation. In many such practices, what we see is not merely a division of ritual labor, but even in some instances a division of agentive responsibility. Consider, for example, the Mexican and Peruvian procession goers in Nepo's study of Latino Catholics who carry heavy effigies on behalf of themselves and their families. Or Sara, a twenty-three-year-old pilgrim in Peña's study on trans-national, Mexican–US devotion to the Virgin of Guadalupe, that recounts how Sara performs pilgrimage, wearing a white t-shirt covered in hand-written requests for protection from her many friends and relatives unable to make the journey themselves. In such cases, one pilgrim's body literally carries the intentions of many other individuals. Or consider my friend Dave Pechota, who calms his Catholic mother about his religious practices by saying, "Don't worry, Mom, I am riding Mike McCallion's coattails into heaven!" He could be in for a surprise. And then finally, this conference has awakened in me, once again, and in a more profound way that we should be careful not to operate out of a deficit model of Catholicism when we are talking and preaching the New Evangelization in parishes and on the streets. These good folks may not be deficient. They may be riding their relatives' or friends' religious coattails at this point in their life, and that they might be okay. We should therefore proclaim in the New Evangeliza-tion more abundantly the love of God for us all.

Dr. Ralph Martin: I don't know who chose the theme for the confer-ence, "Enter through the Narrow Gate: The Urgency of the New Evangeliza-tion," but it comes from Luke, chapter 13. And I thought that we shouldn't depart from here without actually looking at the theme very directly. So, I'd like to read to you that text and just offer a few comments on why I think it's so important for the New Evangelization. "Jesus went through the towns and villages teaching as he made his way to Jerusalem. Someone asked him, 'Lord are only a few people going to be saved?'" Now that's a pretty direct question. And, you know, you might think, "Well, gee, how's Jesus going to answer this?" Well, he doesn't give numbers. He doesn't give percentages. But he also doesn't say, "Oh, sorry for stressing you out. I mean, don't you remember your Scripture classes? This is literary form. I mean, this is Jew-ish hyperbole, relax." No, he didn't say that either. What he says, though, is very direct, very sobering. He said to them, "Make every effort to enter through the narrow door because many, I tell you, will try to enter and will not be able to." That's a pretty shocking statement. "Once the owner of the house gets up and closes the door, you'll stand outside knocking and pleading, 'Sir, open the door for us.' But he will answer, 'I don't know you or where you come from.'" Then you'll say, "Hey, Jesus, wait a second, we ate and drank with you. And you taught in our streets, we came to your healing services, you know, we hung out with you." But he will reply, "I don't know you or where you come from, away from me, all you evil doers. There will be weeping there and gnashing of teeth." And it goes on.

I think what this says is that it's not just enough to know about Jesus, to be positively disposed towards Jesus. These people were positively disposed towards him. But they didn't enter into relationship with him. They didn't repent. They didn't believe. They didn't decide to obey the teaching of Jesus. Sometimes Jesus says that it's not enough to hear the Word of God, but you need to *hear* the Word of God. Or the Letter to the Hebrews says that Jesus became the source of salvation for all who obey Him. We don't talk a lot about obedience today, but we need to obey Jesus. Now, the underlying Greek word for "try very hard" to enter by the narrow door is where we get our English word, "agonize." Try very hard. So, you don't drift into the kingdom of God by just going along with the culture. You don't drift into the kingdom of God, and just say, "Hey, God is so merciful that all will be saved." No, that's a deception. That's a lie. We need to respond to the mercy. There needs to be a yes to the mercy. There needs to be repentance, there needs to be faith, there needs to be obedience. This is pretty important. And this isn't an isolated text. I'm doing a Bible study with a bunch of people in my office right now at Renewal Ministries. We're going through Matthew's Gospel and we're looking for a particular thing. We're looking for what Jesus says about the eternal consequences of not responding to him. We found 64 instances, either implicitly or explicitly, where Jesus talks about the eternal consequences. This isn't a game. Jesus is really serious about this. He set his face like flint towards Jerusalem. He's focused on his mission. And his mission is to seek and to save those who are lost. If we don't believe people can be lost, if we don't believe that many are on the way to destruction, there's going to be a real laziness about our response to the call of the New Evangelization. And quite honestly, if people hear any more about the New Evangelization without hearing about why it matters, I don't think there's going to be a lot of people responding. Because they're going to say in the back of their heads, "You know, wait a second . . ."—I would say that how most people look at the world today, including many of our fellow Catholics, is something like this: "Broad and wide is the way that leads to heaven. Almost everybody's going that way. But narrow is the door that leads to hell and difficult the road, and hardly anybody's going that way."

It's exactly the opposite of what Jesus himself said. So how did something just the opposite of what Jesus himself said get into so many people's minds and hearts? Deception, false teachers, false prophets. Jesus warns about false teachers and false prophets. Paul warns about the doctrines of demons being infiltrated into the Church through plausible liars. So, there's a huge deception that's gotten into the minds and hearts of many Catholics. What did Jesus say in Matthew, chapter seven, and other places where he talks about the narrow gate? "Broad and wide is the way that leads to destruction, and many are traveling that way. But narrow is the door that leads to life and difficult the road, and few are finding it." This isn't because this is how Jesus wants it to be. He doesn't like it. He's weeping that so many are on a path to destruction. And everybody who's on a path to destruction doesn't have to stay on that path. But this is where evangelization comes in. This is where prayer and fasting comes in. This is where zeal for the Father's house comes in. This is where zeal for the salvation of souls comes in. This is where every missionary and every saint for 2000 years had the biblical worldview in mind. They knew that something serious was at stake and that people's eternal salvation was at risk. And unless we restore the biblical worldview, unless we restore a serious understanding—not only the possibility of being lost, but if you drift away with the culture and right now, then you're on your way to destruction in this life and for eternal life. There's a tremendous pressure these days not to tell people the truth. There's a tremendous pressure to cover this up. There's a tremendous pressure not to talk about the eternal consequences. And we can't cover this up if we're going to be faithful to Jesus, and if we're actually going to love people.

Dr. Scott Hahn: Thank you, Ralph. I feel like we need to invent a new category besides "cradle Catholics" or "converts." We need to designate the category "complacent Catholics." And so, the urgency of the New Evangelization. Well, stepping back and looking at evangelization in the Catholic tradition, I'm always struck by how different it is than from my own evangelical upbringing and formation. For evangelicals, evangelizing was something over and done in a moment, a minute. It consisted of the four spiritual laws: God loves you, you sin, Christ died, and you can choose to believe. And, of course, all of that is true for us as Catholics. But evangelization is so much more than a personal relationship with Jesus, though it's no less. I'm always reminded of that evangelization is a two-way street. It's the old evangelization: you share the good news with people who don't know it. And then once they experience initial conversion, in the ancient tradition, you would enroll them in the catechumenate. And as catechumens, they would learn how to pray the Our Father, they would learn what to believe and memorize the creed. They would also hear a lot about Sacred Scripture in terms of typology, the Old and the New, if St. Cyril of Jerusalem's catechetical lectures are any indication of that rich teaching that catechizes toward God. But the finish line, the third stage is the initiation: Baptism, Confirmation, and First Holy Communion.

It reminds me of the personal relationship that I had with Kimberly when we were dating. After courtship came engagement. Then after engagement came our marriage, and that was, in a certain sense, the goal. And yet 40 years later, we realized that there was still a lot of growth and development needed. I think this is where the other side of the street comes in that the New Evangelization is not just evangelizing those who haven't heard, then catechizing them, and then sacramentalizing them. It's really evangelizing or re-evangelizing those who are baptized—those who are sacramentalized but who have drifted off, either as "non-practicing inactive," "complacent," or what have you. It seems to me that the analogy applies because a lot of married people are lonely and miserable and alienated. And so there needs to be a kind of reinvigoration—a renewal—not just of the vows, but of the love. It strikes me that this is the mission that we face right now in the New Evangelization with so many millions—tens of millions—of non-practicing Catholics, "fallen away," or whatever you want to call them. The examination of the demographic is such that, when you look at the younger ones, you see much larger percentages of those who have departed. So, what I had hoped to do this morning was to show that you don't stop evangelizing when you catechize. You don't stop evangelizing when you sacramentalize. If anything, the good news just continues to grow and get better. So that what we're doing in Holy Eucharist, what we're doing, as a communion of sinners wanting to become saints, is almost too good to be true, except it is the Gospel. It is the good news reaching a new level.

I find that, what Cyril of Jerusalem would refer to as mystagogy, the mystagogical catechesis, is what was given only after the Easter Vigil, after you were baptized and confirmed. Because apart from the supernatural grace—the sacraments—you cannot understand the sacred mysteries. But once you have those sacraments, then you're invited to really delve into these depths. And it seems to me that a whole lot of Catholics are taking a whole lot of grace for granted, and that the New Evangelization ought to consistent largely of what we call mystagogical catechesis—post-baptismal instruction—where you go back over the good news, as well as the Lord's Prayer and what it means to grow spiritually through prayer and studying Scripture and all of that. But that when we celebrate the Mass, whether you knew it or not, the good news is almost too good to be true, and yet, it's even better than that. So, I would propose that what we need to do in a way that is truly urgent, and not just to get more people in to heaven and less people to hell, is to get more people to plunge into the depths of what is heaven on earth. That is this communion of angels and saints, this medicine of mercy.

Thinking back to what John Cavadini said about a New Evangelization requiring a new apologetic, that new apologetic needs to be rooted in a new theological logic of love. That alone explains the Incarnation, the Paschal Mystery, and all of the other things that we are called upon to believe and do. The inner logic of God's love is almost too great to fathom. It's almost too good to be true. But this again, I think, is the only thing that explains everything that we're called upon to believe and to live. Retrieving that new apologetic, or actually developing it, is not something that is in place that we just have to rediscover, it really calls for a kind of reconstructive effort on the part of many. And I think the collaboration has already begun this weekend here. But I do believe that the Trinity, that revelation that focuses on the God–man, God incarnate, it's more than just a doctrine. It's more than just religious rhetoric. It's more than a mathematical abstraction. The idea that God is a Father more than I am to my six kids—that this is more than mystical—this is metaphysical. This is the reality that is going to be for us the reality long after the Westin Hotel is nothing but dust.

I think that majoring on the majors and focusing on those mysteries allows us to reawaken a sense that we are called upon to think the un-thinkable, to contain the uncontainable, to be not only saved and healed but divinized. It's a call for me to constant conversion, not just for me to call you to conversion, and for us to reach "them," but to recognize in a deep and true sense that we are "them." This morning, when I woke up, I needed to be reached, I needed to pray, I needed to be renewed in the Word of God every bit as much as anybody else does. And again, that isn't like, "Oh, holy hyperbole!" No, that is the plain and simple truth of what it means to be me. You know, people think I'm a saint, or whatever they think a celebrity is these days. And if I didn't know me, I might be impressed. We're Catholics. We don't need celebrities. What we need is to be saints. And I found that becoming a Catholic thirty-three years ago, was a whole lot easier than becoming a saint. But this grace of ongoing conversion is something that we don't just give to others, we inhale in order to exhale, we breathe in the Spirit of God in order to express the Word of God. And I think that this call to constant conversion is, for us as professors, a need to do something more than recycle our notes from the last few semesters, but to really allow the subject matter to be renewed within our hearts and minds. I mentioned to a couple of my friends that this weekend has been for me a rediscovery like a kid in a candy store who discovers that there are more rooms, there are more vaults, more flavors, that the good news is sweeter than I could have imagined. And to continue to discover that in an ever-deepening way is, to me, that striving to enter by the narrow gate. It's not easy, but it sure is worth it.

Panel Question #1: How should we address the irrelevancy of faith for those who look only to this world—to what is material and temporal?

Dr. Ralph Martin: I think we need to proclaim the glorious good news—the shocking event of Jesus in the power of the Holy Spirit. And it's not a matter of techniques. It's a matter of being in the Lord and speaking from the Lord in the anointing of the power of the Holy Spirit. There's a power to the Gospel. There's a power to the Word of God and I honestly think that's the center of any real conversion.

Dr. Mary Healy: It made me think of a brief talk I once heard by a priest who was in charge of Boys Town. It was very striking. He said, "When we get these adolescents who come to us from juvenile court, this is the technique that we use to really grab them: First, we have to help them see: 'Your life is miserable. You may think it's great because you're doing whatever you want. But, you know, you're heading for thirty years in the penitentiary. You're heading for broken relationships. You're heading for drug addiction.' So, we have to start with that. Then we tell them what their life could be, which they don't have a clue about: 'You could have a stable job that's fulfilling. You could have a family where you really love your wife and children that you're raising.' And finally, the third step is 'We want to help you get there.'" And he talked about how Martin Luther King used a similar technique when he was helping Americans see the terrible state we're in now with racial relations. This is where we are now: it's deplorable. This is where we could be: I have a dream. And now we want to help you get there. I think that's what we need to do with the people of this generation. This is where you are right now. Are you really happy when you look at your life right now? No God in your life, broken relationships, narcissism, all kinds of self-centeredness leading into all kinds of addictions and depression and various problems. In contrast, this is what your life can be in Christ, and we want to help you get there.

Dr. Scott Hahn: Building on what the two of you just said, if people say, "Well, it's not relevant," or, "It doesn't matter," I think you could turn the question around and just say, "Well, what do you think does matter?" It's not that hard to show that what they think matters doesn't really matter in the grand scheme of things, if there is a God, and if there is an eternity. Everybody would like to be Switzerland these days and just kind of stand on neutral ground and not have to choose sides . . . but if, in fact, that sort of choice is inevitable, and far-reaching in terms of consequences, I think we can trust that the Holy Spirit is going to awaken those who seem to be too deeply slumbering even to hear us, because it really isn't always up to us. It really is up to the Holy Spirit to allow us to become the instruments.

The other thing I would say is that we have to reawaken a sense of the bad news, to build on what you were just saying. If it's choosing between the Democrats and the Republicans, I can understand why you want to be Switzerland. But I'm going to be with Fr. John Ricardo in about forty-five minutes, and we're going to be meeting together, and he speaks so passionately and eloquently and biblically about the dominion of darkness—that, in this reality, there is no Switzerland. You're either on the side of the Lord or you're not, and you don't know it. And so, it seems to me that the urgency of the task of the New Evangelization doesn't depend upon the sociological statistics about how many people think it's relevant, or how many people think it matters. I think it depends upon us to show them how much it matters.

Dr. Michael McCallion: One more thing: Parishes need to be open every night of the week with a host of activities and devotions, etc.

Panel Question #2: How does the New Evangelization meet ecumenism? What can we learn from non-Catholic Christians?

Dr. Scott Hahn: There is ecumenism with non-Catholic Christians, as well as interreligious dialogue with non-Christians. But since the question is the ecumenical conversation, I think we have to begin, again, by stepping back and assessing, what is truth and reality? That is, we agree on so much more than where we disagree with regard to the creed and the twenty-seven books of the New Testament, the truth of the Incarnation, the death and resurrection of Jesus, the miracles, and so on. I would say about, well, at least 85 percent of our beliefs as Christians are shared in common, and that's a lot of common ground to stand on. Like any dysfunctional family, we tend to look at our separated brothers and sisters and fixate on our differences— obsess and argue about those sorts of matters. I think the differences are significant, very significant. And yet they pale in comparison to the greater significance of our common commitments, the creed, and so on. So, I think what we ought to do is to really focus on why we diverge based upon where we converge. That God is a Father almighty, and he sent Jesus who promised to build a Church. He didn't say, "Peter, go build me a Church, and I'll try to preserve it or bring it back together." The promise that God almighty is fathering a family, that Christ is fulfilling the promise on this Rock: "I will build my Church, and the gates of hell will not prevail against it."

And likewise, the Holy Spirit is what makes the Church one, holy, catholic, and apostolic in spite of all of my best efforts as a sinner. Those seem to me to be more than just a rhetorical high ground on which we can win more than we can lose in terms of debates. It really is the holy ground on which we stand with brothers and sisters in Christ. And since it is holy ground that we share, I think we have to overcome the downward tendency of human pride: to just want to engage constantly in quarrels, some of which might be fruitful, but most of which I think are not. The more we stand shoulder to shoulder or on our knees together, and the more we face the common task of re-evangelizing our culture that is becoming so extraordinarily secular at a fast pace, the more I think we're going to recognize the common ground and how substantial it is. Yet we recall a supernatural grace that has ended up showing, as of now, well over 1200 Protestant ministers, pastors, missionaries, and professors in the Coming Home Network. When Marcus Grodi and I founded this twenty-six years ago, we never in our wildest dreams imagined that the Holy Spirit would stir up this kind of thing. But it really isn't about winning arguments. It's about winning brothers and sisters into the fullness of the faith, which is nothing less than the family of God.

Dr. Ralph Martin: I want to say amen to that, but also add that the Decree on Ecumenism from Vatican II, as well as the Declaration on the Relation of the Church to Non-Christian Religions and the Dogmatic and Pastoral Constitutions on the Church, really give a good balanced approach to all of the questions dealing with ecumenism and interreligious dialogue. We believe that the Catholic Church is the fullness of the means of salvation. And we believe that God's will is for everybody be joined to that Church. But we also know that there's lots of misunderstandings amongst us and that reducing those misunderstandings and helping each other to appreciate each other more is a good in itself. So, there's a time and a place for bringing people into the Catholic Church. There's a time and a place for removing obstacles to us loving each other more, which will open up the ability of the Holy Spirit to move us more into greater unity, however that might be expressed.

Dr. Mary Healy: Just to add something brief to the last part of the question, which was, "What can we learn from our non-Catholic Christian brothers and sisters?" They, of course, don't have the fullness of the apostolic heritage that we have in the Catholic Church. But precisely because they have less in a certain sense—a stripped-down Christianity, if you will—they have a certain talent for presenting the kerygma, the good news of Jesus Christ, in its simplicity. Scott Hahn mentioned the four spiritual laws, which he boiled down to about eight words, which is great. Of course, that's only the first step in evangelization. But it's the step that, as Pope John Paul II mentioned, we Catholics have tended to skip over. And we tend not to see clearly the distinction between *kerygma*—that initial proclamation of the glorious good news of Jesus—and *didache*—teaching the whole edifice of doctrine and devotion that follows on the initial kerygma and the response of love and surrender to Jesus Christ. I think it's one reason why Alpha has had such a huge success around the world and why, as Catholics, we're using Alpha, because they are helping us rediscover that gift of the simplicity of the initial proclamation of the Gospel.

Panel Question #3: How can we overcome the idea that the laity should take a more passive and non-participatory approach to the life of faith?

Dr. Michael McCallion: You need to be in relationship with them. And in being in relationship with them, you can help to dissipate the idea that they should be as passive as they are. But maybe they're not so passive. Maybe we think that they're passive, but maybe they're not. I'm sure there are passive Catholics, but one thing is just to be in relationship with them. And in doing that, you can show them Christ. Again, it would help if the parish was open every night, because then you could bring them to a five-minute prayer within the community or in front of the tabernacle.

Dr. Scott Hahn: Let me state the flip side of the coin. It might be stating the obvious, but lay people are called to be a kingdom of priests. And the common priesthood of the laity is to sanctify the temporal order. And that isn't like, "Well, that's easy compared to the sacramental work of the ministerial priesthood." It seems to me that without the sacraments, we can't do it, but what it is we're called upon to do goes beyond passivity. It goes to an apostolate that is something that is huge and almost entirely untapped. And yet the universal call to holiness runs like a golden thread throughout all of the sixteen documents of Vatican II, along with the call of the lay people to recognize their parish or their diocese is the world and to not sanitize it, but to sanctify it. That's a mission. Those are marching orders. I'll just identify one study. Dr. Andrew Willard Jones wrote—a book called *Before Church and State*, looking at the Christian Kingdom of King Saint Louis IX, back in the twelfth and thirteenth centuries. Most historians study this in terms of the Church—"the clergy, and the state of King Louis"—but in the actual primary sources, you never find such language employed because the Church consists of clergy and laity. The clergy had an active role, but, at the same time, Saint Louis IX was baptized, confirmed, and married in the Church, and he saw himself as an apostle, and everything that he was doing with the poor, with justice, with the kingdom, was his mission as a baptized and confirmed Catholic, and a recipient of the sacrament of holy matrimony as well. And so, it's not Church and state. It's clergy and laity. What we call High Medieval civilization was a kind of sacramental organism that didn't have a confessional state. It had an apostolic laity, who were conjoined at the heart of Christ, to the sacramental or ministerial priesthood. And I think it's time for us to reconstruct that part of the temple.

Panel Question #4: Considering the child sexual abuse scandals within the history of the Church, how can we respond to people's concerns responsibly, going beyond the gloss that "we all are sinners"?

Dr. Ralph Martin: What I say to people, which I think is helpful, is found in 2 Corinthians: "We have this treasure in earthen vessels." One contemporary translation says, "We have this treasure in cracked pots." We leak. So, yes, there are a lot of imperfect people in the Church—all of us—and there's some grievously sinful people in the Church. But the treasure of the Church is Jesus. The treasure of the Church is God himself. Don't throw out the baby with the bathwater. Don't throw out baby Jesus with the dirty bathwater.

Dr. Mary Healy: Dr. Cavadini made a point that is very relevant to this question last night when he talked about what makes the Church. What makes the Church is nothing we bring to it. He spoke facetiously about how he told his bishop that he was going to form his own church, and that all the members of this church would be people who are worthy to be there. But of course that's a farce, because the Church is what she is precisely because she's composed of people who are not worthy to be there, but who are there because the Church is the Sacrament in the world of the love of Christ who bent down to give everything to those who deserve nothing. So, I think part of the reason for the terrible longevity and severity of the sex abuse crisis is that too many of the leaders of the Church were bent on upholding the institutional good reputation of the Church, rather than humbly, repentantly and contritely acknowledging the grievous, grievous sins of her members, and particularly her shepherds, while at the same time upholding the true vision of the Church as she is: the Bride of Christ, redeemed by his blood, not a museum for saints, but the hospital for sinners that we all need. If the bar was set too high for membership in the Church, none of us would be there. But we're there precisely because we need that infinite grace poured out in Christ.

Dr. Scott Hahn: If I could say, a couple things, building on what you've just shared. I think saving the appearance has been the *modus operandi* for decades. Or, the Italian expression is *bella figura*—that we want it to look good in a formal external way. But instead of saving appearances, what we really need to do is save sinners and we're all that, and so we're not out to make more allegations. But we also are not ostriches, called to bury our heads in the sand. We see what Jesus did in choosing Peter, who he knew would deny him, and Judas who would betray him, and so it shouldn't shock us if there are still Judas-priests or Judas-cardinals, as it were. I think that simply laicizing a prelate who preys upon young kids and seminarians and protects others who do so, and promotes them as well—being laicized, I think, sends the wrong signal. It obscures the plain fact that Vatican II identified the universal call to holiness as something belonging to the saints, to the laity. You don't want to communicate, "Well, if you're clergy and you prey upon young people, and you promote and protect others who do so as well, that simply qualifies you to be a lay person." I don't think anybody intended that message to be conveyed, but I can't help but to think it was conveyed anyway. There is no way to directly address all of the bad news because it's much worse and it's not over and it's not going away tomorrow or the next day. I think the only way to drive out this kind of darkness is through prayer and fasting and deliverance, but also to find a light switch and to flip it on because the good news is so much better than I realize. After thirty-some years of being a Catholic, the good news of the fullness of the Catholic faith shines in such a splendor that I'm still discovering. I think we have got to awaken that sense of childlike awe and wonder, or what John Paul II called Eucharistic amazement—that kind of light alone will drive out the darkness, along with prayer and fasting and deliverance.

Panel Question #5: Is it enough simply to be kind to other people, to do kind things, and to take care of the planet, without any reference to God?

Dr. Scott Hahn: I'm working on a book called *It Is Right and Just*, pointing out that Cicero, who didn't have the Scriptures, recognized that *religio*—religion—is a virtue of the natural moral law. In fact, for him, and for the classical tradition of the natural moral law, religion is the highest form of justice. If justice is giving to others what you owe them, then there's distributive and commutative justice. But there's also *pietas*, where you honor your parents because you can't give them back life like they gave you—*patria*—to your own people, your homeland, patriotism, but *religio*, which is giving God thanks and praise, particularly in the form of sacrifice which you offer to God, and to no creature. And so, it seems to me that if it's a matter of the natural moral law, and if it's right and just to give him thanks and praise, it is profoundly wrong and unjust not to. What we do without realizing it, is that we back ourselves into a kind of complicity, where inadvertently we're acknowledging that the humanitarian, the horizontal, the works of mercy, especially the corporal ones, these alone.

Well, the fact is, there are lots of good reasons for people to embrace unbelief. But there are even better reasons for us to be able to help them reach belief, through creation, the mirror by which we come to know the Creator. But also, I just sense that the Holy Spirit is waiting upon us to wake up to proclaim the word of the cross, which is always going to be foolishness to those who seek wisdom, a sign of weakness to those who are looking for power. And yet it is the wisdom and the power of God. God wants us to do more with less. I think that we would prefer to have the philosophical, the historical, and the academic chops to share credit with our Lord. But I think, in the poverty of Christ and the poverty of what we call the word of the cross, and in the poverty of the Eucharist, it isn't really a banquet in any natural sense, as Cardinal Wright once said. A meal? It's not even a snack. But it is the marriage supper of the Lamb. And so, I think there's a need for us to allow God to do more with less, and to make his strength known in our weakness and to call people back to a full awareness that not only, "There is a God, and here are his existence and attributes," but, "He is providential. He provides for us to make it to him." I sense that if we could hear the heart of Christ, we would discover that he longs for that more passionately than all of us put together.

Dr. Ralph Martin: This is a very common attitude, and it's a very good question. Is it good enough just to be a good person, to be kind and things like that? Well, how do we know whether it's good enough or not? We need to hear what God's Word says: No, it's not good enough because, as Jesus said, "Call no man good." No man is good in the eyes of God. The only one that is good in the eyes of God is Jesus, and those who participate in the goodness of Jesus. And then also Jesus tells us, "Love your neighbor as yourself." But that's the second commandment. The first and greatest commandment is, "Love the Lord, your God, with your whole heart, your whole mind, your whole soul, your whole strength, and your neighbor as yourself." For the creature not to worship the Creator, for the creature not to adore the one who created him, for the creature not to hang on every word that comes from the Master's lips, can really cloak a very profound kind of arrogance and pride and self-satisfaction and self-reliance and self-salvation—self-righteousness. "I feel like I'm righteous enough, I don't need to pay attention to what God tells me, I don't need to pay attention to Jesus." That could be a very profound form of rebellion.

Index

CPSIA information can be obtained
at www.ICGtesting.com
Printed in the USA
FSHW010331190221
78716FS